QUANTITATIVE TECHNIQUES IN MANAGEMENT

QUANTITATIVE TECHNIQUES IN MANAGEMENT

S.K. Murthy

ANMOL PUBLICATIONS PVT. LTD.
NEW DELHI-110 002 (INDIA)

ANMOL PUBLICATIONS PVT. LTD.

Regd. Office: 4360/4, Ansari Road, Daryaganj,
New Delhi-110002 (India)
Tel.: 23278000, 23261597, 23286875, 23255577
Fax: 91-11-23280289
Email: anmolpub@gmail.com
Visit us at: www.anmolpublications.com

Branch Office: No. 1015, Ist Main Road, BSK IIIrd Stage
IIIrd Phase, IIIrd Block, Bangalore-560 085 (India)
Tel.: 080-41723429 • Fax: 080-26723604
Email: anmolpublicationsbangalore@gmail.com

Quantitative Techniques in Management

First Edition, 2010

ISBN 978-81-261-4574-4

PRINTED IN INDIA

Printed at Mehra Offset Press, Delhi.

Contents

Preface

This textbook covers an important area of study in business management. Quantitative skills and competency building program. Many academics are concerned with the better ways and means of teaching in this area. The chapters on"Linear Programming"are very interesting and figures that are presented with the graphical method are helpful to readers.

The textbook comprises of Dynamic Programming. PERT/ CPM, Inventory Management, Safety Stock. It is a comprehensive, student-focused textbook designed primarily for undergraduate business students taking an introductory course on quantitative methods. Starting with no assumptions about students' knowledge, the textbook uses examples that support the students with all abilities.

Author

Chapter 1

Introduction

HUMAN RESOURCE

Full strategic partnership requires a "decision science" that enhances decisions about talent resources; finance and marketing enhance decisions about money and customers. We describe the historical lessons from finance and marketing, and how they reveal the elements of a new decision science for talent resources, and a logical framework to support the decision science.

Then, we provide an example showing how organizations can use this framework to gain new insights about the talent decisions that are most critical, and enhance the strategic insights and influence of those decisions.

People, intellectual capital, and talent are ever more critical to organizational strategic success. This observation is so common today that it almost goes without saying. Digitization, labour shortages, growth through acquisitions, simultaneous downsizing and expansion, workforce demographic changes, and globalization are just a few of the trends that have made talent a top priority. Today, top executives are quick to point out that managing talent well is their personal concern; it is perhaps the most difficult issue preventing their organization's maximum success.

Yet, when we ask them if their decisions about the talents of their people are made with the same rigor, logic, and strategic connections as their decisions about money, technology, and products, they readily admit that their talent decisions are much less rigorous. Business leaders are increasingly frustrated with traditional HR, even when it is executed well or bestin-class.

One CFO (now the CEO of his organization) put it well: "I value the hard work of HR, but I worry that our organization may not know which talent issues are the important ones, versus which are mostly tactical. I know how to answer that question in finance, marketing, and operations. I'm not sure how to do it for talent. I wish HR had more to offer here."

Frustration with the current state of traditional HR, and hopes for something more, are reflected in questions like these: "Why is there so little logical connection between our core business management processes and our talent management processes?

Our strategic planning, marketing, operations, and budgeting processes connect deeply and logically with how we create competitive success and shareholder value. Yet, at best these processes reflect only general talent goals like headcount, labour costs or generic HR programmes. At worst, people issues appear only as a headcount budget at the end of the plan."

"We invest heavily in the latest HR measurement techniques: HR scorecards, HR financial reports, ROI on HR programmes, and studies of how HR programmes enhance attitudes, skills, and abilities. Yet, these HR measures seldom influence key business decisions, such as acquisitions and entry into new markets.

They provide little insight on how well we compare with our competitors in creating competitive advantage through people. Can talent measures truly drive business decisions and investments?" "Not all investments are equally important in all situations.

Marketing would never get away with a strategy to 'provide 40 hours of advertising for every product.' Yet, our HR programmes typically apply similarly to everyone, such as '40 hours of quality training.' Shouldn't we deploy our HR investments with greater precision and distinction, to have more impact and less wasted effort?"

"HR spends a lot of time showing the value of HR

programmes. Yet, in Finance, Marketing, and Operations we judge their value through results: How much they help our leaders make better decisions about those resources to drive organizational effectiveness. Why is HR different?" The recent surge in HR measurement systems suggests that many believe the solution lies in better metrics. Finance, marketing, and engineering appear to have better "facts and figures" than HR does.

HR measurement systems typically strive to show the return on investments in HR programmes, or apply scorecards and six-sigma techniques to HR processes; however, research shows that two important goals for HR measurement, (1) to enhance decisions about human capital and (2) to connect human resources to strategy, are rarely met. HR measurement cannot solve the problem alone, because today's measurement systems typically adapt measures designed for other resources and apply them to HR. For example, six-sigma initiatives often apply accounting -based cost-efficiency or operational measures.

The best result is less costly and quicker HR processes, but not necessarily better talent. At worst, six-sigma processes achieve gains in efficiency (which is measured) at the expense of significantly reduced quality of talent (which is often unmeasured). The same pattern emerges when measures designed for finance, marketing, or process improvement to are applied indiscriminately to HR.

Examples such as "HR accounting," "HR quality," "HR branding," "HR balanced scorecards" can be useful systems if applied properly, but they typically fail to address the fundamental challenge of improving talent decisions.

Today's HR has advanced significantly in its sophistication and strategic planning; however, the majority of today's HR practices, benchmarks, and measures still reflect a traditional paradigm: excellence defined as delivering high-quality services in response to client needs. For years, writers have advocated more "strategic" HRM, or adopting a more outside-in rather than inside-out approach.

Market-based HR and accountability for business results

are undeniably important; however, in practice these ideas are often implemented simply by asking strategic clients what services they want (leadership development, competency systems, Board governance, etc.) and delivering them. Marketing principles are used to convince clients of the value of HR services, or financial calculations are used to correlate HR practices with business results.

These all reflect a traditional service-delivery paradigm that is fundamentally limited, because it assumes that clients know what they need. Fields such as finance have a different approach. They have augmented their service delivery paradigm with a "decision science" paradigm that teaches the frameworks to make good choices.

Significant improvements in HR decisions will be revealed not by applying finance and accounting formulas to HR services, programmes, and processes, but rather by learning how fields like marketing and finance evolved into the powerful, decision-supporting functions they are today. Their evolution provides a blueprint for the new paradigm for HR.

PROFESSIONAL PRACTICES

At least three markets are vital to organizational success:

1. The financial market
2. The customer/product market
3. The talent market.

In the financial and customer/product markets, there is a clear distinction between the professional practice associated with how organizations operate in the market, versus the decision science that supports analysis and deployment of the resources within that market. There is a clear distinction between accounting (the professional practice) and finance (the decision science).

Accounting is vital for management reporting and external requirements yet very different from the financial tools used to decide about appropriate debt structure, internal rate-of-return thresholds, et cetera. There is an equally clear distinction between the professional practice of sales and the decision science of marketing.

Excellent sales practices and measures are vital, but very different from the tools used to make decisions about customer segmentation, market position, product portfolio, et cetera. Today, the differences between accounting and finance are so clear that we seldom even consider them. The competencies of a successful accountant are related to, but clearly quite distinct from, those for a successful financial executive, and professional curricula reflect this.

The industry itself has segmented this way: Large accounting firms are very different from investment banking firms that focus on finance. Similarly, the competencies and activities of sales are clearly distinct from those of marketing. This does not mean that the professional practice is merely "administrative," or less important.

The decision science cannot exist without the professional practice. In fact, the professional practice must precede the decision science. Few organizations survive with great marketing and ineffective sales, nor great finance without highly professional accounting. Today, the synergy between accounting and finance, or between sales and marketing, is so strong that it is easy to overlook how decision science evolved from professional practice, and how they are both inextricably related, yet distinct. A closer look at this symbiotic relationship between the professional practice and the decision science reveals insights about the evolution of HR.

HR, like finance and marketing, helps the firm operate within a critical market—in this case, the market for talent. Organizations cannot succeed without effective decisions and professional practices for operating in the financial and customer markets, and they also increasingly require effective decisions aligned with professional practices in the talent market.

Organizational decision processes and tools employed in the talent market are far less mature and refined than those used in finance or marketing. Although accounting and finance are clearly distinct, as are sales and marketing, perhaps the most valuable insights can be drawn from their synergy, and how decision science evolved from professional practice.

Accounting is about 500 years old, and was a well-developed profession long before the decision science of finance showed how accounting measures could support decisions based on concepts such as relative returns on capital, and how different factors (margin, asset productivity, and leverage) affect those returns.

Finance emerged in the early 1900s and is largely credited to the duPont organization, with the duPont model still in wide use today. Why the early 1900s? Because that is when capital acquisition and deployment became an important source of competitive advantage, and the ability to differentiate which types of businesses could generate an appropriate return on capital was vital to making effective decisions.

Before that, organizations typically consisted of business units that, even if quite large, had generally consistent capital returns. For example, Sears was a large organization, but the capital model varied little from location to location. With advancing industrial production, capital investment decisions took on more importance within companies and across capital markets, and the tools of finance evolved to improve these decisions.

Similarly, sales is as old as trade itself, and sales practices were a well-developed profession long before the decision science of marketing used sales information to create decision models such as customer segmentation and product life-cycles. When Sloan restructured GM by aligning specific brands within the portfolio to specific customer segments, a new course was charted.

In the years that followed, the decision science associated with marketing made rapid advancements, as the size and sophistication of customer and product markets made systematic decisions a competitive factor for organizations. Marketing evolved from an almost exclusive focus on advertising practices to recognizing advertising as only one of many tools to be synergistically deployed to achieve strategic success and increased value.

During the 1950s, the management of the customer competitive space moved from being advertising-research-oriented to being decision-oriented. Top management became accountable and was provided tools to integrate marketing with the overall business objectives through strategic deployment decisions. Management of the talent resources is at a similar inflection point today.

The HR function creates tangible value in organizations by focusing primarily on delivery of HR practices (staffing, development, compensation, labour relations, etc.), based on professional and often research-based principles. These practices are important, and research indicates that when they are done well they add tangible value to the organization.

Professional practices alone do not systematically address the increasing sophistication and importance of talent markets and decisions to today's competitive challenges. For all their contributions, good professional practices are not the same as having a logical and deep decision science for talent. Today, such a talent decision science is a source of competitive advantage, just as decision sciences for financial and customer markets were in the previous century.

Today, HR faces the challenges from business leaders described in the introduction. Similar challenges characterized the capital and customer markets, at the point in their evolution when they had achieved a sophisticated professional practice, but lacked a fully developed decision science to give it context and direction.

The historical lessons from finance and marketing suggest that today's HR challenges will not be addressed simply by incremental improvements in the professional practices of HR, nor by measuring them more precisely, nor by asking clients what they want. The next step in the evolution of HR is a new paradigm, based on a decision science for talent.

DECISION

What does decision science do? It provides a logical, reliable, and consistent framework that enhances decisions about a key resource, wherever those decisions are made. Decision science does not rigidly prescribe actions, but instead provides a system to identify and analyse key decision issues, adapting to the unique information and characteristics of the specific context.

For example, in finance, the duPont model allowed organizations to allocate financial capital across business units using more than the traditional accounting measure of profit. It revealed a new insight at the time: Allocating financial resources to the areas of highest return on capital, not simply the highest profit, was a path to superior performance.

Perhaps more important, it articulated the necessary conditions for high returns, such as higher asset utilization, and it showed how to anticipate the effectiveness of financial investments, not simply account for their outcomes after the fact. In marketing, customer segmentation enabled organizations to allocate their customer and marketing capital not merely equally to all customers, nor to the customers with the highest sales, but rather systematically to choose the appropriate marketing investments and methods for each market segment, and to identify in advance the segments with the greatest potential impact on the organization's success.

Finance creates organizational value by enhancing decisions that depend upon or affect financial resources. Marketing creates organizational value by enhancing decisions that depend on or have an impact on customer or product resources.

Finance and marketing provide reliable and deeply logical frameworks that connect financial and customer capital to the organization's sustainable strategic success. Strategic decisions must go beyond generic best practices to create a unique and sustainable competitive position for the organization.

VALUE OF DECISION

The finance and marketing decision sciences certainly have important effects on the professional practices of accounting and sales, as when different sales efforts are matched to different customer segments. Paradoxically, the most important effects of decision sciences are outside the professional function itself, as managers, employees, shareholders, and others learn to reliably and consistently improve their own decisions about the financial and customer resources that they affect.

For example, the logic of return-on-investment (ROI) is something every manager learns, and can be applied to decisions as diverse as investing in new equipment, marketing initiatives, production improvements, or mergers. ROI does not force managers to follow a rigid programme imposed by accounting or finance.

Rather, ROI provides a framework that helps managers identify and logically analyse the relevant success factors for deploying financial capital in these diverse decisions. Such decisions are made by countless managers and leaders throughout the organization, mostly outside the fields of accounting and finance. Thus, the decision sciences of finance and marketing support and structure decisions, wherever they are made. Finance and marketing provide a "teachable point of view" about how financial and customer resources create sustainable organizational value. Ultimately, the success of finance and marketing is judged less by the quality of their programs, than by the quality of decisions throughout the organization, about financial or customer resources.

Today, HR seldom has a teachable point of view, so HR processes often feel controlling and dogmatic to line managers. It is often difficult for managers to connect what HR is asking them to do (the professional practices) with the competitive business issues that determine the organization's success.

TALENTSHIP

The lessons from marketing and finance tell us that the goal of a talent decision science would be "To increase the success of the organization by improving decisions that impact or depend on talent resources." We have coined the term "talentship" to describe the new decision science, and to reflect the notion of stewardship for the resource of employee talents. Talentship is to HR what finance is to accounting, and what marketing is to sales.

As talentship evolves, organizations will increasingly succeed not simply through HR practices, but by the quality of decisions about talent resources, throughout the organization. Just as with decisions about financial and customer resources, talent decisions reside with countless strategic managers, leaders, and employees, deciding about the talents available to them, and their own personal talents.

When we ask business and HR leaders to think of a decision that depended on or affected talent, but was not made well, even companies with "best in class" HR functions have little difficulty generating examples. The examples carry a remarkably consistent message: The talent decision mistakes are NOT being made by HR professionals.

Poor talent decisions seldom focus on HR programmes, but instead reflect well-intentioned leaders making decisions without fully understanding the talent implications. So, the greatest opportunity to improve talent decisions is outside of the HR profession.

There are two choices:

1. Try to control these decisions (such as requiring that they be made by only HR professionals)
2. Equip those outside the HR profession (line managers, employees, executives, etc.) to better understand the talent implications of the decisions they make.

HR programmes are only one way to enhance talent decisions, just as accounting and sales programmes are only one way to enhance decisions about financial and customer resources. Today's HR functions typically define themselves in terms of their practices. HR textbooks and certifications are organized around the practices and functions that HR delivers, not the strategic decisions that HR supports.

HR careers typically involve broadening expertise in the HR disciplines (staffing, compensation, labour relations, training and development, etc.), on the way to becoming "HR generalists." HR professionals are urged to develop competencies as "partners in strategy execution," "change agents," and "employee advocates", but, unlike in finance and marketing, such competencies are not logically linked to a decision-making framework.

Enhancing the strategic role of HR means equipping HR to improve talent decisions throughout the organization. Automating administrative work or shifting it away from high-level HR professionals can be helpful, just as separating bookkeeping away from accounting was valuable, but it is not the same as incorporating a decision science into talent decisions wherever they are made.

CONTROL SYSTEMS

A typical reaction to the idea of talentship is that many HR frameworks are already used by organizations, and they certainly affect decisions.

One example is salary grades. Virtually everyone knows the salary grade to which they belong, and employees and managers routinely use salary grades in their decisions about budgeting, head-count planning, merit pay, and other rewards. Because salary grades are often the only available framework for mapping the organization's talent resources, it becomes the default framework for things such as signature authority, participation in leadership programmes, parking space allocation, and many other decisions unrelated to the original purpose.

The salary grade system certainly affects decisions, but it is not a decision science. It is a control system, similar to the accounting and sales frameworks that existed before their decision sciences developed. The salary grade system in HR is like the chart of accounts in accounting. It provides a classification system to organize large amounts of data, and it improves the consistency of decisions (it limits the amount of merit increases to provide budgetary and salary structure control). Like most HR systems, salary grades are "control" frameworks that create value mostly by limiting discretion to prevent mistakes.

Strategic decisions require discretion and uniqueness, not merely consistency and control. Lacking a decision science when such decisions present themselves, leaders are motivated to "work around" control systems. For example, faced with the imminent loss of key talent to high-paying competitors, managers may inflate the job grade because it is the only way to comply with the control system and still achieve the pay increase necessary to the key talent. These "work arounds" undermine the credibility of the HR systems. A true talent decision science would provide a rational and logical framework to determine where and why off-grade pay increases are needed.

Ironically, the lack of a decision science creates a greater need for control, because without a more rational framework, decision makers will use fads, benchmarks, tradition, et cetera. Such frameworks produce decisions of lower quality, so the organization must use control systems to restrict the range of action. Managers, in turn, often resent such systems, because they imply that managers are not to be trusted with talent decisions. This is one reason that HR is seen as administrative, or even obstructive. HR managers are often perceived to be effective business partners only when they help business leaders work around the HR control systems. They are good partners within a bad system.

TALENTSHIP AS PARTNERSHIP

Today many HR professionals lament that they are "at the table" but not influential in the strategy and business planning process, when key decisions are made, such as mergers and acquisitions, entry into new markets, expansion globally, and introduction of new technologies. Interestingly, sales and accounting are usually not at the table either.

The decision sciences of finance and marketing are at the table. The professional practices of accounting and finance reflect the implications of the strategic decisions that rely on finance and marketing frameworks. To participate fully in the strategic discussions, HR must have a unique, talent-focused perspective for improving decisions, not just a process for implementing decisions.

Improving decisions requires teaching more than telling. Finance and marketing are effective because they are taught to business leaders and become a part of their work. Likewise we envision that the future talent decision science will be taught to others, becoming a natural part of their work and improving their talent decisions.

A decision science improves reliability, consistency, and shared understanding. Give several finance professionals the same business challenge, and they likely will approach it with similar logic, and develop reasonably similar analyses. This is one reason that finance and marketing have such strong functional "brand identification."

In contrast, when several HR professionals attack the same business challenge they often produce inconsistent solutions, quite often reflecting their different HR professional practices (e.g., compensation, development, organizational design), or a different individual's particular experience (e.g., "this is how they did it at GE"). Each solution may be good, but by definition they cannot all be optimal. Lacking a consistent logical framework, talent decisions will be made using frameworks influenced by politics, fads, or fashions. Alternatively, talent decisions will be made by applying existing decision frameworks, such as focusing only on HR programme costs because that is what the accounting decision system recognizes.

To teach others to make better decisions requires a shared point of view that provides a common language and structure for decisions. It is a fundamental component of every successful decision science. In finance, this includes concepts such as return on investment and free cash flow, and the models that trace the implications of organization decisions on them.

Economic value added (EVA) and return on invested capital (ROIC) are not rigid reporting systems. Rather, they provide a logical starting point that helps decision makers reliably and consistently focus on the important elements. Business units adapt the generic models to reflect the specific challenges that they face.

For example, one organization may decide to use ROIC to evaluate new capital investments while others may use EVA, internal rate of return, or even payback period. In all cases, the framework is consistent, teachable, and focused on decisions, not programs. It can be explained and taught to those who manage financial resources throughout the organization, who are usually outside the finance or marketing profession.

In the organizations that we work with, there are almost always a few HR professionals who effectively demonstrate how talent connects to strategic success, and are known for improving the talent decisions of the managers and employees they support. Typically, these are rare individuals, well-known, and business units feel rather lucky to have them. These HR professionals invariably admit that they learned to provide decision support on their own, and in their own way, with little systematic instruction or development.

Their success is difficult to reproduce in their HR colleagues, employees, and business managers. One HR professional put it well: "This capability is critical to our future, but it doesn't 'scale' because everyone does it and learns it differently." A talent decision science contributes to scale by lending consistency to the strategic logic, and how it is learned and used by HR professionals.

Although a talent decision science certainly improves specific HR decisions, plans, and strategies, an even more significant contribution of talentship is developing, using, and teaching a consistent logical point of view about how talent resources connect to strategic success.

A logical point of view provides a consistent script for an ongoing dialogue about talent and strategy, allowing more reliable and consistent diagnosis, analysis, and action on talent issues throughout the organization. This improves talent decisions within the HR function and outside it, where the opportunity for impact and improvement is the greatest.

What will be the elements of the decision framework that supports talentship? Nearly all decisions that depend upon or affect people within organizations can be described in terms of three elements: impact, effectiveness, and efficiency. Moreover, these elements have useful analogies within existing decision sciences, such as marketing.

In talentship, "impact" concerns "How much will strategic

success increase by improving the quality or availability of a particular talent pool?" The analogy in marketing is "How much will organizational profitability increase by improving market share or sales success with particular customers or customer segments?"

In marketing, customer segmentation determines how much strategic success would increase by improving sales to a particular customer segment, and thus which segment should get more attention. Answering the impact question for talent resources requires what we call "talent segmentation," a term we coined to describe the logical differentiation of talent pools by their importance to strategic success.

The analogy to customer segments in talentship is "talent pools." Traditionally, organizations describe work in terms of jobs. Sometimes a talent pool is completely contained in one job, but usually talent pools combine elements from several jobs or skill sets. Examples of talent pools are "those with customer contact at the point of service," "those who integrate product lines to support cross-selling" or "leaders."

Organization leaders sometimes say that they already know which talent pools are most crucial, and that the "impact" question is so obvious that their opinion will be shared by everyone; however, when we actually ask several business leaders to name the high-impact talent pools, their answers are so different that they could not possibly support reliable and consistent talent decisions.

For example, some believe the highest-impact talent pool must be front-line leaders, because they touch so many employees and processes; others believe it must be salespeople because you cannot have profits and growth without sales; still others believe it must be top executives, because their scope is so broad and the market rewards them so highly. There are two reasons for this inconsistency.

First, business leaders and strategists typically focus only on business processes and market outcomes, and rarely connect strategies to human capital or talent. Human resource leaders typically focus on designing and gaining support for HR programs, rarely asking which talent pools would be the most productive targets for those programs. The connecting point between strategic business process and the HR programs is the talent pool, and it is often overlooked by both groups.

Second, business and HR leaders typically consider talent pools in terms of their average importance. Traditional HR systems divide jobs into categories based on their average value to allocate pay, training, and other resources equitably. Salary grade midpoints are a good example. Identifying the talent pools in which investments will pay off most handsomely often requires focusing on the effects of changes in talent value, not the average value.

We coined the term "pivotal talent pool" to capture this idea. Talent pool "pivotalness" is the difference in competitive success that would be achieved by improving the quality or availability of that talent pool. In marketing, customer segments with the highest average sales or profits may not be those in which improvements in market share most improve sales and profits. When business leaders consider only the average value of talent, they routinely overlook talent pools that could have a significant effect on strategic success. Lacking a good sense of talent pool differences, organizations frequently adopt a "peanut butter" approach, spreading programs across everyone equally, such as "40 hours of quality training for everyone" or "stock options for everyone."

The marketing decision science is so well developed that recommending "40 minutes of advertising for every product" would never be tolerated. Differentiating among customer segments is fundamental to marketing, just as "impact"—differentiating among talent pools based on their importance to strategic success—must be at the heart of talentship.

EFFECTIVENESS

In talentship, "effectiveness" concerns "How much do HR programs and processes affect the capacity and actions of employees in talent pools?" The analogy in marketing is "How much does an advertising or pricing programme change the behaviour of the customers in a customer segment?" "Effectiveness" is independent of "impact."

Traditionally, HR organizations are more adept at "effectiveness" than "impact," tracking the effects of HR programs on such things as performance ratings, competencies, climate, and attitudes.

For example, we worked with several organizations that carefully tracked their sales training and compensation programs against the associated changes in sales behaviour, only to realise upon more careful analysis that the biggest reason for low sales was outside of the sales talent pool (i.e., product was unavailable when it was promised).

Although sales training did effectively improve sales behaviour, the "impact" was significantly limited by the quality of a different talent pool: back-office employees who operated the supply-chain. Because "effectiveness" was the focus, back-office employees received much less attention than the front-line sales group did, and "impact" suffered. Today's widespread desire to calculate the "return on investment" in HR programs reflects "effectiveness rather than impact."

The sales training described probably produced an ROI well above the minimum hurdle rate, but that ROI was still much less than the potential return from directing training resources to the more pivotal talent pool, back-office employees. Ignoring impact in favour of effectiveness can produce well-meaning HR programs that have large "effectiveness" on low-"impact" talent pools.

EFFICIENCY

In talentship, "efficiency" concerns "How much HR programme and process activity do we get for our investments (such as time and money)?" The analogy in marketing is "What programme activity (advertising, sales, etc.) is generated for a certain investment of resources?" In marketing, typical efficiency measures include the number of television programme segments acquired per advertising dollar, or the number of billboards acquired per region.

"Efficiency" is independent of "impact" or "effectiveness." Most of today's HR measures focus on efficiency, such as ratio of HR staff to total headcount, cost per hire, training hours per employee, benefit costs per employee, HR functional costs as a percentage of revenues.

Attending only to efficiency can produce extremely lean advertising or sales organizations, that have only small effects. This is the typical dilemma of trying to "shrink to success." Some HR functions have shown impressive cost savings, for example, by outsourcing their activities. Relying solely on such input-output measures risks fixation on lowest-cost, often by standardizing and centralizing HR programs.

Many organizations realise too late that although outsourcing saved money, it also reduced the distinctiveness of their HR systems and practices compared to competitors, decreasing both effectiveness and impact far more than the original tempting cost savings. The effectiveness and impact of the talent decisions are not readily captured by typical accounting and finance measures. Without a point-of-view that clearly articulates all three elements, HR efficiency may get more than optimal amounts of attention.

LINKING TALENT

Making the talentship decision science actionable requires having processes and tools that encourage and enable the organization's decision makers to ask the right questions about their talent. That requires a framework that integrates "impact," "effectiveness," and "efficiency," articulates the connections between HR, talent, and strategic success, and provides a consistent approach to talent decisions and a common language to communicate about those decisions. Lacking such a framework, it is easy to drown in a sea of data and opinions, and to lose sight of the key issues.

In finance, decision frameworks such as EVA are made actionable with models and tools that show the elements of the calculation, and how to combine them. Such frameworks also make it easy for decision makers to identify elements where data exist versus where they do not, and to see clearly the effect of gaps in data on the assumptions and conclusions they reach.

EVA did not simply evolve from hundreds of accounting

measures, but from a systematic analysis of how returns on capital create value. Yet, routinely HR organizations proudly present business leaders with systems or "HR scorecards" containing hundreds of indices and data elements, with no guiding framework, hoping that business leaders will invent the required decision science to use them wisely.

Talentship becomes actionable through a framework that defines the components of impact, effectiveness, and efficiency, explains how they relate and combine logically to connect HR, talent, and strategic success: the HC BRidge[R] Decision Framework. In this framework, impact, effectiveness, and efficiency are defined more explicitly through a set of linking elements. The framework is an outline, like EVA or ROIC in finance, with each linking element representing deeper logic and analysis. It does not prescribe actions, nor does it describe a particular business or strategic situation. Rather, the framework spans different situations and decisions, providing a logical way to organize the information, describe different situations in similar ways, create deeper understanding, and improve decisions.

The framework is useful as a planning tool, working from sustainable strategic success at the top, to derive implications for HR practices and investments at the bottom. This is the traditional approach, typically adopted by business and HR leaders, textbooks, and consulting firms.

Our work has shown, however, that the framework is also useful in guiding execution, by starting with HR investments and practices at the bottom and clarifying how they connect upward to business processes, resources, and sustainable strategic success.

We also find it useful when talent questions "start in the middle." HR professionals are often confronted with a request such as "we need to get our manufacturing employees to be more innovative." The framework guides a dialogue beginning with this element ("human capacity" in the form of innovation), identifies how it connects to key aligned actions, talent pools, and business processes/resources (moving upward).

If innovation is found to be a high-impact human capacity, the model can help to identify the HR practices that will most enhance it (moving downward from "human capacity"). For example, one HR manager met with a business leader to come up with a standard headcount budget and expected number of employment requisitions for the coming year.

Rather than simply focusing on headcount gaps, he used the decision framework, asking: "What do these employees do that makes the biggest difference to your business?" (aligned actions), "How does their activity blend with others in the organization to create that value?" (talent pools), "What are the key processes in the business where these activities have their biggest effect?" (business processes), and, finally: "How does doing these processes well contribute most to our ability to build and sustain an advantage in the marketplace?" (sustainable strategic success).

The line manager said: "This is certainly a different conversation than I usually have with someone from HR. I never before saw headcount planning as so strategic!"

DECISION FRAMEWORK

Federal Express in the Asia-Pacific region is useful for illustrating the framework, because it is a familiar organization that offers some interesting insights into the model. Impact concerns "How much will strategic success increase by improving the quality or availability of a particular talent pool?"

Most HR and business leaders asked to identify the key talent at Federal Express will name pilots, logistics designers, and top leaders. No one can deny their importance. At Federal Express Asia Pacific, some of the largest opportunities to improve on-time performance and customer satisfaction might lie with a relatively "undervalued" talent pool: couriers and dispatchers.

Our investigation showed it was not unusual for couriers to encounter a customer who said something like the following: "Can you wait 15 minutes, because I will have eight more packages for you." The quality of courier responses, multiplied across hundreds of incidents every day, contributed significantly to the effectiveness or ineffectiveness of the entire system. Waiting at the wrong time could cause a truckload of packages to miss the timing window at the airport hub, and be delivered late.

Not waiting, when time is available, caused needless customer dissatisfaction. Improving the quality of the courier/ dispatcher talent pool on this important aligned action was actually more pivotal even than improving pilot quality. A traditional analysis would identify pilots as a more valuable talent pool on average, and we would concur.

Pilots have higher salaries, higher educational requirements, and handle aircraft worth millions of dollars. Yet "talent pool pivotalness" focuses on how improvements in talent enhance strategic success. Pilots are important, but little gain would be achieved by improving pilot performance. The framework revealed that there was more opportunity to advance the strategy by improving the performance of couriers than that of pilots. Moreover, it identified precisely what elements of courier performance mattered most.

Effectiveness concerns "How much do HR programs and processes affect the capacity and actions of employees in each talent pool?" Capability (can employees contribute?), opportunity (do employees get the chance to contribute?), and motivation (do employees want to contribute?) are the elements of "Human Capacity".

At Federal Express Asia-Pacific, the "aligned action" would be the correct response to the customer request. Understanding this reveals new opportunities for HR programs to create aligned actions through capability, opportunity, and motivation.

For example, in Asia, unlike in the United States, common social status differences often mean couriers expect to defer to the customer, and might find it inappropriate to say "No" to a customer request. Considering the impact of this action, creating for couriers the motivation, capability, and opportunity to say "No" may be one of the most strategic investments the organization can make.

For example, "opportunity" can be created by adding additional shipping trucks to handle overflow. Couriers could then say "No, I can't take your additional packages now, but I can send someone who can." Thus, a deep and logical analysis of the courier talent pool's aligned actions can reveal improvements in the design of the ground operations system.

Efficiency concerns "How much HR programme and process activity do we get for our investments (such as time and money) in HR programs, practices, and functions?" In the Federal Express example, HR might have benchmarked its efficiency by measuring cost-per-hire, pay-per-employee, or time-to-train. Usually, such benchmarking suggests where costs/time can be reduced, or where volume of HR activity can be increased, without spending more.

The more complete analysis suggests that it might make sense to spend more resources than their competitors, to get the right couriers and dispatchers, precisely because of their strategic importance. Competitors battling to reduce HR expenses by hiring those who will work most cheaply may be overlooking the strategic opportunity that better-qualified workers can produce in these pivotal roles.

PUTTING TALENTSHIP INTO ACTION

The new paradigm of talentship and decision frameworks are effective when they improve decisions that matter most to sustainable strategic success. That requires not just a decision science, but also integrating the decision science within the organization's ongoing processes.

The framework often has its greatest value as a guide to reframing talent issues within existing strategy discussions, budgeting processes, or talent management and performance processes. Our experience suggests that it is often tempting for HR leaders to announce the framework as a "new HR planning model," with a host of forms to be filled-in by HR and business leaders.

Such attempts rarely work well. Instead, the most successful organizations integrate the principles of the framework into their existing decision processes, just as they integrate basic financial models such as EVA and ROIC. The framework provides a way to organize and synthesize data from different organizational systems (strategy, capital budgeting, operational budgeting, financial reporting, product line analysis, etc.) to inform better talent decisions.

Many leaders dub this a "stealth" approach, because it avoids rigidly imposing the decision framework, or any model, as something that must be "completed" or "filled in." Instead, wise managers use the framework to suggest new questions, to reframe existing data and questions, and thus to develop a collaborative point of view about how talent connects with organizational strategic success. In the end, it is about raising the quality of the "conversations" that take place when talent decisions are made. This embeds talentship within the organization's existing processes and provides an unthreatening engagement for the organization's strategic and business leaders.

Many organizations already use models that contain several components of the framework like HC BRidge[R] in Exhibit 1, but organizations often use them only to describe what HR does or intend to do, or to rationalize investments in HR processes after decisions are made. Talentship, like other decision sciences, reveals the power of applying the decision framework when it can have the greatest effect: Before making the decisions.

It is also important to embed this paradigm shift within the processes of HR itself. Talentship has significant implications for virtually every element of human resources, including measurement, strategy, competencies, leadership development, and HR infrastructure. This transition can be daunting if it implies that leaders inside and outside of HR must change immediately.

Fortunately, the new paradigm can begin from many points, and often with the issues with which HR organizations are already engaged. Many organizations have found that they can make significant improvements by working through one HR process at a time. As each process is redesigned within a common decision framework, opportunities for enhanced integration and communication can arise to create new synergy for the organization.

The new paradigm for HR requires more than knowing the business or applying financial and marketing principles to HR programs and services. It requires extending the traditional service paradigm to become accountable for great decisions about talent, wherever they are made, and where they matter most.

This requires building decision frameworks that logically connect decisions about talent to strategic success, and provide the language that HR leaders use to collaborate with, have deeper conversations with, and teach their colleagues to find new answers to strategic questions—answers that reflect a unique perspective based on human behaviour and the principles of talent markets.

This new paradigm based on talentship, a decision science for talent resources, is a significant opportunity for organizations to achieve sustained competitive success through one of their most important resources: the talents of their people. Historically, decision sciences such as marketing and finance were paradigm shifts. The time has come to embrace and build the new decision-based paradigm in human resource management.

Chapter 2

Growth of Economy

CHARACTERISTICS

Since the early 1990s, the world has witnessed the spectacular growth of the economies of China and India (averaging 10.2 and 6.2 per cent annually from 1992 to 2005, respectively). Associated with this growth has been the dramatic development of the service sectors in the two Asian giants. However, a comparison of China's and India's economic structures demonstrates that the role of the service sector (or, the tertiary sector as it is known in China) is very different. In India, the service sector has become the dominant contributor to the Indian economy, accounting for 54.2 per cent of GDP in 2004.

The success in this sector is regarded as"India's services revolution". In China, however, the service sector has lagged well behind the manufacturing sector (or the secondary sector, according to Chinese terminology), though its role in the economy improved slightly in the last 15 years.

From 1990 to 2004, the service sector as a proportion of China's GDP increased modestly from 34.3 per cent in 1990 to 40.7 per cent in 2004. Why have the two countries taken very different trajectories in developing their service economies? What are the implications for future development in the two Asian giants? Which factors affect demand for services in China and India? These are some of the questions which are investigated in this chapter.

To date there have hardly been any comparative studies of services in China and India. However, several studies have focused on the service sector in the individual countries. For example, Gupta and Mohan both examine productivity in the Indian service sector in comparison with other Asian economies. Chanda discusses service trade in the world, particularly in India, and its implications for the World Trade Organisation (WTO) negotiations in services, while Gordon and Gupta present a detailed study explaining India's service growth in the past decade. Examples of studies on China include Li and Hou who produced an edited volume on China's WTO entry and the implications for the service sector, Jiang who edited a book focusing on growth and structural changes in services with some marginal coverage of international comparison, and Li who conducted a comprehensive investigation of China's service sector. Thus, it is the goal of this study to extend the existing literature by comparing the growth in and demand for services in China and India.

First there is a brief review of developments in the service sector in China and India. This is followed by a discussion of the determinants of the demand for services. Three empirical models are employed to examine the factors affecting demand for services internationally, as well as in China and India. Subsequently, the chapter discusses the growth outlook for services in the two countries. The final section summarises the findings.

DEVELOPMENT

Following the conventional classification, an economy is divided into three sectors, that is, agricultural (or primary), manufacturing (or secondary) and service (or tertiary). The agricultural sector consists of farming, forestry, animal husbandry and fisheries. The manufacturing sector is composed of mining, construction and manufacturing. All other economic activities which are not covered by the agricultural or manufacturing sectors are broadly defined as services and hence belong to the service sector.

They include services provided for the agricultural sector, activities associated with the supply of water, electricity and gas, transport and communications, wholesale and retail trade, finance and insurance, business and personal services, and community and social services. Services can be broadly distinguished between two types, that is, old and new. The old or traditional services include petty trading, domestic services, catering and hotel services. The new services are generally associated with communications, business and legal practices, culture, research and education. The latter are tradable internationally and hence are also called tradable services.

SERVICE SECTOR GROWTH

From 1978 to 2004, the service sectors of China and India achieved high annual growth averaging 10.8 per cent in China and 7.0 per cent in India. The difference in these growth rates matches the difference in the rates of GDP growth in the two countries. During the same period, an average annual growth rate of 9.7 per cent was recorded for the Chinese economy compared to 5.4 per cent for India. At the disaggregate level, the structures of the service sector in China and India are very similar.

In both countries, the service sector is still dominated by the traditional or old services, followed by business services (finance, insurance and real estate) and transport and communications. However, the new service sectors are catching up rapidly. From 1999 to 2003, communication services showed the strongest growth in both countries (with an average annual rate of 16.8 per cent in China and 23.9 per cent in India), followed by education (8.6 per cent) and research (11.9 per cent) in India, and real estate (8.8 per cent) and research (8.9 per cent) in China. Though growing rapidly in recent years, research-related services are still relatively small in both countries.

OUTPUT AND EMPLOYMENT SHARES

The development of the service sectors can also be examined by analysing the sectoral shares of output and employment over the national totals in the two countries.

Output shares of the service sector in China and India have grown steadily since 1978. The role of services in the Indian economy is clearly more significant than that in the Chinese economy. Accordingly, since 1990, India's service sector has grown faster (annual growth rate of 7.5 per cent) than the manufacturing sector (6.0 per cent) while the opposite is true in China where the manufacturing sector grew at 12.1 per cent and the service sector, at only 8.4 per cent.

In contrast, the employment share of India's service sector has grown very slowly according to available statistics covering the period from 1983 to 1999, though the absolute figure was much higher than that in China in the 1980s. The employment share of China's service sector has, however, been growing steadily since 1978, in particular since the early 1990s. As a result, China's service sector has absorbed relatively much more labour than India's since the mid-1990s.

In terms of creating new jobs, services have played a vital role in both economies. For example, during the decade of 1995 to 2004, more than 62 per cent of the new jobs created in China were in the service sector while India's services provided about 54 per cent of new jobs in the country from 1994 to 1999. As both countries must relocate a large pool of rural surplus labour, further employment growth in the service sector will be indispensable.

SERVICE CLASSIFICATION

REGIONAL VARIATIONS

In terms of the level of development of the service sector, there is considerable variation across the regions of both countries. "Regions" here are defined according to the official administrative units, that is, they mean China's provinces, autonomous districts and municipalities and India's union states and territories. Several observations about service development among the regions can be made. First, regional development in services follows the national trend. In general, the service sectors at the regional level in India are on an average more developed than those in China. For example,

Beijing has China's most advanced service sector, accounting for 61 per cent of GDP in 2001, while Delhi has India's most advanced service sector with a share of 77 per cent in the same year.

Second, the service sector tends to be more important among relatively more developed regions in both countries. There is clearly a positive relationship between the level of service sector development and GDP per capita in both Chinese and Indian regions. Finally, the service sector plays a more important role in regions where the level of urbanisation is high, such as in Delhi and Chandigarh in India, and Beijing and Shanghai in China.

GROWTH IN INTERNATIONAL PERSPECTIVE

The experience of economic development shows that when a country expands its manufacturing capacity, its agricultural sector declines, and that over time the service sector grows and eventually overtakes the manufacturing sector to become dominant. For example, the share of services in total GDP in 2003 amounted to 71 per cent in Australia, 72 per cent in the United Kingdom and 75 per cent in the United States. This process of change follows the stages of economic development.

However, in comparison with countries at a similar stage of development, China's service sector development is slightly below the average while India's is slightly above it. These are clearly demonstrated which illustrates service sector GDP shares against per capita income among nations with per capita GDP less than USD2000 in 2003. Information at the disaggregate level also implies that services in China and India are still at the early stage of development which is represented by the dominance of the old services, as well as weakness in real estate, education and research services.

The relative backwardness of services in China is also reflected in the role of service trade. In 2003, China was the world's fourth largest merchandise exporter but its service exports ranked only tenth. The share of service exports over total exports in China (9.6 per cent in 2003) was much smaller than the 28.4 per cent in the United States, 32.4 per cent in the United Kingdom, 22.4 per cent in Australia, 13.9 per cent in Japan and 18.6 per cent in the world as a whole during the same period. Not surprisingly, China is currently a net importer of services.

In contrast, India's service exports accounted for 30.9 per cent of total exports in 2003 making the country a net exporter of services according to the World Bank. This is largely due to India's success in information technology (IT) service exports and India's relatively small value of merchandise exports (equivalent to only 12 per cent of China's in 2003). In 2003, India's total merchandise exports ranked 31st in the world but its service exports ranked 20th.

In addition, among the service exports in 2003, the share of finance and insurance amounted to only 1.0 and 1.5 per cent in China and India, respectively, while this share was 7.8 per cent in the United States and 22.6 per cent in the United Kingdom in the same year according to the World Bank.

To sum up, the service sector as part of the national economies of China and India achieved substantial growth in recent decades. However, from an international perspective, China and India are outliers, i.e., India's service sector over-performed while China's under-performed. In addition, new services are still weak in both China and India with the exception of India's IT export sector. At the regional level in each country, the pattern of service development is similar to the national trend. In particular, service development seems to be closely related to the level of urbanisation. These features are further explored in the following sections.

It is argued that service sector growth is determined by several factors such as production specialisation, income level and urbanisation.

These factors are interrelated. As an economy grows, productive activities become more specialised and urbanisation accelerates due to the rising level of income. In the meantime, as a result of the increasing specialisation of production, firms tend to outsource many service activities such as legal, accounting and security services. Some authors call this process "specialisation splintering". The main source of demand for services comes from producers.

At the household level, Engel's law shows that, as income rises, consumption of food and durable goods becomes saturated over time and demand for services such as healthcare, travel, communications and finance increases. Growth in income also boosts demand for away-from-home consumption of food and services. Furthermore, urbanisation contributes to the growth of the service sector in two ways. Unlike farmers who, to some extent, are self-sufficient in service provision, urban consumers rely on commercial suppliers to provide most services. They are also more likely to enter the urban informal sector for employment if there are no job opportunities in the formal sector.

Services account for the lion's share of the informal sector. Thus, urban residents are both consumers and suppliers of services. It is expected that the service sector grows as the level of urbanisation increases. This is confirmed by preliminary analysis of both China's and India's regional data in the preceding section. In addition, the participation of women in the workforce has an impact on service demand as well. More women in the workforce can lead to an increase in demand for services, ranging from babysitting and catering to tuition and beauty treatments. Furthermore, regulatory policies also affect the development of the service sector. A good example is the rapid growth of telecommunications services after deregulation in many countries.

This phenomenon can also occur in other areas such as insurance, banking, health care, etc. Regulatory environments can also affect international trade and foreign investment in services. Finally, apart from the factors discussed above, service sector growth in China and India may also be affected by development strategy and historical experience. Divergence in the latter may contribute to the different role of services in the two countries. For example, India's service industry may have benefitted from the country's early and prolonged linkage with the West, in particular the UK. In the meantime, when the communist government took office in China in 1949, it adopted a biased policy towards the development of heavy industry initially, and labour-intensive manufacturing more recently, while the movement of rural-urban labour was restricted for some four decades and hence entry into the service sector (mainly old services) was very limited. Thus, China's historical development policy was anti-services and this partly explains the underdevelopment of the country's service industry. In the empirical analysis presented in the following section, the factors just discussed are taken into consideration to the extent that quantification is possible.

THE EMPIRICS

To examine the determinants of growth in services in China and India, three models are applied to Chinese provincial, Indian state and cross country databases, respectively. For panel data models, several optional models are considered, e.g., without group dummy (the same intercept for all groups), fixed effect (different intercept for each group) and random effect models (intercepts vary by a random error).

SER in equation (1) is measured as the GDP share of services in a country or region. The choice of the variables (X) in the models is dictated by the availability of data. In the three optional models considered here, X includes per capita income (I), urbanisation (U), service export shares in total exports (EX) and the proportion of women in the total non-farming workforce (W). EX and W are not available for the regions of China and India, and are therefore incorporated in the cross-country model only. The Chinese data cover 31 regions and the period 1993 to 2003. The Indian statistics are available for 31 union states and territories out of 35 for nine years. The cross-country database has one year (2003) data for 93 countries.

The estimated coefficients of both per capita income and urbanisation are positive and statistically significant, implying that both variables are important factors affecting the development of the service sector, especially in China and India. In addition, it is found that external demand also has a positive impact on service development among the countries.

This partly explains the phenomenal growth of IT service exports in India. The cost of services is shown to have a negative effect but the estimated coefficient is statistically insignificant. Thus, further investigation is needed. The findings here are of course subject to qualifications due to data limitations.

SERVICE MARKETING

GROWTH OUTLOOK

Both the Chinese and Indian economies have entered a phase of rapid growth. It is commonly agreed that this growth will last for decades. It is also anticipated that per capita income in both countries will rise over time and that urbanisation will subsequently accelerate. These factors imply that the Chinese and Indian service sectors will expand further. This growth will also be boosted by globalisation. From 2006, China's WTO commitments will allow greater foreign participation in the service sector including telecommunications, banking, insurance, etc.

Economic openness will also create more jobs for accountants, lawyers and other financial specialists. Further economic liberalisation and deregulation in India will ensure sustained growth, including growth in services. Both China and India will also benefit from the WTO's General Agreement on Trade in Services (GATS). Therefore, the growth prospect for services in both countries is bright and will be associated with the following features.

Service sector growth in China will continue while the manufacturing sector remains dominant. Both sectors will show some gain in terms of both GDP and employment shares at the expense of agriculture. According to one set of forecasts, the GDP shares of the agricultural, manufacturing and service sectors in 2020 will be 5.0, 45.8 and 49.2 per cent, respectively, while the employment shares will be 34.2, 22.4 and 43.4 per cent, respectively. By then, China's service sector will be larger than the manufacturing sector. However, China will still have a long way to catch up with the advanced economies in the world. For instance, the service sector in 1997 accounted for 58 per cent of total GDP in Japan, 64 per cent in the US, 53 per cent in Germany and 60 per cent in the UK, while the employment shares were, respectively, 62 per cent in Japan, 74 per cent in the US, 62 per cent in Germany and 72 per cent in the UK. In China, the service sector contributes to national economic growth largely through the shift of labour from agriculture into services. This shift of labour will eventually be replaced by the shift from manufacturing to services.

The current growth momentum in India's service sector will continue in the near future. However, growth in the manufacturing sector will be accelerated. This trend is already clearly demonstrated in the latest statistics. From 1994 to 2003, the manufacturing sector grew at an average annual rate of 6.6 per cent, though the growth rate increased to 8.1 and 9.0 per cent during the financial years of 2004-5 and 2005-6, respectively.

The consequence of such growth is that the GDP shares of both the manufacturing and service sectors will expand at the cost of agriculture. For example, the GDP share of services was estimated to be 57.6 per cent by the end of the 2004-5 financial year.

The dilemma for India at present is that services account for more than a half of GDP but employ less than 30 per cent of the total work force. According to the experience of developed economies as cited in the preceding section, these shares should match. A study of the Pacific Basin countries also shows that without concomitant progress in industrialisation, growth in services in terms of both output and employment is not sustainable. The same argument can be applied to India as well.

In addition, recent expansion of India's service sector, to some extent, is boosted by the IT service exports but, the IT sector employs mainly educated, urban youth, potentially leaving most of India's population further behind. Furthermore, the numbers employed in India's IT sector are relatively small (under one million) and Konana et al. argue that its rapid growth has not generated sufficient linkages with the rest of the economy. Thus, India will need growth in both services and manufacturing.

It is found that the role of services in both China and India has been rising, with China starting from a lower base. Growth has been driven in both societies mainly by increasing specialisation of production, rising living standards and accelerated urbanisation. There are also some non-economic factors which are difficult to quantify in empirical analysis but have played important roles in service development, including biased development strategies in China, India's early linkage with the West and the recent boom in Indian IT exports.

India's service sector is now the dominant contributor to GDP growth but employment absorption is not very high. India's service sector will continue to grow, but the country needs industrialisation even more as millions of rural workers have to be employed. The IT sector is not large enough to significantly affect the growth of the national economy. In comparison with India, China's service sector is lagging behind. Even by international standards, China's service sector is below average and it can be anticipated that services will expand further as Chinese companies outsource their communications, legal and accounting services and as urbanisation accelerates in the coming decades. In addition, the service sector has been the main provider of new jobs in China where there still exists a sizable pool of surplus rural labour.

The first draft was completed while the author was visiting the East Asian Institute, National University of Singapore. The author is grateful to its Director Professor Wang Gungwu, and Research Director Professor John Wong for the generous support provided. He also thanks three anonymous referees, as well as Elspeth Thomson and participants at an EAI seminar for helpful comments and suggestions.

QUALITY GAPS MODEL

Since the end of World War II, jobs in the service sector have steadily increased from a little less than half of all jobs in the U.S. economy to nearly 80%. One of the most important industries found within the service sector is transportation, which in recent years has accounted for over 20% of the nation's gross national product (GNP).

The importance of service quality in any service industry cannot be disputed. Recent political, economic, and technological changes affecting the transportation industry have made service quality a major concern for carriers and shippers alike. Shippers have increased expectations concerning the quality of service they receive and carriers are struggling to meet these expectations. This struggle between shippers and carriers would suggest that there is room for improvement in carrier managements' understanding of how shippers define service quality. This study is an attempt to analyse service quality within the industry and to determine potential areas of improvement within the carrier/shipper relationship.

DEFINING SERVICE QUALITY

A recent Gallup survey indicated that executives ranked the improvement of service and tangible product quality as the single most critical issue facing U.S. managers. But how do we define service quality Zeithaml, Parasuraman, and Berry tried to answer this question as early as 1983. Their research showed that service quality can be defined as the extent of discrepancy between customers' expectations or desires of service and their perceptions of the service they actually receive. These same researchers have developed a model of service quality that focuses on possible communication and control gaps within the "consumer-marketer" system, which can lead to a breakdown in service quality. These gaps have been tested and supported in earlier research using several types of service organizations. Since transportation is such a vital segment of the U.S. service economy, it would seem fruitful to examine the industry to discover whether it suffers from a breakdown in service quality. This study will assess these service gaps and offer solutions to any service quality problems.

SERVICE QUALITY MODEL

The service quality model, as adapted to the transportation industry. The first gap represents differences in expectations between shippers and carriers. This gap indicates the amount of discrepancy between what service shippers actually expect and the service carriers think shippers expect.

Shippers may be saying to carriers, "We want on-time delivery" and carriers may be hearing "We don't want any late deliveries." In this case, there could be a significant difference between what the shippers are saying and what the carriers are saying. If carriers really understand and communicate well with their customers, misunderstandings should seldom occur, and gap one should be quite small.

The second gap illustrated in the model is found only on the carrier side. This gap occurs when management incorrectly translates shipper expectations into service quality specifications. For instance, management may define on-time delivery as any shipment arriving within four hours of the scheduled arrival, while the shipper may expect delivery as scheduled plus or minus two hours.

The third gap is caused when service delivery does not meet service quality specifications. This gap is also found only on the carrier side of the model and represents a breakdown in customer service implementation within the organization. According to Zeithaml, Parasuraman, and Berry, this can be caused by a lack of teamwork (employees and management not working toward a common goal), or confusion surrounding control (who is accountable for quality control). Managers must communicate standards and quality specifications clearly to employees and reward those who implement them.

For ease of analysis, gaps two and three have been condensed into one gap, which will measure the difference between what the carrier believes the shipper wants and what the carrier actually delivers. Should this study reveal a significant gap 2/3, it will be necessary to examine both gaps separately in future studies.

Gap four of the service model is the difference between the service delivered and the external communications from the carrier to the shipper.

For example, if the carrier sales representative promises 90% on-time delivery (external communication), and the carrier delivers only 80% on-time, this difference will appear in the fourth gap.

The two main causes of this gap, according to the model's authors, are lack of horizontal communication (i.e., a breakdown in communication between sales and operations personnel), and the propensity to overpromise (i.e., the sales force making promises to shippers that they know cannot be met). Sometimes salespeople misunderstand the fact that unless operations can deliver on their promises, the entire organization suffers.

Gap five says there is a significant difference between the customers' expectations of the service quality and the quality of service the customer receives. This gap is the direct and indirect result of adverse effects in the four prior gaps in the model. It measures the cumulative impact of the differences in any or all of the first four gaps.

Based on this service quality model, the following hypotheses will be tested in this study:

- *H sub* 1: The service that shippers expect is significantly different from the service carriers believe shippers expect. (Gap 1)
- *H sub* 2: The service that carriers actually deliver is significantly different from the service carriers believe shippers expect. (Gaps 2/3)
- *H sub* 3: The service that carriers actually deliver is significantly different from the service promised to shippers. (Gap 4)
- *H sub* 4: The service perceived by the shippers is significantly different from the service shippers expect from carriers. (Gap 5)

According to the service quality model, if hypothesis one, two, or three is supported by the study, indicating gaps in the shipper/carrier system, hypothesis four will also be supported.

If there are no gaps in the system, then shippers are receiving the service quality that they expect.

SERVQUAL, a multiple-item scale for measuring perceptions of service quality, was the survey instrument used in this study. This scale, which was developed and tested by Parasuraman, Xeithaml, and Berry, was found to have Total-Scale Reliability coefficients ranging between .87 and .90 for the various dimensions of service quality. Details about how the survey instrument was developed and tested can be found in the article cited in the reference section of this chapter. Questions from the survey were used to test the four hypotheses formulated for this study. Each question uses a seven-point, Likert-type scale, ranging from strongly agrees to strongly disagree. The survey was mailed to attendees of a national transportation educational seminar, and members of a national transportation professional organization.

The sample could be considered a "quasi" random sample. It represents a "cluster sample" or cross-section of the industry, and includes representatives of most modal classes, as well as shippers who use various modes within the industry. This method of sampling was used due to the prohibitive cost of obtaining a listing of all carriers in the industry and a comparable listing of all the shippers who utilize the services of these carriers. Of the 950 surveys mailed, 148 usable responses were returned. The 66 respondents employed by carriers and 82 respondents employed by shippers represent a response rate of nearly 16%.

The respondents are representative and knowledgeable about the industry. The carrier respondents have been involved in transportation for an average of 17 years (modal response 10 years) and the shippers have been involved an average of 15 years (modal response 20 years). Job titles reflected in this sample include president/vice president, director, manager, supervisor, and a general category called other.

Transportation modes represented by both carrier and shipper include air cargo, motor carrier (general commodities and household), rail, and sea cargo. The questionnaire was based on the reactions of shippers and carriers to various statements reflecting features of service quality. These statements are based on a survey developed by Zeithaml, Parasuraman, and Berry. The authors describe twenty-two statements that were designed to measure service-provider gaps and their causes. Statements applicable to transportation were selected and adapted to specifically analyse possible gaps in the transportation industry. Data from the questionnaires provided information on what the service shippers expect, carriers perceptions of their shippers' service expectations, the actual service delivered, external communications to shippers, and the service shippers actually perceived that they received.

Dependent and independent t-tests were performed to test the hypothesized differences and to examine the gaps as explained in the service quality model. The results of these tests and their conclusions will be discussed in the remaining portions of this chapter.

To measure the existence of the first gap of the model, shippers were asked to rate what they believe to be important features of an excellent carrier (expected service quality) and carriers were asked to rate the features the carriers were actually providing the shippers (perceptions of expected service). Respondents were asked to assign a number from one (strongly disagree) to seven (strongly agree) for each statement, representing the degree of importance they attach to each feature of service quality.

It might seem logical that, initially, one would expect differences to exist between what the shipper expects and how the carrier understands these expectations. However, the service model dictates that if the carrier is to provide excellent service, it must clearly understand the customer's (shipper's) expectations and then provide service consistent with these expectations. Therefore, we would not expect significant differences between shipper expectations and how the carrier understands these expectations when excellent service is being provided.

It is interesting to note that only six statements showed the expected and perceived results to be significantly different (alpha < .05). Modern equipment, personal and individual attention given to shippers, error-free records, and convenient operating hours were all judged to be more important by carriers than by the shippers. Carriers' delivery on promises was the only statement judged significantly higher by shippers than carriers. This finding emphasizes how important promises are to shippers.

These results may indicate that the first gap in the model is a function of carriers no understanding the importance shippers place on promises. If true, this should be reflected in the remaining four gaps in the model.

The data supports the first hypothesis—that there is a significant difference in expected and perceived service quality. However, this difference is only apparent in six of the nineteen statements, and in only one is the carrier underestimating the importance of a feature of service quality.

GAP TWO/THREE

Gap 2/3 is measured as the difference between what the carriers believe they are actually providing (perceptions of carriers), and what the shippers believe they are actually receiving in service quality (service delivery). However, the shippers are asked not what they want, but what they are actually receiving from their primary carriers. The differences between shipper and carrier responses appear much greater in gap 2/3 than they appeared to be in gap 1.

Not only are responses to all but three of the statements significantly different, the difference favours carriers with the higher mean score in all cases, in all of the statements, the carriers overestimate the quality of service they are providing to the shippers as compared to the shippers' estimate of that same service. It is interesting to note that while the carriers were much closer to the perceptions of what the shippers expect, what the carriers provide is much further from the target. This may be explained in terms of the service quality model as the size of gap 2/3 being much larger than that of gap 1. If this is true, it would indicate that improvement should focus on translating perceptions into quality specifications and standards, then making sure these quality specifications and standards are met.

These data strongly support the second hypothesis of this study: the service quality carriers actually provide is not the same as the service quality carriers believe that shippers expect from them.

GAP FOUR

Gap four of the service quality model is the difference between service delivery and external communications. One of the major components of external communications is the making of promises; carrier sales representatives me promises to their shipper customers. Therefore, this gap is measured as the difference between how both the carriers and the shippers judge how well the carriers keep those promises.

There is a significant difference in both comparisons, particularly the comparison of shippers' expectations versus their actual experiences. It would appear that the data supports the third hypothesis of this study: the service carriers actually deliver is not the same as the service promised.

GAP FIVE

Since all four hypotheses have been supported by the analysed data, it would follow that Gap 5 should also be confirmed by the data. The last gap reflects the cumulative effect of the first four gaps, and represents the difference between the service quality the shippers expect and the service quality the shippers actually receive from the carriers. The size of this gap is critical because it is this Fifth gap that forms the basis of customer dissatisfaction. It is in this fifth gap that the effects of all of the previous gaps are revealed to the shipper in the form of unfulfilled expectations.

To measure the size of Gap 5, the same statements were again given to the shippers. This time the respondents were asked to assess each statement in terms of the service they would expect from an excellent carrier and then in terms of the actual service they receive from their primary carrier.

All but one of the statements show significant differences

between what the shippers want and what they believe they are receiving. Convenient operating hours is the only feature of service quality in which expectation and perception are approximately equivalent. Modern equipment shows a significant difference. However, the negative mean difference implies that the perceived service is actually superior to the expectation.

Results of the remaining seventeen of nineteen statements indicate that shippers' expectations of service quality are higher than the perceived service they are getting from their carriers. This would imply a large gap between service expectation and service receipt, and could arguably be the basis for customer service problems within the transportation industry.

The fourth and final hypothesis of this study was also strongly supported by the data; the service perceived by the shippers is not the same as the service quality expected by the shippers. As the previous three hypotheses were all supported, it follows that support for the final hypothesis would also be found.

The statement with the largest mean difference expectation and perception is "carrier delivers on promises." This may suggest that carrier sales representatives who make promises to shippers that cannot be kept are the major source of shipper dissatisfaction.

Based on the results of the analyses, support was found for all of the four hypotheses proposed in this study. In terms of the service quality model, the data also confirmed the existence of all five theorized gaps in the carrier/shipper system within the transportation industry.

Identifying and understanding the gaps in the carrier-shipper relationship will be a firs step in allowing individual carriers to focus their attention on areas specifically needing attention. Results of this study suggest that carriers understand what shippers expect from a carrier. This implies good communication between the shippers and carriers, a definite strength for the industry.

However, there seems to be a breakdown somewhere on

the carrier side. The carriers know what service quality the shippers expect, and yet it would seem that the carriers are not providing that quality of service to the shippers.

Why is his happening? Do the carriers feel it is too costly, or are they failing to translate what they know of shippers' expectations into measurable quality standards and specifications that their employees can follow? Or are carriers no communicating standards and specifications clearly to their employees? These questions remain to be answered by the individual carrier. The next step in this stream of research is to examine the three gaps to determine more precisely where and why the breakdowns ate occurring.

The size of Gap 5 is consistent with the literature that states that shipper expectations of service quality are not being met. This research suggests that the gap includes many features of service quality that appear not to meet expectations and points to many areas in need of improvement. The most conspicuous offender is in the area of promises and lack of delivery on those promises. By concentrating on keeping their promises, carriers may be able to improve the service quality they offer their shippers.

Because the keeping of promises is important in shaping shipper expectations, a small improvement in this area could make a significant difference in the shippers' perception of service quality. Focusing on this one area may afford carriers dramatic results in their effort to improve service quality. This in turn may translate into a significant positive impact on profits.

Several other features of service quality bear investigation. The data indicate that modern equipment is overrated by the carriers, and is of less interest to the shipper. To better meet shipper expectations, carriers should emphasize other service features in lieu of modern equipment.

Other areas in need of improvement appear to be performing service on time, being more interested in shipper's problems, and error reduction in records. Again, future studies should focus on each of these areas to discover the fastest and most efficient methods for improvement.

SERVICE MARKETING MIX

It is important to note that this study assumes that the respondents are characteristic of the industry as whole, individual shippers and carriers may vary in how well they conform to these results. Nonetheless, it is useful for all carriers to address these issues within their organizations to ensure that the service quality they provide is the best that they can possibly provide, given their individual constraints.

The results are useful to individual carriers in several ways. First, it is hoped that the results will prompt individual carriers to constantly monitor their customers' (shippers') expectations and make sure they know how well they are being met. One way to do this would be to administer the SERVQUAL instrument regularly or develop a questionnaire. The results from the questionnaire could be used in conjunction with customer comments and other sources of information to tell the carrier how well it is doing.

Second, the results of this study should motivate the individual carrier to determine how well its representatives keep the promises they make to shippers. This may entail developing new performance measures to evaluate carrier representative effectiveness. The literature emphasizes how critical keeping promises are to customer satisfaction.

Lastly, the results of this study indicate that from an industry vantage point, carriers can always try to improve the service they provide. As we currently find ourselves in the midst of a significant downturn, excellent service can make the difference in a carrier's survival. Whether the carrier is a trucking company or air freight company or any model, the principles embodied in the service quality model apply to each and every mode. Although the results are combined to reflect the state of service quality in the industry, it must be remembered that individual carriers and modes make up the industry.

By concentrating on the problems disclosed in this study, and evaluating their performance relative to the findings, individual carriers should be able to discover ways to improve their service quality. Findings of future research should help to pinpoint problem areas better and to offer definitive solutions to the improvement of service quality in the transportation industry. This in turn will enhance the profitability of the industry as a whole.

Quality may be the most critical component in satisfying an organization's customer. The elevation of quality as a component of customer satisfaction started with the teachings of Juran, Crosby, Deming and Feigenbaum and continued with the development of programs such as Total Quality, Continuous Quality Improvement and Total Quality Management. Total Quality Management positioned quality as the "meeting or exceeding of a customer's expectations". Further, Garvin and Parasuraman, Zeithaml and Berry put forth the proposition that while quality was multidimensional in nature, it could be enhanced or lost unidimensionally. While this continued focus on quality contributed to a general improvement in products and services, it did not encompass all phases of a business's competitive position. Quality programs helped define which dimensions contributed to a customer's initial perception of quality, however, they did not identify how and whether t he importance of those dimensions could vary; from the customer's initial interest in the provider's product through the product's useful life, i.e. the transaction cycle.

In order to successfully compete in the unending race for a customer's business, in an economic manner, an organization and its management must develop a competitive edge. This edge may come in the form of understanding how a company's customers value a given quality dimension (relative to the other quality dimensions) and when and if that quality dimension can increase (or decrease) in importance over time. Therefore, to clarify understanding of these quality dimensions and their interrelationships, a comprehensive model would provide operational guidelines in these competitive struggles.

In 1987, Garvin proposed a framework to describe overall product quality that consisted of eight separate dimensions. In 1988, Parasuraman, Zeithaml and Berry identified five generalizable factors (dimensions of quality) for service industries. These quality dimensions became the foundation on which much current quality dimensional research has been founded.

A review of current literature identifies a continued separation of product and service quality dimension research, an interest in service quality gaps, the relevance of these dimensions in various industries and industry-specific interpretations of these dimensions. Unfortunately, very little research has been conducted to incorporate these two sets of quality dimensions and, most importantly, no work has been done to determine the effect timing would have on the relative importance of these quality dimensions.

If timing does affect the desirability of these dimensions, then the current quality models are incomplete. This chapter is an attempt to highlight the importance of managing this comprehensive set of quality dimensions over time.

This chapter will integrate the generally accepted dimensions of quality into a general model, which can guide future research related to the interrelationships attributable to a typical transaction cycle. A general model encompassing quality dimensions and their relative importance within the transaction cycle would offer value to both academicians and practitioners. As a last step, a quantitative methodology is offered to operationalize and/or assist in the management of quality.

DIMENSIONS OF QUALITY

Quality has traditionally been viewed as: 1) conformance to requirements; 2) fitness for use; and 3) innate excellence. In 1987, Garvin suggested that product quality is not a single recognizable characteristic; rather, it is a multifaceted characteristic that appears in many forms. He observed eight dimensions of product quality: performance, features, reliability, conformance, durability, serviceability, aesthetics and perceived quality. He also maintained that different users would require different mixes (combinations of varied amounts) of the quality dimensions. In other words, quality is in the eye of the beholder.

In 1988, Parasuraman, Zeithaml and Berry identified five quality dimensions for service industries: tangibles, reliability, responsiveness, assurance, and empathy. These dimensions and the SERVQUAL instrument, from which they were derived, have received considerable support from Carman and Fick and Ritchie and some criticism from Crosby and LeMay.

Crosby and LeMay argued that price should have been added to the quality dimensions derived from the SERVQUAL instrument, thereby forcing choice and stability.

Few transactions can be identified as purely product (no service involved) or purely service (no physical product involved). Rather, most transactions provide a combination of product with accompanying service or service with some product. Goods composed of a combination of both product and service require an evaluation of both product and service quality dimensions. It, therefore, seems reasonable to merge the lists of quality dimensions from product- and service-based research.

To assist in operationalizing this dual list of quality dimensions we are suggesting a time- based approach. We, therefore, are grouping the dimensions by stages in the transaction cycle; i.e., distinguishing between those established at the time of exchange (E) and those added throughout the relationship. The transaction cycle for a product and/or service traditionally starts with the perception of demand (customer needs), moves through product/service design, manufacture and/or provision, transaction and/or sales, use of product (including support services) over its useful life and, finally, through the thought processes that may or may not lead to a repeat purchase from the same source.

The first group of quality dimensions would be established upon delivery (embedded, as it were), while the second group supports the package of delivered product/ services over the usage period in the transaction cycle (supporting). Finally, price, an estimation of the value of all attributes, will cause the customer to choose a level of each quality attribute they need or want, but not more than they want.

By including price into the model, a major problem encountered during previous uses of the SERVQUAL questionnaire would be eliminated. The instability introduced into the SERYQUAL factors, due to their desirability and non-cost, would be reduced by forcing choice. Price causes the buyer to make tradeoffs between the various quality attributes and money.

THE GENERAL MODEL

As put forward in this configuration, three components - those embedded, those supporting and their price -- contribute to customer satisfaction. The provider builds the embedded dimensions into the product before the exchange. This component is divided into two subsets of dimensions.

The first subset -- performance, features, conformance, serviceability, aesthetics and perceived quality -- can be determined at the time of exchange and cannot be augmented after the exchange. The second subset -- reliability and durability -- can only be fully established (measured) after waiting long enough to allow the purchaser to evaluate the product's performance.

The second component, supporting dimensions, is explicitly or implicitly part of the transaction.

It consists of the package of dimensions that:

- Supports the exchange process itself.
- Supports the customer's use of the goods over their life, as covered by the initial transaction.

This set of dimensions may include the appearance of any facilities where the sale and any support services take place (tangibles), willingness to help customers (responsiveness), knowledge and courtesy (assurance), and apparent degree of caring about the customers (empathy). This set of dimensions can and probably will change over the usage portion of the transaction cycle. The value of this set of dimensions can be increased, held the same, or decreased according to the seller's desires and capabilities.

Price, the third component in this model, is established at or before the transaction, representing the product/service's expected value. Whether the price fairly represents the value received by the buyer cannot be ascertained until much later in the transaction cycle, when value received is compared to value expected. The buyer cannot easily modify price after the exchange, so it is established at the time of the transaction, but value is not.

DIMENSIONS OF QUALITY

At the time of exchange information concerning features, aesthetics, perceived quality and tangibles are observable while performance, conformance and serviceability are available with additional effort on the part of the customer. However, reliability and durability are largely unknown for the specific product, but can be identified for the category of product.

Experience with the product or service is required to establish the extent of those latter dimensions. Further, responsiveness, assurance and empathy are generally available but are still under the on-going control of the seller, and therefore are subject to change over time.

The"Customer's Perception of Quality Dimensions over Time" was compiled by a focus group of several academics/ consultants to industry. The level of each dimension's importance and the information available to the customer were determined based on the focus group members' many years of experience. A series of empirical research projects are necessary to determine if these findings are generally held to be true by companies in one or more industrial SEC codes.

Further evaluations of these patterns and their availability would afford insight into the customer's level of satisfaction with its product or service purchases over the expected period of usage. A service provider may be chosen based on evident embedded dimensions, promised supporting dimensions and the price charged. However, repeat business comes from satisfaction

SATISFACTION

The desirability/importance of quality dimensions could

be depicted from the time of exchange to the end of the product/service usability. Each of the three groups of quality dimensions can be classified respectively by: dimensions embedded in the product/service, support dimensions for the product/service, and price. The correct combination and/or level of these three groups of quality dimensions would contribute vastly to any particular customer's degree of satisfaction derived from the transaction.

Certain EB1 dimensions (performance, features, conformance, serviceability and aesthetics) will be prime contributors to customer satisfaction at the time of the transaction due to the immediacy of sight, feel, sound, smell and taste of the product/service itself.

These will diminish as the product loses its feel of newness. EB2 will become more important to the customer's satisfaction as the positive or negative value of the product's reliability and durability play out. The second component (support), depicted by (SP), can increase or decrease in importance due to the continuing presence or absence of the supporting quality dimensions.

QUANTITATIVE METHODOLOGY

Traditionally, managers of the selling firm tend to view quality as inherent (embedded) in the product and/or service being sold. This leads to the mind-set that quality has been established when the product and/or service has been delivered to the buyer. Therefore, if the product did not live up to the advertised, expected levels of quality, the buyer was stuck with it and the seller's reputation "takes the hit".

This chapter takes the position that some of the dimensions of quality are still under the control of the seller and therefore can still be augmented after the point of sale or delivery.

If some of these embedded dimensions do not live up to their billing, then other dimensions can be modified or enhanced to preserve the perception of overall quality of the product and the provider. For example, if an auto manufacturer found that an unusually large percentage (i.e.,

5% versus 1%) of their transmissions developed a significant problem that required those transmissions to be replaced within 75,000 miles of use, the auto manufacturer could do one of four things:

1) Do nothing;
2) Test all transmissions currently in stock before installing (if possible);
3) Remove all the transmissions in stock from the assembly process;
4) Enhance the warranty on all transmissions.

The first option would create a frustrated, angry customer that most likely would not become a repeat customer for the auto manufacturer.

The second and third options would be very expensive, and while the cost of these actions could be passed along to the customer, it may place the auto manufacturer at a price disadvantage. The fourth option would be the best for the auto manufacturer as it would require action only on those transmissions that failed and would preserve their quality reputation while the problem was researched, resolved and incorporated into the transmission's design.

This quick, no-questions-asked service, would create a customer that is confident in the auto manufacturer's ability to handle future problems (they would be WOWED!). The enhanced warranty would represent a modification of a controllable dimension of quality that would allow the auto manufacturer to preserve the customer's perception of the overall quality of the purchased product (automobile) and the provider (auto manufacturer).

Chapter 3

Policies and Role

FUNCTIONS, POLICIES AND ROLES

Historically, it was taken for granted that public services would be delivered by a staff of career civil service employees, working within the structure of centralized public agencies budgeted with appropriated funds.

Today, none of these are true - public programs are more than likely performed by alternative organizations or mechanisms rather than by public agencies; and when public agencies are used, they are more likely to be staffed by contingent workers hired through flexible employment mechanisms rather than permanent employees protected by civil service regulations and collective bargaining agreements.

Purchase-of-service agreements with other governmental agencies and non-governmental organizations (NGOs) have become commonplace. For example, Metropolitan Dade County, FL now provides fire and rescue services to almost every small-and medium-sized municipality in Dade County (the exceptions are the cities of Hialeah, Miami Beach and Miami). 0These arrangements were negotiated because they offer persuasive advantages for Dade County and municipalities. For Dade County, there is the opportunity to expand services within a given geographic area using economies of scale. For municipalities, the arrangement offers the opportunity to reduce capital costs, personnel costs, and legal liability risks. In addition, because fire fighters are heavily unionized, it offers the opportunity to avoid the immediate political and economic costs associated with collective bargaining. As another example, many local governments contract with individual consultants or private businesses to conduct personnel services such as employee development and training.

The use of outside consultants and businesses (hired under fee-for-service arrangements on an "as needed" basis) increases available expertise and managerial flexibility by reducing the range of qualified technical and professional employees that the agency must otherwise hire to provide training.

The costs of service purchase agreements may actually be lower than the same function performed by in-house personnel, in that the government agency pays no personnel costs or associated employment taxes and reduces its own legal liability risks. Privatization is the performance of a formerly public function by a private contractor.

It differs from service purchase agreements primarily in philosophy and scope. While service purchase agreements contract for delivery of a particular service to a public agency, privatization means abolition of the entire public agency, replacing the infrastructure with an outside contractor who then provides all services formerly provided by the public agency.

MECHANISMS FOR DELIVERING SERVICES

Privatization has become commonplace over the past 15 years because it offers all the advantages of service purchase agreements, but on a larger scale. Privatization has become commonplace in areas such as solid waste disposal, where there is an easily identifiable "benchmark" (standard cost and service comparison with the private sector), and where public agency costs tend to be higher because of higher pay and benefits.

But privatization is spreading rapidly in other areas that have previously been almost entirely the prerogative of the public sector: schools and prisons. In 1994, the school board of a working-class Pittsburgh suburb was facing desperate problems. It had the highest tax rate in the county; only one of 40 students who took the Scholastic Achievement Test in the year from June 1993 to June 1994 scored above the national average of 950 on math and verbal test results; and the number of high school graduates plummeted from 225 in 1978 to 60 in 1994.

It sent layoff notices to teachers at one of four schools and hired a Tennessee company to pick its own teachers and run the school. Not surprisingly, it made this decision over strong opposition from unionized teachers and school administrators, who intimated that the purpose was union-busting rather than educational reform. A state court issued an injunction forbidding the contact; the district is considering an appeal.

In 1990 a record of over one million people were incarcerated in federal and state prisons. Despite heavy increases in prison construction, most states have been at capacity for the past five years. Privatization is one option for increasing government performance while attempting to hold down costs.

During the past five years, a number of private corporations have gotten in to the business of managing prisons, halfway houses, boot camps, and detention facilities. These organizations offer elected officials an alternative to public construction and management of prison facilities, which is a soaring cost for most state governments.

Franchise Agreements often allow private business to monopolize a previously public function within a geographic area, charge competitive rates for it, and then pay the appropriate government a fee for the privilege. Examples are private shuttle bus companies in many major cities using vans instead of buses.

The vans frequently duplicate public transportation services by "skimming" riders off of popular bus routes; but municipalities often encourage the procedure because it reduces their own costs, provides some revenue in return, and results in a continuation of a desirable public service. Subsidy Arrangements enable private businesses to perform public services, funded either by user fees to clients or cost reimbursement from public agencies.

Examples include airport security operations (provided by private contractors and paid for both by passengers and airlines), some types of hospital care (for example, emergency medical services provided by private hospitals and reimbursed by public health systems), and some higher education programs.

For example, a state may choose to subsidize a private university by paying it to operate a specialized programme, rather than to assign responsibility and resources for it to a public institution.

It is because of subsidy arrangements that a private institution with a prestigious (and expensive) medical centre, receives more appropriated funds from the state of Florida than does Florida International University, the state university in Miami. Or, local housing authorities may choose to subsidize rent in public housing projects based on tenant income to encourage occupancy by low-income residents. Vouchers enable individual recipients of public goods or services to purchase them from competing providers on the open market.

Recent public opinion has focused on educational vouchers as a possible alternative to public school monopolies. Under this system, parents receive a voucher that could be applied to the cost of education for their child at a number of competing institutions - public schools, private schools, etc. Another variant is housing vouchers as a substitute for publicly constructed and managed housing. These vouchers allow public housing recipients to purchase the best possible housing on a competitive basis from available private landlords.

Volunteers are widely used by a range of public agencies to provide services that might otherwise be performed by paid employees. These include community crime watch programs, which work in cooperation with local police departments. Volunteer teachers' aides provide tutoring and individual assistance in many public schools.

Self-Help is common in community development programs and correctional facilities. Community development programs frequently use residents on a volunteer basis to provide recreation, counseling, and other support services for a community. Frequently, such contributions are required to "leverage" a federal or state grant of appropriated funds. Contrary to the popular image of prisons as vacation resorts, prison inmates are usually responsible for laundry, food service and facilities maintenance.

Regulatory and Tax Incentives are typically used to encourage the private sector to perform functions that might otherwise be performed by public agencies with appropriated funds. The Job Partnership Training Act (JPTA), for example, was a tax incentive-based national system for manpower training that replaced CETA.

CETA (the Comprehensive Education and Training Act, was a federally-funded programme that passed money through to state and local governments for assessment, training and job placement activities. Its successor, the Job Training Partnership Act, offered income tax deductions for corporations that hired, trained and retained disadvantaged employees. The intended effect - human resource development and employment - was the same as with CETA, only the mechanism was different.

Regulatory incentives include the zoning variances granted to condominium associations. Frequently, construction requires variances for roads, parking, waste collection and disposal. In return for these variances, the condominium association agrees to provide many services normally performed by local government.

These include security (if the condominium has a gated entrance), waste disposal, public works (maintenance of common areas), etc. This may seem an unfair arrangement to the residents, who pay both maintenance fees to the condominium association and local property taxes for the same services (which are not provided by the municipality).

But it does explain the increasing popularity among builders and residents of condominiums - their lower unit cost often makes them the only low or moderate housing available; and they would not be approved by local planning councils or zoning boards unless the contractor agreed in advance to require the condominium association to be responsible for services that otherwise would be the municipality's responsibility.

FLEXIBLE EMPLOYMENT RELATIONSHIPS

All of these mechanisms are used for providing public services without using public employees, and in many cases through other funding sources besides appropriated funds. Yet even in those cases where public services continue to be provided by public employees working in public agencies funded by appropriations, massive changes have occurred in employment practices.

Chief among these are increased use of temporary, part-time, and-seasonal employment; and increased hiring of exempt employees (those outside the classified civil service) through employment contracts. These two devices, along with the increased use of outside contractors, have markedly changed the face of the public work force.

Increasingly, employers reduce costs and enhance flexibility by meeting minimal staffing requirements through "permanent" employees, and by hiring "contingent" (temporary, part-time or seasonal) workers to meet peak workload demands. These positions usually offer lower salaries and benefits than career positions.

And employees can be hired and fired "at will" (without reference to due process entitlements of civil service employees, or collective bargaining agreements). Skill requirement of these jobs are reduced by job-redesign or work simplification. Where commitment and high skills are required on a temporary basis, employers may seek to save money or maintain flexibility by using contract or leased employees to positions exempt from civil service protections.

Exempt positions are classified, in that positions must be created and funded before they can be filled. But they are not classified within civil service systems, so their incumbents are not "permanent" (at least, not in the sense of having a property interest in their positions).

Instead, the terms and conditions of these positions are

specified through performance contracts specifying pay and benefits, and limiting the term of employment. While contracts may be routinely renewed with the approval of the employee and the employer, employees may also be discharged "at will" in the event of a personality conflict, a change in managerial objectives, or a budget shortfall.

Frequently, once employees become exempt, they lose their "bumping rights" back into a classified position in the event of a reduction in force (RIF).

Increasingly, managerial and technical employees are hired into these types of contracts. They increase the salary and benefits that can be offered to highly qualified employees, and they enhance managerial flexibility to trim personnel costs quickly, should this be necessary, without having to resort to the bureaucratic chaos precipitated by the exercise of "bumping rights" during an RIF situation.

The impact of these two devices is accelerated by retirement "buyouts," which offer employees close to retirement age an incentive to retire early within a limited period of eligibility ("window").

In a typical example, employees with 17-20 years of service (in a jurisdiction with a 20-year eligibility requirement for retirement) may be offered, for a limited time period of two months, the opportunity to resign and receive retirement benefits equal to those they would have received with three additional years' service.

And the employer may even "sweeten the pot" by offering to pay its share of the cost of employee and family health benefits during the early retirement period (before the employee is eligible for Medicare). If the plan is designed properly so that enough employees retire to save substantially, but enough stay to provide for organizational continuity and skills, both employer and employee benefit.

The employee gets an option to retire early at close to current salary; the employer gets to fill the vacant position with an entry-level employee at a much lower salary. The major drawback for the municipality is unexpectedly large lump-sum payments for accrued annual leave or sick leave.

IMPACT ON THE ROLE OF PUBLIC

The emergence of alternative personnel systems has meant changes in the role of the public personnel manager, and the comparative importance of personnel functions. First, historical traditions emphasize the technical side of personnel management, with less emphasis on policy-related analytical work, relationships with outside organizations and conflicting values. In addition, both employees and line management are seen as clients, and are perceived as being served through the merit system. The traditional department's work includes record keeping and the processing of personnel transactions, especially in smaller government agencies or units.

A more contemporary view emphasizes different activities and relationships. While the traditional functions continue to be important, they are relatively less important than the "brokering" or mediating of conflicts among competing personnel systems.

For example, the modern personnel director might be called upon to prepare cost-benefit analyses of alternative pay and benefit proposals related to collective bargaining with employees in the solid waste department. At the same time, he or she might also be asked to evaluate the comparative feasibility, productivity and cost of privatizing or contracting this entire function out (thus making the collective bargaining analysis obsolete).

Or, since the majority of employees in the department are minorities, the director might be asked to assess the impact of contracting out on the city's overall level of affirmative action compliance.

Modern personnel directors do not work in isolation; rather, they work closely with other officials within their own agency (budget directors, attorneys, collective bargaining negotiators, affirmative action compliance officers, and supervisors) and outside it (legislative staff, union officials, affirmative action agencies, civil service boards, health and life insurance benefit representatives, pension boards, ethics commissions, and employee assistance programs dealing with substance abuse and other personal problems).

Most public personnel departments have moved cautiously into the modern era because of their traditional reluctance to be identified with or become involved in "politics." Yet as their function is increasingly viewed as the development and management of human resource systems involving the reconciliation of value conflicts, they are overcoming this reluctance and working outside the confining environment of the civil service system.

And they are finding that this expanded role brings benefits as well as risks. They are able to bring their expertise to bear on a range of critical human resource issues in a variety of contexts - issues traditional personnel managers might define as falling outside their area of responsibility. For example, they can work with legislators on privatization and benefits issues, with labour negotiators on alternative pay and grievance procedures, and with affirmative action compliance agencies on affirmative action proposals or minority business contracting procedures.

By continuing to assert their central role in the most critical issues of agency management, they are developing not only their own professional status, but the status of their profession.

CHANGES IN JOB DUTIES

The use of non-governmental organizations reduces the absolute number of public employees, thereby diminishing human resource functions of the personnel department - especially those functions related to acquisition, development, and sanction of public employees.

However, it does increase the importance of planning, that is necessary to estimate the type and number of contract employees needed to provide a desired level of service; share in developing contract proposals for outside organizations; and evaluate responses to proposals by comparing costs and services.

The use of volunteers and self-help means that personnel directors work increasingly with citizen volunteers and community-based organizations, much as personnel directors for not-for-profit organizations (community recreation programs, hospitals, and schools) have traditionally used volunteers to supplement paid staff. In these cases, public personnel managers need to become more skilled in recruitment, selection, training, and motivation of volunteer workers.

Flexibility in employment relationships is achieved primarily by the increased use of temporary, part-time, and seasonal employment; and by increased hiring of exempt employees (those outside the classified civil service) through employment contracts.

Use of contingent employment relationships generally means less emphasis on planning and employee development, at least for these employees. The organization is typically staffed at minimum workload levels, and additional employees are added as needed based on fluctuations in workload.

Development of employees (through training, performance evaluation, or motivation) is largely irrelevant. Contingent workers are hired with the skills needed to perform the job immediately. Performance evaluation is unnecessary - if they do their jobs adequately, they get paid; if not, they get fired. Their motivation is financial, perhaps augmented by the chance of being hired into a civil service position if any vacancies become available.

Nor is the sanction function particularly important for public personnel managers with respect to these workers. Of course, employers are required to maintain a safe and healthy workplace; but compliance with the Americans with Disabilities Act, the Family Medical Leave Act, and the Fair Labour Standards Act are not required for temporary, part time, or seasonal workers.

Nor is it at all difficult, from the employers's perspective, to maintain the terms of the employment relationship - "at will" employment means just that. Like political appointments, but unlike their civil service counterparts, "at will" employees have no right to retain their jobs. They can be discharged for any reason, or for no reason, without management having to give a reason or to support it.

CHANGES IN JOB OBJECTIVES

The evolution of public personnel management values and systems has meant corresponding changes in the fundamental objectives of public personnel management. During the development of public personnel management as part of the transition from patronage to merit systems, public personnel management functioned as the champion of merit system principles.

The growth of public personnel management regulations and procedures occurred within the context of civil service systems whose development was characterized by a bipolar dynamic of competition between political patronage appointments (the "spoils system") and civil service appointments (the "merit system").

In this context, the public personnel manager was viewed as a moral guardian responsible for protecting employees, applicants and the public from the evils of the spoils system. This required knowledge of civil service policies and procedures, and a willingness to apply them in the face of political pressure.

During Stage Three, public personnel managers sought to maintain compliance with civil service rules and regulations and limit patronage appointments, and legislators and chief executives sought to maintain bureaucratic compliance, efficiency and accountability through budgetary controls and position management. Through such devices as personnel ceilings and average grade level restrictions, it became the role of public personnel management to control the behaviour of public managers and to help assure compliance with legislative authority.

In effect, it was the responsibility of public personnel managers to synthesize two distinct values (bureaucratic compliance as the operational definition of organizational efficiency, and civil service protections as the embodiment of employee rights). There was tension between them because they were both symbiotic and conflicting.

Taken to extremes, either would diminish the other; in moderation, both supported the concept of a qualified and effective public service that was at the heart of bureaucratic theory and scientific management. During Stage Four, due to a variety of political and economic pressures, the focus of public personnel management shifted to work management as managers and public personnel specialists continued to demand flexibility and equitable reward allocation through such alterations to classification and pay systems as rank-in-person personnel systems, broad pay banding, and group performance evaluation and reward systems.

This trend coincided with employee needs for utilization, development, and recognition. In addition, because this period was characterized by a dynamic and self-correcting equilibrium among four competing values, the role of the public personnel manager involved political (mediating and conflict resolution) skills in addition to technical knowledge.

During this period, public personnel managers functioned as interpreters and mediators of four conflicting values. Intuitively, maintaining an acceptable balance among four conflicting pro-government values was difficult, yet it gave value to the profession because of the political, professional, and technical skills it demanded of personnel managers.

Because the current period (Stage Five) has emerged so recently, the ways in which it is changing the role of the public personnel manager are not yet entirely clear. But it is possible to predict their probable impact. Public personnel managers will still be required to be good managers under Stage Five, but the definition of "good management" is narrow by previous standards.

First, public personnel managers are required, more than ever, to manage government employees and programs in compliance with legislative mandates for cost control. Given the common legislative presumption that the public bureaucracy is an enemy to be controlled rather than a tool to be used to accomplish public policy objectives, public personnel managers in the future may have less opportunity to exercise professional responsibilities in balancing conflicting values. The scope of their authority may be diminished by legislative micromanagement, or the value of cost control may be so dominate as to preclude other considerations - even concern for employee rights, for organizational efficiency, or social equity.

Second, "good management" may in time comprise skills that are more directed to minimizing maximum loss (such as risk management and contract compliance) than to maximizing human development and organizational performance for permanent employees. "People skills" will continue to be important.

For example, public personnel managers will increasingly be responsible for developing and managing a range of public employment systems for contract, temporary, and "at will" employees. They may be required to work increasingly with volunteers and community-based not-for-profit organizations that increasingly constitute the social safety net by which the value of community responsibility is carried out.

Civil service and collective bargaining continue to be important, for many public employees (particularly school teachers and administrators, police and firefighters) are still covered by union contracts and collective bargaining agreements. But risk management, cost control, and management of other types of employment contracts will become more important than ever. In this sense, substituting a calculating perspective for an optimistic view of the joint possibilities for organizational productivity and individual growth represents a narrowing of the public personnel manager's perspective.

It is noteworthy that the search and screen process for the personnel director of a mid-sized Florida city resulted in the highest ranking being given to a person with no previous civil service personnel experience. Instead, this person was a labour attorney with extensive private-sector experience negotiating and administering employment contracts with outside vendors and contractors.

It is evident from this analysis that the field of public personnel management is turbulent and transitional. Some traditional public personnel departments continue to function as technical staff agencies within an environment characterized by agreement on values. This role is most common for personnel departments or civil service boards operating within civil service systems in homogeneous political environments.

More progressive departments might be called upon to take a more active role in designing, implementing, or evaluating human resource management systems within an agency that operates in an environment characterized by disagreement on personnel systems and values. A good example of this type of environment is the personnel systems found in some state court systems.

First, state judges are elected, and appoint their primary administrators. Second, some court administrators are appointed "at will" to exempt positions by the Chief Judge. However, these are not political appointments, in that applicants must meet stringent qualifications. Third, some court employees may be covered by county civil service systems (including probation officers).

Fourth, some court employees (such as process servers) are officers of the court because they discharge official functions, yet they are paid on commission by private attorneys. Fifth, family law cases are often assigned to court-appointed mediators selected at random and paid by the court as independent contractors. It is important to recognize that the court administrator is the chief administrative officer, responsible among other things for budget and personnel management. This means dealing with multiple levels of government, multiple funding sources, and multiple personnel systems simultaneously.

These activities usually require the use of analytical human resource management information systems. For example, they might conduct analyses like the cost of absenteeism, sick leave abuse, and fringe benefits for the agency. They might distribute and evaluate ratings on employee performance evaluation systems to measure their effect on productivity.

They might experiment with new techniques for selecting employees (such as assessment centres), or new techniques of job design intended to meet employee needs and increase employee productivity (such as job sharing or flextime). They might be responsible for developing policies and procedures for substance abuse testing; for developing proposals for establishing EAPs (employee assistance programs) to help employees maintain productivity while resolving personal problems; or for encouraging QCs (quality circles), groups of employees responsible for proposing and implementing changes in procedures to make the organization more productive.

They might be called upon to monitor the frequency of turnover in various departments, "cost out" proposed changes in pay and benefits, and monitor the compliance of benefits contractors with previously negotiated contracts.

CHANGES IN REQUIRED KNOWLEDGE, SKILLS AND ABILITIES

Traditional public personnel management requires that personnel directors know the laws and regulations that control practices within a particular system, as well as the techniques used to perform personnel functions within that system. For example, traditional civil-service-oriented personnel management requires knowledge of civil service rules and regulations (such as competitive examination procedures, or how to select from a list of eligible applicants), as well as how to develop and administer examinations, write job descriptions, administer pay and benefit programs, and process personnel actions.

Contemporary public personnel management requires these skills and more. It requires a knowledge of public personnel management techniques, an understanding of historical developments in the field, and the ability to resolve ethical dilemmas among competing values under conditions of change and uncertainty.

Personnel rules and procedures are not value-neutral; rather, they are the implicit or explicit implementation of a particular public personnel system (or compromises among several such systems). This means that each selection or promotion decision must be viewed not merely as a technical exercise, but as a case that reflects and exemplifies this historical conflict over alternative values, power and public personnel systems.

Public personnel directors must be sensitive to the need for administrative systems to be responsive to legitimate political values and public participation in governance, especially in local government. These kinds of changes inevitably challenge the shield that the rhetoric of "merit" has provided the traditional manager.

Now there is no escaping the political pressure personnel managers must face. They work under consent decrees and with unions that traditionally have set barriers to hiring women and minorities. At the same time, they are expected to respond to their political leaders while maintaining the integrity of the civil service system they oversee. Yet they have no guidance from within the traditional civil service system for how to integrate these increasingly insistent and conflicting demands.

Given that the emergence of two new alternative public personnel systems has brought about changes in the duties, objectives, and skills required of personnel managers, it might be useful to assess how well prepared they consider themselves to function in this new environment. What follows is the results of a focus group discussion held among 19 public managers and officials, primarily public personnel managers, to discuss their use of alternative systems, their actual and desired extent of involvement in choosing these strategies, the amount and source of their information about these systems, and desired topics for further training. A complete focus group questionnaire and copy of the responses is provided at the end of the chapter.

Of the 19 participants, the typical participant was a local government personnel director with a graduate degree, working for an agency with over 500 employees. All of the participants' employers use some alternatives to traditional civil service systems, with purchase of services from outside vendors being universal. Most use purchase of service from other government agencies, privatization, volunteers, self-help, and regulatory and tax incentives. Some use franchise agreements and subsidy arrangements. Almost none use vouchers.

In the future, most respondents predict about the same usage of part-time civil service and exempt employees, less usage of civil service employees, and more usage of full-time exempt and contract employees. The typical respondent reported that they had shared responsibility, though not primary responsibility, for choosing these alternatives to civil service. This was consistent with their expectations. Most reported that the most important decision-maker had been elected/appointed officials, followed in second place by managers and budget directors, with human resource directors ranked third.

Most participants reported that they needed some or much information on these alternatives to function effectively. Their main sources of information are professional associations and journals, classes and seminars, and other human resource professionals. This is as they think it should be. But a majority reported having received no formal training on the subject during the past two years. Those who reported receiving formal training indicated that it was for the most part self-initiated, and paid for by themselves rather than their employer.

When asked what topics should be covered, they responded as follows: Because civil service at some level will always be present, some comparison of benefits and costs with those of alternative personnel systems is necessary. Public personnel managers should be taught how to deal with political and union opposition to changing a civil service system, including getting rid of it as an option. Elected and appointed officials should also be trained on civil service systems and alternatives.

Beyond civil service, personnel managers need training in how to select outside contractors and administer outside contracts. Training should include more detail on actual case examples. Closer to home, more attention should be given to alternatives for performing the human resource function itself.

Outside vendors should be trained in how to prepare responses to RFPs (requests for proposals) developed by government agencies.

Most importantly, this issue should be looked at from all angles with a view toward long term objectives for a viable system, not a bandaid or quick fix. These findings are quite preliminary, consisting as they do of the results of one focus group in one locality. However, some conclusions seem evident, at least as working hypotheses for further study. First, local governments' use of alternatives to civil service delivery of public programs is already widespread, and expected to become more prevalent in the future.

Second, as they expect, public personnel managers have considerable involvement in the choice of these alternatives. Third, because formal training in public personnel management is usually based around civil service systems and collective bargaining, public personnel managers do not consider themselves adequately trained in this area.

Fourth, existing organizations and mechanisms (particularly other human resource managers, professional associations, training, and professional journals) are considered sufficient for this training, though most have not had training in this area.

Beyond this, it is clear that public personnel managers themselves are aware that the change to alternative personnel systems is a significant choice for public agencies.(15) They wish that elected and appointed officials, those they consider as having the primary role in making these decisions, had more training and insight into the comparative advantages and disadvantages of alternative public personnel systems, including civil service.

Chapter 4

Organizing Management Functions

The functions, functional change, and human potential of lower-level and middle-level managers (LMM) have recently received increased attention in conceptual and empirical analysis. There are various reasons for the special attention devoted to these organization members, who have traditionally been neglected by microeconomic research.

Thus, changed economic, technological, and sociopolitical factors have induced firms to formulate new strategic aims and to secure their implementation through functional policies. LMM play a dual role in these processes of strategy formulation and, especially, implementation. They are both "change masters" and the recipients of change.

They are the targets of top management's human-resource management (HRM) measures, and at the same time actors, initiators, and sponsors of HRM measures applied to their own subordinates. Caught in the middle, they have the difficult task of mediating a firm's policy decisions downward through the hierarchy. As the purveyors of ideas and information from new strategies, they run the risk of setting into motion aggravating processes of change with regard to their own traditional functions and their accustomed work situation. As the persons affected by change, they are often an important source of resistance to change in the phase of strategy implementations. Thus, uncooperative LMM are often blamed when strategies, once formulated, are—so goes the almost universal complaint—not implemented, or are found to be incapable of implementation. Consequently, the buildup, cultivation, and development of the human potential of LMM, and especially the development of the qualifications needed for change, are of decisive importance for successful implementation of strategic goals. The human potential of LMM is in this respect a strategic success factor. Various theses on the content and the extent of the functional change of LMM have been described in the literature. Some authors expect—especially in connection with the increasing networking of information technology in and among organizations—not only a functional change, but a loss of function for LMM.

Accordingly, managerial capacity becomes partly superfluous on these levels, or at least undergoes a quantitative thinning out. Nonetheless, those managers who remain are regarded as an important human resource whose relative importance for the growth of a firm is increasing. In most cases, however, it is expected that freed manager capacities will be utilized for expanded and/or new jobs, and not eliminated. This presumption is supported by our own empirical studies.

The two approaches, however, have two points in common that are of relevance for the present study: (1) in both approaches, LMM are regarded as valuable human potential by firms, a potential that is indispensable in order for a firm to be able to cope successfully with future problems; (2) a functional change is accordingly expected for these managers, and that change will place new demands on the activity they perform in their jobs. Against this background, the acquisition of new qualifications by LMM for successfully coping with the new challenges becomes critically important. An analysis of the change of function and the consequent qualification needs for LMM was the object of an international empirical research project whose results are presented in the following sections.

CHANGES IN THE REQUIREMENTS PLACED ON LMM

PROJECT DESIGN

The results presented below are part of an international

comparative study in six European countries: the United Kingdom; Denmark; Holland; France; Italy; and Germany. The project was titled: Study on changing functions of lower and middle management.

It was financed by the European Foundation for the Improvement of Living and Working Conditions, located in Dublin. This foundation is an autonomous EC institution established by the Council of Ministers in 1975 to furnish the EC Commission with scientifically based proposals for improving living and working conditions in the EC member nations. The set of assumptions guiding research (agreed upon by the international research team) was structured as follows: changed background conditions for economic action require new firm strategies; the implementation is dependent on a set of measures and changes regarding organizational structure and personnel policy.

This process of development of organization and personnel entails changes in the functions and requirements of LMM, which in turns puts pressure on these managers to acquire new qualifications (new qualification needs). The acquisition and practical application of new qualifications are to be secured through appropriate personnel development (PE) and organization development (OE) measures.

Among the essential external factors are economic (competition), technological (microelectronic revolution), and sociopolitical factors (transformations in values, for example).

The purposes of the research project were:

- To describe the changed demands and functions of LMM and to identify the possible causes of this change.
- To describe personnel and organizational options that are realised or planned for these levels of management in firms.

The acquisition and application of functionally necessary new qualifications by LMM, and how this process is conducted within the firm is regarded in this context as a crucial precondition for ensuring flexibility and efficiency in firms. The following is a report on the German part of the study.

DEMARCATION PROBLEMS

Since there is no generally valid demarcation between "lower-level," "middle-level" and "top-level" management, the conceptual limitations were established as guidelines for our study. The basis for demarcation between the upper- and middle-level management is the legal definition of a managerial employee.

Since management functions are in some cases clearly exercised in the staff domain, all staff workers with responsibility for personnel management are classified as middle-level management in accordance with the above definition. Lower-level management is restricted to employees with only one hierarchical level under them.

The results of the interviews, however, revealed that in practice the demarcation of management levels is sometimes made along these lines, sometimes along others, and sometimes is not made at all. Thus, in many firms the first and second levels of the hierarchy are regarded as top management when they work very closely together; in smaller firms, on the other hand, top management usually comprises only the executive level. A distinction between middle-level and lower-level management is generally not made. A comparison of the interview results thus proved to be extremely problematic because of these different defining criteria. It was therefore necessary to diverge from the original standard guidelines and conform to the practices specific to each firm.

CHANGE IN STRATEGIC GOALS, AND IN OBJECTIVES BEARING ON ORGANIZATIONAL STRUCTURE AND PERSONNEL POLICY

CASES AND METHOD OF STUDY

During the first phase of the empirical investigation, eleven case studies were made. The most important precondition for including a firm in the sample was that information either on its management problems or on how it approached such problems had to be available as far as it was relevant to the questions posed in the study.

The pertinent specialized literature, specialized periodicals, and the economic press were used as sources for this. Cases discovered in a literature search and regarded as interesting were selected so that the sample on the whole satisfied the following criteria:

- To include a range of firm sizes.
- To have a sample that was a representative cross-section of over several economic branches.
- If possible, to include several firms within one branch, in order to permit comparison.
- To include at least one multinational firm.

Eleven firms were chosen for the study on the basis of these selection criteria: three from the service sector; four from the electrical industry; three from the automobile industry; and one from the chemical industry. Semistruct-ured interviews with personnel managers were carried out in each firm (a total of fourteen); these managers were drawn from the top or the second highest management level.

Since the LMM problem situations have not yet really been defined and formulated by research, and hence there are no standardized research instruments available, we chose an explorative method to reconnoiter the problem (comparative case studies).

The most essential aspects of changes, both external and internal to firms, that result in new functional and qualificational requirements for LMM are shown. Increased competition is most often mentioned among the changed background conditions of a firm's business operations.

Two aspects should be distinguished: first, markets are becoming increasingly internationalized, and this is associated with intensified competition; second, on the other hand, there is a constraint to compete because of growing saturation on particular markets. These two aspects are not mutually exclusive. Further, rapid technical progress and the associated rapid obsolescence of products (especially in the data-processing industry) are stressed. Competition-related pressure to innovate grows as the time between technical innovation shrinks.

As for socially relevant factors, it is noteworthy that the growing ecological consciousness among the population (e.g., within and toward the automobile industry, the chemical industry, etc.) was mentioned several times as a relevant background condition for business operations. The transformation of values that has long been discussed in the literature, and is particularly important for shaping the managerial and supervisory structures and processes within an organization, is now ascribed relatively minor importance by the managers surveyed.

Change in economic, technical, and social factors entail new strategic goals for firms, with a view toward establishing as close a connection as possible between external change and organizational activities, and, over the long term, toward ensuring company survival.

Among these goals are:

- Growth of the firm, also internationally (especially in the automobile industry, data-processing firms, media firms, paint manufacturers);
- A growing orientation toward the market and toward customers (especially in the service branches);
- Securing technical advantage over competitors (automobile and data processing industries); and
- Improvement in organizational and individual flexibility (this is mentioned as a strategic goal by highly bureaucratized firms especially).

Changes in organizational structure and personnel policy that alter the internal structures and processes of control, operations management, and personnel management, are mentioned particularly as top priority for implementing strategic options.

The organizational level: There is a discernible tendency toward decentralization in many firms. Decentralization is intended to facilitate the delegation of responsibility, which is desired by all the firms studied. Delegation of responsibility is supposed to relieve the burden on top management, and to enlarge the tasks and responsibilities of lower- and middle-level managers.

The motivation and job satisfaction of those concerned should thereby be enhanced. Further, delegation of responsibility should increase a firm's flexibility, since it should allow decisions to be made more quickly and competently. The delegation of tasks and responsibilities also increases proximity to the customer, especially in the service sector. Most of the firms studied are striving for a flatter, less drastic hierarchy, with a view toward adapting organization to the changed situation. The view is heard in some cases that the elimination of one hierarchic level could combat incrustation in bureaucratic structures.

The personnel level: Firms are trying continually to adapt the management capabilities of their managers to the changed demands. Personnel-oriented management is a central principle of management in almost all firms. For managers, this means being required to give more attention to the expectations of those they manage.

In all cases we found that firms are ascribing increasing importance to organizational culture and corporate identify. The end pursued with these two concepts is to bind employees and relevant groups outside the firm more tightly to their organizations. Managers' identification with the firm must especially be strengthened.

Another essential focal point is improving information policy for all employees. The presumption is that the better informed the employee, the more he or she will be inclined to identify with the goals of the firm. The informed employee is an essential building block of the desired corporate identify. In one firm, an open-door philosophy, including top managers as well, is practiced.

There was also a discernible tendency in the firms studied for managers' attitudes toward work and/or toward other areas of life (family, mobility, etc.) to be an increasingly important hiring criterion in personnel recruiting. Adequate specialized qualification is now regarded only as a basic precondition for hiring new employees.

To sum up, we can say that from the standpoint of the managers surveyed, the increasing dynamics of technical economic development and the associated heightened competition on markets are the most salient background conditions of business operations; the strategic objectives and the requisite molding of a firm's internal structure must be oriented to these conditions in the future. The results related to these central points in the German study are considerably similar to the assessments of British, French, Dutch, Danish, and Italian managers who were asked the same question.

This development may be interpreted as an increasing loss of practical market certainties. Coping with the related socioeconomic risks and uncertainties becomes a central challenge to organizations and their members, with a view toward ensuring the organizations' further development and their ability to survive.

The changed background conditions heighten the requirements placed on the control functions of persons and organizations. This development is discernible in the search for new organizational forms and new hiring and behaviour models for an organization's members, which altogether tend toward debureaucratization and increasing individual flexibility, with an eye toward increasing the ability to act and react, with regard to the market and society (i.e., a firm's problem-solving potential).

The principles of mass production, organized bureaucratically to achieve efficiency, are losing more and more of their problem-solving powers, given the new, changed background conditions of economic action. The new quality of the demands on the control functions of firms is also evident in the fact that the ensuing problems of practical economic development, the externalization of which was long regarded as the expression of the capital logic of an individual business, are now themselves becoming an economically conditioned (because they are dependent on the ups and downs of the market) object of a firm's management (e.g., in ecologically sensitive branches such as the automobile and chemical industries).

It is to be expected that new qualification needs for LMM will arise with the changed external problem situation and the internal firm structures caught up in a process of change. In addition to specialized skills, which all the respondents regarded as a precondition for assuming management positions, attention is focused especially on social and communicative skills.

The personnel managers of all eleven firms surveyed and the middle-level managers themselves see particular deficiencies in these skill domains. The connection between external change, strategic objectives, structural change, and the qualificational needs of LMM will now be illustrated on the basis of four selected examples.

DIMENSIONS OF THE QUALIFICATION NEED

CHOICE OF CASES AND METHOD OF STUDY

Four of the eleven cases in the first research phase were chosen as further intensive case studies to explore certain aspects of the need and acquisition of qualifications. Group discussions and semi-structured interviews were carried out with a total of forty-nine LMM.

The following questions were taken up in each group discussion:

- What new or changed qualifications other than those you now have do you think you will need in the upcoming years?
- What difficulties do you see in the acquisition and application of the new qualifications?

Our questions concerning the group were as open as possible to spur the participants to intensive collaboration. We were able to structure the group discussions roughly in the same way in all three firms. However, the different compositions of the groups must be taken into account in comparing the results:

The managers of the paint manufacturing company were especially sensitized to the importance of social skills, compared with the other respondents, because of prior business experience (network management). The strong heterogeneity of the groups showed up in a positive way, thus contributing to obtaining a differentiated response to the questions.

All the members of the credit institution have the same function (branch managers) and belong to the same hierarchical level. Compared to the firm structure, this random sample is nonetheless a relatively representative segment of the lower-level and middle-level management of the firm. The questions were answered relatively summarily.

The composition of the group from the computer manufacturer displayed no relevant distinctive features. The participants belong to different functional spheres and different hierarchical levels. There was also nothing exceptional as regards the group's cooperation.

Two other questions were asked in the semistructured interview over and above the themes touched upon in the group discussion. These questions had to do with how the needed qualifications were identified, their acquisition within the firm, and organizational support in acquiring and using these qualifications.

"Major" problems, however, that went beyond the individual situation, often punctuated the group discussion, whereas in the interviews the individual, everyday situation of the respondents was stressed. Questions concerning the difficulties in acquiring and using new qualifications elicited responses asserting a lack of learning skills, especially in the interviews.

This may be due to the fact that this point was in particular need of explanation, and to the social control at work during a group discussion. The complaint of "eternal yesterday," which often cropped up in the interviews, is much more difficult to put fort within a group of colleagues.

On the other hand, there is a considerable convergence of methods, especially in regard to qualificational needs and difficulties in acquiring and using them, inasmuch as these needs and difficulties went beyond the particular firm and were common to a certain extent to all. We will therefore forego presenting these points separately to help keep things in perspective.

The results of the studies show that the interviewed managers expected a multileveled qualificational need because of changes both internal and external to the organization, and not in the last instance in regard to the internal EC market in 1992.

In addition to peculiarities specific to particular firms, qualificational needs that go beyond the particular firm are discernible for LMM, listed below in order of priority:

- Development of social skills.
- Development of strategic knowledge, strengthening market-oriented and customer-oriented thinking.
- Acquisition and broadening of knowledge of languages.
- Development of systematic, holistically oriented thinking.
- Development of individual adaptability and flexibility.

In terms of the first requirement, development of social skills, one outstanding result of the study is that the requirements concerning social skills are ranked in all firms as having the greatest importance for the future. The acquisition of comprehensive social skills thus exceeds all other domains in importance.

The term "social skills" refers broadly to the ability to communicate human closeness and emotional warmth in dealing with colleagues, and so to stress the human side of the job. Employee-oriented management and the ability to communicate, with one's superiors as well, are also regarded as important.

The managers of the different firms repeatedly stressed the necessity and importance of teamwork. Within one of these organizations, however, the question comes up to whether social skills are learnable, and if so, to what extent. The view is expressed that an individual must possess a willingness to assume social responsibility, and that this is a basic precondition that cannot be learned.

In the transport firm, the assumption of responsibility and the willingness to "go into other people's problems" are classified, for example, in this domain. Ability to encourage employees, and to counsel them, as well as to mediate in cases of conflict, is regarded as important in the sphere of interaction between superiors and employees.

Concerning the second requirement listed above—development of strategic knowledge, strengthening of market-oriented and customer-oriented thinking—an enhanced market orientation is regarded as important by all the surveyed manager groups. It is necessary in order to be able to recognize and make better use of available opportunities.

To achieve a better market orientation, the credit institution, for example, is planning certain complementary structural changes: the branches will henceforth be run as profit centres. The transport firm has already completed a reorganization (decentralization).

The respondents working for the paint manufacturer, the credit institution, and the transport firm all stressed that strategic capabilities and skills, as well as strategic thinking, will have a larger role to play among management tasks. The acquisition of these skills will therefore be a focal point in the near future. The respondents of all firms pointed to the necessity of thinking more in international dimensions. Thus, for example,international standards, as well as divergent trends on markets, must be taken more into account in product development.

Because of the changed social background conditions (e.g., the influence of citizens' action groups, a greater environmental consciousness, and legislative restrictions on firms), organizations today interact much more intensively with various strategically relevant interest groups.

The managers of the computer manufacturer especially stressed that intensive consideration of the field of force between a firm and its environment is becoming increasingly important for individual managers as well. Since it must be assumed that the demands made of a firm, and hence of its employees, by different social groups will continue to grow, the respondents regarded the ability to deal with these demands as an important skill requirement in the future.

The third requirement—the acquisition and broadening of knowledge of languages—is included because deficient knowledge of foreign languages is mentioned as an important problem in all firms. This does not seem so egregious where Europe 1992 is concerned, but it does show that there is a an elementary need for better language skill qualifications, given the essential changes that may be expected to take place at that time.

Regarding the fourth requirement—the development of systematic, holistically oriented thinking—thinking in terms of contexts and relations is regarded as a new important requirement, especially in the paint manufacturing and computer manufacturing firms. The complexity of tasks is increasing so abruptly that an intelligent approach is only possible if the overall relational context is taken into account. This also requires of managers an ability to think in networks, that is, to include other domains and departments of the firm in the planning and execution of tasks.

In terms of the fifth requirement—the development of individual adaptability and flexibility—on the whole, the respondents of all firms noted that the requirements with regard to individual mobility and flexibility will increase for a variety of organizational contexts. A continuous adaptability to altered situations, a fundamental willingness to learn, and geographic mobility, are some of these requirements.

The assessment shows that technical and specialized know-how are not regarded as top-priority qualification needs. It must be presumed that the relative importance of these qualifications for LMM will decline. Nonetheless, these qualifications are still regarded as important and are considered by the surveyed managers (and personnel directors) to be part of an indispensable basic knowledge.

The meeting of this qualificational need will also be a precondition for the success of European market integration. These integrational trends can be expected to further accelerate technical economic development, and heighten the demands placed on the control functions of organizations and their employees as the protective functions of national markets and the barriers to market entry are gradually dismantled. Social and strategic skills, knowledge of languages, and flexibility must then be seen as necessary individual and organizational prerequisites for dealing competently with openings and networkings in markets as well as in society.

These results are also confirmed by a study done by the personnel consulting firm of Korn and Ferry. These international consultants have analysed the national strengths and weaknesses of managers. Compared to an "ideal Euromanager profile," German managers are weak with regard to team orientation, thinking in international contexts, and motivational and communicative skills. Personal characteristics such as mobility, tolerance, humour, creativity, and understanding of other cultures are also too weak. German managers also have an inadequate knowledge of languages. In light of these findings, the broad agreement with the diagnosis of the managers we surveyed is noteworthy.

CONSEQUENCES FOR HUMAN-RESOURCE MANAGEMENT

The empirical findings make it clear that developing a systematic and coordinated concept for the development and cultivation of the human potential of LMM is a top-priority task, if the changed economic background conditions are to be addressed with maximum effectiveness and if strategic objectives are to be realised. Remarkably, our studies, as well as Anglo-American studies, show that the LMM themselves—who are directly concerned—consider the need for such a concept more urgent than do top-level managers. This presumably explains why, as is often lamented, it is so difficult for new human resource management concepts to gain headway among top management.

The results of our study should therefore serve as an orientation for the top management of firms. The concept of human-resource management, currently the focus of considerable attention in academic discourse, can therefore provide useful guidelines for a firm's personnel policy and for relevant decision making.

Human-resource management is an American concept of resource-oriented personnel management that has recently entered into the German dialog. The view of personnel as potential, as human capacity, and not merely as a cost factor—that is, as a potential that must be systematically planned, maintained, and developed—is central to HRM. But it has been an integral component of German personnel management theory for a long time as well.

Over and above the rhetoric about recognition (the individual is in the centre point of the firm), the HRM concept displays some structural characteristics that are novel for German personnel management theory, at least regarding the clarity of its formulations, and that hence can be useful for the purposes of the present study.

The special characteristics of the HRM concept are:

- Measures of personnel recruitment and development, that hitherto have been separate, are systematically interlinked.
- HRM is locked into a firm's strategic and structural decisions.
- Human resources is seen from the perspective of general management, not from the perspective of some functional sphere (e.g., personnel department).
- Assembly-line management is incorporated into HR responsibility.

The first characteristic alludes to the need for better coordination between the domains of traditional personnel and organizational work (this is the consistency equals efficiency hypothesis). An avowal by top management of the benefit of more participation requires relevant measures of personnel selection, further education, remuneration, and job structuring. Further opportunities for participation for middle-level managers should not be countermanded, for example, by an objective loss of function.

A reciprocal linkage and temporal parallelism of decisions concerning corporate strategy, organizational structure, and human-resource measures is necessary to ensure that the successful implementation of strategies does not founder on the deficient human-resource potential of the organization. This perspective has also recently been assimilated by German personnel-management theory.

One task of strategic human resource management is, in the view of the authors, to derive, from in-firm strategies and business units strategies, personnel policy guidelines and measures to serve the strategic goals.

The strategic character of these human resource measures is reflected, for example, in the fact that they are geared not to short-term requirements (adaptational measures), but rather to the growth of success potentials and the creation of the personnel prerequisites for this.

The linkage between personnel policy (HRM) measures and changes in organizational structure also reflects the interconnection of measures for organizational and personnel development, repeatedly called for in the literature, that represent the preconditions for successful change.

To ensure that HRM has a strategic orientation, this function must be integrated into the sphere of responsibilities of top management. This should counteract the additive, uncoordinated planning and realization of personnel policy that is ubiquitously observed at the firm level (e.g., policy confined to particular departments or functions). Operational HRM measures, however, are (again) the task of every line manager.

In addition to the structural characteristics of the HRM model,. which go beyond the traditional approaches of personnel management, four central policy areas may be identified with regard to content.

- Employee influence (participation philosophy);
- Human-resource flow (personnel recruitment, use, and dismissal);
- Reward systems (incentive, remuneration, and participation systems); and
- Work systems (job structuring).

These policy areas are influenced by the interests of participants in the organization (stakeholders), shareholders, management, employees, trade unions, the government and the community, as well as by situational factors, such as employment structure, business strategy, management philosophy, labour-market conditions, trade-union requirements, technology, laws, and societal values.

Human-resource management decisions have both immediate organizational outcomes (commitment, competence, congruence, cost-effectiveness) as well as certain long-term consequences (individual well-being, organizational effectiveness, societal well-being).

Beer et al. stress especially the differential efficiency of the integrating coordination and consistency of the four political policy fields among themselves and with the business strategy. It is clear from the standpoint of strategic HRM that HRM measures must be applied complementarily to ensure the buildup and development of human potential.

INTEGRATION OF HRM MEASURES

From the standpoint of the managers interviewed in our study, the deficient integration of discrete measures of personnel policy into a tenable general concept is a weak point that makes the requisite acquisition and use of new qualifications more difficult. The following difficulties, which are beyond the particular firm, or beyond our particular case studies, reflect this:

- Lack of support from top management;
- Lack of career planning; and
- Lack of incentives.

The first problem, the lack of support from top management, is a point of criticism heard consistently from the respondents, who refer both to the distribution of authority and responsibility at the lower level as well as to the poor example offered by top managers in their thinking and action.

Top management must recognize that they function as models and make sure that the values, norms, and principles that are regarded as organizationally correct are also made visible. If personnel have the opportunity to see organizational norms lived out by others, it is easier for such norms to become a force guiding the action of all of an organization's members;

this is also one of the central assumptions of the concept of organizational culture and a guideline for culture-conscious management.

Lip service alone is not enough. Some examples of top-management activities that are conductive to the development of a model function, coupled, of course, with the development of the requisite skills, are:

- Giving LMM margin for maneuver in the use of new qualifications; creating free spaces for experimentation.
- Not permitting (e.g., by systematic rationalization utilizing new information and communication techniques) the centralization of information and decision-making structures to undermine how important the organization considers it that LMM acquire qualifications to improve their management abilities.

The second problem, systematic career planning, gives direction to individual action, in respect to acquiring the requisite qualifications, and supplants incidental, improvised job taking.

If career planning is to have any prospects of success, certain preconditions must be met: planning must be couched in the broader framework of planning quantitative and qualitative needs for personnel to firm up the credibility of career planning and to avoid exaggerated promises and frustrations.

Career promises by superiors or by the personnel department are perceived by some of the managers surveyed as a "motivation trick" if it is obvious that there are far fewer upward mobility positions available than there are persons who have been promised such a promotion.

For this reason, the managers concerned must also be told that planning of careers does not exclude divergences from the plan. Career planning must not be equated with career guarantees. Whereas systematic career planning has the function of providing long-term direction in the acquisition of qualifications (indirectly effective HRM measures),

measures affecting the organization of labour create a direct incentive for the acquisition and practical application of new qualifications.

For example, replacement arrangements for the time a manager attends further education are such a measure. Also, managers may be offered assistance to improve their individual time management and their individual work techniques, permitting a more efficient individual organization of their work. This can ease the burden of routine and creates free time that could then be used to acquire and or to apply new qualifications. Relief from routines is ranked as a desirable structuring objective by LMM of all four firms.

The results of the survey show clearly that the managers concerned see the personnel policy of the firms studied as highly fragmented. Inconsistencies between particular personnel policy measures reduce or counteract the efficacy of these measures in their target groups' own estimation. Measures focusing on participation and development should thus be internally consistent with strategic and organizational measures. Where shaping the work situation of LMM is concerned, this means a methodical endeavor to expand their room for action.

The case studies also clearly show that the requirement that strategic, structural, and personnel measures be interlinked is justified from the standpoint of efficiency, but is rarely realised in firm practice (as yet).

The reason for this may be that the responsibility for HRM measures still rests to a large degree exclusively with the personnel departments, and is still too little regarded as a top-management task.

The consistent criticism of the lack of support from top management, which detracts from the effectiveness of relevant personnel policy measures, is an unequivocal argument for increased involvement by top management in HRM responsibility.

PROSPECTS

The findings of the present case studies and the conceptual

considerations presented could contribute to a common understanding, both internally, among an organization's members, as well as between researchers and practitioners concerning basic personnel policy problems, and encourage the devising of ways to develop personnel policy practice.

The next step of firm practice, however, cannot be derived deductively from the hypotheses produced by industrial management research. Scientific results can, however, contribute to the systematization of organizational problem situations, and provide guidelines for company decision makers.

But the promotion of human resources is not solely the task of a company's management, or indeed of companies in general. If human resources are seen as a competitive advantage of countries poorly supplied with raw materials over countries rich in raw materials, the development of these resources becomes a task of the society as a whole and one of growing importance as well.

Generally speaking, current developments in society and the economy, and in the organization of labour, can from the standpoint of LMM be interpreted as a thrust toward individualization, entailing new risks for those concerned. And among these risks are the loss (due to technical economic factors) of traditional certainties with regard to professional practical knowledge (qualification) and the consequent creation of insecurity and uncertainties.

Also, new qualifications are becoming obsolete increasingly rapidly. At the same time, a new kind of dependency arises: the situation of the individual is becoming more and more dependent on the labour market and hence on education and further education. Traditional certainties are losing their protective and binding force as labour market economies are implemented and the supporting edifices created by welfare and labour legislation are dismantled. Thus, individuals are becoming increasingly institutionally dependent.

The challenges to the social partners (also in the European community) lie in the creation and development of overall background conditions in the labour market, in welfare and labour laws, as well as in education policy to improve LMMs' labour-market mobility and to prevent social dumping. Given this background, the requisite meeting of the qualificational needs of LMM must be joined with the creation of supportive marginal and background conditions at the institutional and social levels.

Chapter 5

Expectation and Perception

Franchising, as a form of market organization, has experienced rapid growth over the last several decades. Both the franchisor and the franchisee can improve performance from a marketing perspective and a profitability context when there is an effective franchising arrangement. Market advantage can be achieved when the franchise system successfully develops an identifiable product or service which assures customers of a uniform and predictable level of product quality and service. The strength of a franchise operation is focused around the dual roles of:

- Excellent management and operations
- Outstanding quality and reliability of the product and service.

A franchisor must therefore be concerned with both the quality of its franchisees and its products.

The franchisor faces a dichotomous problem of marketing to both:

- Perspective franchisees
- End consumers or customers.

In order to grow, the franchisor must recruit additional franchisees. Effective recruitment calls for a market programme targeting perspective franchisees. In addition, the franchisor often has the responsibility of promoting the product or service to the end consumer.

The advantages inherent in franchising systems are often recognized by scholars and practitioners alike. The success that franchising has achieved during the past several decades attests to the merits of franchising. Nevertheless, there still exist within franchise relationships classic problems of control and self-interest. The conflict that arises between franchisors and franchisees may be one of the most difficult and frustrating challenges in franchising. There are often several sources of conflict within franchise channels.

Franchisees may not provide an expected level of managerial talent and energy to properly handle the business. The franchisee may be buying a vision of the American dream with unrealistic expectations of the work necessary to make the business succeed. The franchisee may not desire the hard work or long hours that are expected at the beginning of a franchising operation. The franchisee may be motivated to purchase a franchise to escape from either unemployment or poor job prospects but may not have the skills to manage his or her own business. The franchisee may not have thoroughly investigated the franchisor nor may he or she have sufficient operating capital to start up or run the business. When problems arise, the franchisee's disenchantment may seriously impair the relationship with the franchisor and cause serious harm to the business operation.

Conflict arises when one party believes that its goal attainment is being impeded by another. In a franchising relationship, the franchisor and franchisee usually have different objectives. The franchisor generally will be considering performance of the entire system while the franchisees are focusing on their individual outlets. Both franchisor and franchisee will attempt to maximize profits for themselves.

As each organization within the franchise system strives to meet its own goals, the problem of self-interest can create serious difficulties for the harmonious operation of the franchise relationship. One problem which must be addressed is the responsibility of the franchisor to properly select those franchisees whose goals complement their franchising system. Training can also be provided on an ongoing basis to ensure that the franchisees' goals remain consistent with those of the franchisor. In both cases, market research can prove to be a valuable tool to understanding franchisees' goals and aspirations.

When a suitable franchisee is enlisted, the franchisor must continue to monitor and analyse the sales and profits of each unit. Such research can provide insight into the customers' buying habits and the demand for the product or service being offered. Of course, franchisors need to adequately understand the end consumers and their desire for the franchisors' products in order to ensure their own survival.

But even more important, the franchisor can collect information which can identify and define the marketing opportunities and problems for a particular business. The ability of the franchisor to understand demand from a total systems perspective yields greater coordination of franchisor/ franchisee effort, greater capacity to take advantage of economic efficiencies in the research process, and more openness and adaptiveness to change on the part of franchisees.

The decision by franchisors to conduct marketing research is generally centreed around a recognized need for specific information and the desire to manage and maintain proper organizational functions. It is generally not thought of as a tool to enhance franchisor/franchisee relationships. It is in this area that marketing research shows great promise. To be effective, however, marketing research should address marketing issues in both target markets. First, it should help the franchisor choose franchisees whose goals will enhance franchise system performance, and second, it should help the franchisee better serve its end consumer.

THE MARKETING RESEARCH PROCESS

There are basically four steps in the marketing research process that franchisors must follow:

- Define the problem and research objectives.
- Develop a research plan for collecting information.
- Implement the research plan by collecting and analyzing the data.
- Interpret and report the findings.

When defining the problem and research objectives, it is important that the franchisors doing the research work closely with the decision makers to determine what research is needed and how it will be used.

If this step is skipped, the results generally will not address the major problem. In a franchise setting, the research people must work closely with those people in the franchise who handle recruitment of potential franchisees. They must also work with the franchisees themselves to understand the needs of the market.

Marketing research is designed to reduce uncertainty and provide knowledge for the franchisor. Thus, marketing research will help determine what is going right and what went wrong. Research can help the franchisor understand consumers' buying motivations and determine the strengths and weaknesses of the products or services.

When developing a research plan, there are three objectives of market research to remember:

- *Exploratory*: To gather primary information that will better define problems and suggest improvements.
- *Descriptive*: To describe the market potential for a product or the demographics and attitudes of consumers who buy the products.
- *Causal*: To understand the cause and effect relationships in market practices.

The three major functional roles in marketing research are descriptive, diagnostic, and predictive. The descriptive role focuses on gathering and presenting statements of fact. For example, what has been the sales trend for the franchise outlet during the last five years? What are the consumers' attitudes toward the product or service? The second role of research goes beyond description and is diagnostic.

A researcher attempts to explain the data. What was the impact on sales when we introduced the new product? Have sales increased as a result of the new product line introduced? The final function of research would be predictive. Will this individual operate a franchise in a manner consistent with franchise philosophy? Can we predict how a new advertising campaign will affect sales? If we replace the manager, will we improve on employee morale and performance?

The third stage of a marketing research project is implementing the research plan by collecting and analyzing the data. The franchisor must determine the best instrument to use to collect data for the project. Interviews, focus groups, and surveys can all be used to collect data, but the costs, ease, and depth of information vary from one method to another. For example, when conducting research about a franchisee's goals, more in-depth information will probably be required than can be provided by a simple questionnaire.

The fourth step in marketing research is interpreting and reporting the findings where conclusions are drawn to the franchisors. The purpose of this research is not to overwhelm management but provide information which will be useful for making decisions.

THE FRANCHISE DILEMMA

The franchise dilemma is that franchisors have two distinct and different target markets, including:

- The prospective franchisee
- The end consumer.

Unlike most major retail or service outlets, the franchisor does not sell directly to an end consumer but through a franchising organization. The franchises are generally owned and operated by franchisees who actually run, manage, or supervise the outlet stores. It is, therefore, important for the franchisor to first develop a success profile for prospective franchisees.

USING RESEARCH TO CREATE A FRANCHISEE PROFILE

The successful franchisee profile is best developed by devising a preference research model. Such an approach involves research using both personal interviews and a general survey instrument. The personal interview is generally completed with existing successful franchisees. The purpose of the interview is to measure franchisees' attitudes toward their managing experience, as well as general demographic information. The franchisees selected for the study are generally among the top quartile or top third in sales or other success criteria as determined by the franchisors.

In addition to the personal interview, a general survey is made of all franchisees concerning what they believe would be a success profile for franchisees. This general survey is often developed by first using focus groups. The focus group generally includes 6-10 people gathered together for a few hours with a trained interviewer to talk about franchisees, managers, and successful management techniques.

These individuals may be the franchisor's franchisees, but they may also include other managers and owners of different types of businesses, as long as they have some understanding of management and ownership responsibilities. The trained interviewer generally begins with broad questions before moving to specific issues. The interviewer encourages open discussion, hoping that the interactions between the participants bring out actual experiences and recommendations for successful franchisees. These discussions are generally taped for future playback and study.

Once a focus group has determined critical factors that lead to successful franchisees, a survey of franchisees can begin. The purpose of the survey is to obtain primary data concerning attitudes toward the franchisor and the franchise system, and goals of the franchisee, as well as demographics. It is with this information that the franchisor can begin to understand where problems with relationships with their franchisees are occurring.

MARKET RESEARCH

One of the most typical functions of a marketing research programme is to understand the habits and attitudes of customers. This information, when provided to franchisees by the franchisor, can build stronger channel relationships. The customer profile is often conducted through exit interviews as well as a general survey.

The exit interview generally is conducted as customers leave a store. At this time, their attitudes about the product or service are measured. In addition, perception indicators can indicate how individuals felt about the quality of the product or service being sold compared to competitors' offerings. Also, demographic information will provide valuable information about the customer segment currently visiting the franchisee's outlet. With the customer profile for each outlet, franchisors may be able to tailor their franchise programme to better meet the unique needs of each franchisee, hence reducing conflict within the relationship.

Additionally, marketing research may be conducted with focus groups which will allow for greater insights into the end consumer. Focus groups may indicate the strengths or weaknesses of a particular company, product, or service. The focus groups may easily be divided up into heavy users, moderate users, light users, or non-users of a particular franchise outlet. Marketing research can play an integral part in proper decision making in a franchising organization. More and more franchisors are recognizing the benefits of implementing a marketing research programme.

Along with the commonly recognized benefits of marketing research, franchisors should also recognize that marketing research can be an effective tool in building strong relationships with its franchisees.

First, marketing research can help franchisors select franchisees whose goals are consistent with system-wide growth. Second, franchisors can conduct customer research and share the findings with franchisees.

Marketing research provides information which franchisors can use to properly determine the profile for both the successful franchisee and the target customer. When both the franchisee and customer profiles have been developed, the franchisor will be better able to select franchisees who can manage the franchising outlet and serve the customer. Marketing research becomes one tool to reducing unnecessary conflict within franchise channels.

The increasing efforts by marketers to target diverse groups of consumers call for a closer examination of the ethical implications of market segmentation and differentiated marketing. Previous research suggests that marketers and consumers often differ in their perceptions of marketing ethics. Based on contingency theory, this research proposes an integrated framework—which includes the nature of the product, consumer characteristics, and market selection—to analyse the ethical complexities of the marketing exchange. Interactions among these factors lead to various contingencies with different ethical implications for marketing managers and public policy makers. Marketers should assess consumer interests and the ethics of marketing programs before their implementation

In the last several decades, targeting distinctive consumer segments with differentiated marketing has been a popular strategy among many marketers. The distinctive nature of various consumer groups such as children, the elderly, women, and ethnic minorities has made them attractive market segments. However, market segmentation and targeted marketing have, from time to time, met with tremendous difficulties. Targeting potentially harmful products at vulnerable and disadvantaged consumers such as children, the elderly, and inner-city residents has received negative publicity and been subjected to damaging litigation. The increasing willingness of some large corporations to exploit vulnerable consumers indicates unfair treatment of these consumers and a lack of justice in the marketplace.

On the other hand, cases of discrimination and redlining still occur in certain product and market areas, such as the discrimination directed at minority consumers by insurance and mortgage companies. Disenchanted consumers are increasingly rallying consumer interest groups to put pressure on firms that they consider to be predatory or discriminatory in their marketing practices. Companies such as R. J. Reynolds, Prudential Insurance, and Texaco Oil Company have suffered from tarnished images, consumer boycotts, and court penalties of hundreds of millions of dollars.

Although the modern marketing concept emphasizes its mission to satisfy consumer needs and wants, that promise, in reality, is sometimes lost or misplaced, resulting in outcomes that are not in the best interests of either the customers or society. A lack of understanding of the ethical issues associated with market segmentation and selection has contributed to these problems, which have tremendous social and economic costs. While targeting harmful products at vulnerable consumers has received harsh criticism, restricting the marketing of certain products and labeling some consumers as vulnerable are considered equally troublesome, suggesting that the ethical implications of marketing practices are complicated.

Although researchers have examined the ethics of market segmentation and selection, effort is lacking in synthesizing various issues to provide a holistic understanding of the ethical implications of the marketing exchange. Based on contingency theory, we integrate previous research and propose a three-dimensional framework--which includes the nature of the product, consumer characteristics, and market selection--to analyse the ethics of market segmentation and related marketing strategies. Interactions among these variables lead to various scenarios with different ethical implications for marketing management and public policy making.

Particular attention is given to areas in which marketers and consumers differ in their perceptions of ethical propriety with respect to the nature of the product and market selection. To avoid ethical conflicts in marketing, we suggest that companies consider consumers' interest and assess the ethical implications of their marketing plans before implementation. In the marketing field, market segmentation and the differentiation of the marketing mix have become so prevalent that they are almost synonymous with competitive strategies.

While targeted marketing has largely been beneficial to both consumers and marketers, cases of consumer discontent from time to time raise questions about the ethical implications of market segmentation and targeted marketing, most notably the targeting of harmful products at vulnerable consumers, such as targeting alcohol and cigarettes at inner-city consumers and churning insurance policies to the elderly. Meanwhile, the opposite of targeting--the exclusion of certain consumers from a company's offerings--is just as controversial.

These problems are not unique to marketers of consumer goods. Business service providers and public and nonprofit organizations are not immune to such challenges. Organizations, including educational institutions and government agencies, that cater to certain segments of society have also become the targets of public scrutiny and face the prominent possibility of consumer discontent and legal actions.

While consumers and marketers continue to struggle with these complicated issues and seek viable solutions, researchers have studied the ethics of market segmentation and market selection. Recent studies have focused on the ethical implications of targeted marketing of harmful products at vulnerable consumers.

TARGETED MARKETING

Targeted marketing, as a popular marketing strategy, refers to the concentrated marketing of a product to a segment of consumers due to the attractiveness of the group, in terms of such factors as its size and growth rate. Theoretically speaking, there is nothing inherently wrong with targeted marketing. When marketers promote a product beneficial to a group of consumers, targeted marketing is largely ethical and welcome by consumers.

For instance, some restaurants and hotels have special promotion programs aimed at children, and indirectly at their parents, with inexpensive toys and special vacation packages. In recent years, however, many cases of targeting potentially harmful products at vulnerable consumers have raised ethical concerns in terms of justice and fairness, such as targeting sweepstakes at the elderly and handguns at women. Even indirect and subtle targeting of potentially harmful products at vulnerable consumers has received criticism, such as targeting children with R-rated movies and using animal characters to promote cigarettes and alcohol.

PRODUCT HARM

Many products in the marketplace, such as wholesome food and medicine, are beneficial or at least beneficial to the target group. However, products that are intended to be beneficial have from time to time been found harmful to some consumers, resulting in"market failures".

For instance, unless a pharmaceutical company tests a new product on everyone (instead of limited clinical trials), it is difficult to determine whether the product will cause any harm. The key issue here is the marketer's knowledge of the product's potential harm, even to a small group of people.

If a company discovers that a small percentage of people may suffer negative reactions from its products and it immediately takes corrective measures, the company may be deemed as acting ethically, believing that it should take responsibility for the incident as part of its business liability.

If the company had prior knowledge of the side effect and it took no remedial measures upon such discovery, it would be considered as intentionally harming the consumers.

Having prior knowledge of the harmfulness of a product and withholding that information have been used as evidence against companies, such as in the Dow Corning case of silicone breast implants and the legal battle against tobacco companies.

However, the evaluation of a product's harmfulness is not always clear-cut. Even the marketing of seemingly beneficial and harmless products can sometimes take an unexpected turn, because such products can be harmful to consumers who have known characteristics. Some products, even though not inherently harmful, can be potentially harmful to consumers due to abuse or misuse.

For instance, targeting alcoholic beverages at poor inner-city consumers is particularly problematic, as this segment already suffers from a greater number of alcohol-related health and social problems than the general population. Thus, ethical evaluations of many products depend on their interaction with consumer characteristics and marketing practices.

VULNERABLE CONSUMERS

Recently, consumer vulnerability has drawn much attention in studies of marketing ethics. In numerous legal cases, the court system in the U.S. has defined vulnerable consumers as a group of people who, due to various idiosyncrasies, are sensitive and susceptible to the potential negative effects associated with using a particular product. For instance, a small group of people, due to their body biology, may suffer side effects from using certain medications.

Moreover, children do not have the same level of knowledge, experience, or maturity as adults to process commercial information. Many elderly people, due to their physical and/or mental conditions, also face challenges as consumers. In addition, some consumers may be prone to addiction or compulsion while others may be disadvantaged due to their social and economic conditions.

Such examples of targeting vulnerable consumers include the targeting of high interest loans of credit cards to consumers with poor credit histories and less financial sophistication. Thus, product harmfulness is heightened for consumers at a risk or disadvantage, and poses ethical concerns.

DISCRIMINATION

While much recent research has examined the ethics of targeting harmful products to vulnerable consumers, some researchers continue to investigate the opposite case: the exclusion of certain consumers in marketing. Discrimination in marketing refers to the practice of denying access to products to a group of consumers due to their racial or ethnic background, age, gender, or other characteristics. Discrimination may also have to do with discrepancies in product quality and variety, and the terms of exchange such as pricing and payment method.

Since the 1960s, many studies have investigated pricing discrimination against the poor and minority consumers. Despite the tremendous progress in the last few decades, discrimination and redlining have persisted in areas such as housing, mortgage lending, and financial services. Here, the important gauge points are the equivalence or proportionality in marketing intensity and the disparate treatment of consumers.

Existing studies have made significant progress in

conceptualizing the ethics of market segmentation and differentiated marketing. In several important respects, their findings have elevated our understanding of the ethical implications of the marketing exchange. First, these studies emphasize that the concern with the ethical consequences of marketing practices in the United States is well grounded in the fundamental beliefs in social and moral equity, fairness, and justice for all people.

Second, researchers have emphasized the ethical risks inherent in market segmentation and differentiated marketing. Dunfee, Smith and Ross suggest that due to the boundary-expanding nature of marketing, ethical concerns may arise in certain situations when marketers cross such boundaries. For instance, marketing products to youth that are intended for mature consumers, such as alcoholic beverages, leads to different ethical evaluations.

According to Star, the social discontent and ethical concerns associated with marketing stem from the functional limitations of the marketing concept. Contemporary marketing practices often rely on market segmentation, which divides consumers into submarkets based on characteristics such as age, gender, race, and nationality. To provide unique values to consumers and to avoid head-on competition, each market segment may require a unique marketing mix. Thus, segmentation and subsequent marketing practices often imply differential albeit unequal treatment of various consumer groups, and raise ethical concerns.

Third, extant studies have found that ethical concerns or dilemmas often arise when a marketer's perception is in conflict with that of consumers or the public. In fact, the customer interface represents the area of marketing in which conflicts in the perception of the ethical propriety of marketing practices frequently occur. Thus, marketers must study the perception of the public when formulating marketing strategies in order to avoid potential misunderstandings.

NEED FOR INTEGRATION

The review of literature reveals several deficiencies in the existing research. First, previous studies have focused on one or another issue of the marketing exchange and lack the integration of disparate perspectives. While much recent research has concentrated on targeting harmful products at vulnerable consumers, the practice of excluding some consumer groups is equally controversial. However, discussion of these two topics has largely been separate in the existing literature.

Theoretically speaking, these two issues are closely related to each other because discrimination and redlining have as much to do with market segmentation and selection as targeted marketing, but in opposite directions. Moreover, insufficient effort has been expended to examine the many positive marketing activities that target disadvantaged groups, such as charity, corporate sponsorship, and public service programs.

Although the existing literature condemns unethical marketing practices, it has not offered consistent guidelines to determine exactly when the marketing of certain products to some consumers becomes ethically problematic. There are also questions as to whether some consumer characteristics are the causes of vulnerability or simply its correlates. For instance, when controlling for education and income, the effect of vulnerability among ethnic groups may be less pronounced.

Thus, several authors have cautioned against the use of race- or ethnicity-based vulnerability. Government intervention to restrict marketing may have some merit, and at the same time finds strong opponents among those who support the free market and free speech. Often, consumer advocates and industry spokespeople find themselves in deadlocks in the heated debate about the ethics of market segmentation and selection.

Recent studies have revealed complex interactions among products, consumer characteristics, and marketing practices in ethical evaluations of marketers, and have recommended that marketers should tread carefully when venturing into certain market segments. Despite these research efforts and the many theories of marketing ethics that have emerged, a framework for comprehensive analysis of the ethical implications of market selection and related marketing strategies remains elusive.

Noting the manifold issues and perspectives, several researchers stress the need for a normative theory of ethics about market selection and marketing strategies. A more integrated approach to analyzing the ethical implications of the marketing exchange can help chart a coherent discourse on these critical issues and a better understanding of marketing ethics for managers and public policy makers.

A CONTINGENCY APPROACH

Since the early 1980s, businesses and researchers have devoted much attention to the ethical implications of business practices, which has signaled the arrival of the "ethics era" in which consumer sovereignty is given more emphasis than marketers' interests, and there has been a decline of the caveat emptor assumption. A creative variety of frameworks and theories has been developed within the marketing ethics literature, such as the general theory of marketing ethics, moral decision-making theory, and social contracts theory. These theories typically rely on one or more of the classical theories, such as Kantian ethics and perspectives of rights, duties, and justice.

Existing theories of marketing ethics have developed various "tests" to examine the ethicality of marketing practices. Some of these ethical tenets are related to product harm, consumer characteristics, and market selection. For instance, Laczniak and Murphy's framework of ethical reasoning elaborates several such tests. The motive test asks whether the intent of the contemplated action is harmful. The consequence test establishes whether any major damage to people or organizations will result from the contemplated action.

The justice test asks whether the proposed action leaves another person or group less well off, and whether this person or group is already a member of a relatively underprivileged class. Although these tests have pragmatic appeals, there may be conflicting responses to their questions due to multiple stakeholders in the marketing exchange.

Despite the frequent ethical problems that involve consumers, few theories have considered the role of consumer perceptions in marketing ethics. The exceptions include the consumer sovereignty test and distributive justice. The consumer sovereignty test (comprising three dimensions) requires marketers to examine whether consumers are vulnerable or disadvantaged, perhaps due to age, education, of income.

Marketers need to establish whether a target market has the capability to understand the benefits and risks associated with a product, has sufficient information to judge whether their expectations for purchases will be fulfilled, and has the choice of going elsewhere. The theory of distributive justice suggests that the unequal and differential treatment of consumers, when it leads to detrimental effects on their well-being, particularly of those who are disadvantaged, may result in a perceived lack of fairness and justice.

However, most normative theories of marketing ethics that have emerged in the last two decades have focused on either defining the fundamental principles of ethics to develop guidelines, or on the moral development and ethical reasoning of managers.

Although this approach undoubtedly has merit in assisting marketers to reflect on the ethics of their decisions, it is less satisfactory in providing definitive ethical evaluations of specific practices. Meanwhile, others have proposed universal codes of marketing ethics, such as those of the American Marketing Association, that deal with various ethical issues in different marketing areas such as advertising, sales management, and marketing research. However, they do not specifically address the complex interplay among consumer characteristics, product types, and marketing strategies.

CONTINGENCY THEORY

Dunfee, Smith, and Ross contend that the pluralistic approaches in current marketing ethics research reflect the inadequacy of general normative theories of marketing ethics to handle the rich and complex context of the marketing function. Thompson argues that making decisions on the basis of the context-independent general principles while disregarding the contextual details can result in socially irresponsible, and even detrimental, consequences.

Although most marketing ethics theories, particularly the classic utilitarian (teleological) theories of ethics, consider the interests of various parties and complex situations, they have been criticized as too abstract and general to provide adequate guidance for managers. Due to the great number of ethical issues inherent in customer relationships and marketing functions, one set of universal rules or principles of ethics may be too simplistic to apply to all marketing situations.

To provide clear guidelines for ethical decision-making in marketing, several researchers have emphasized the role of various cultural, organizational and environmental factors in ethical evaluations of marketing activities, including the contextualist approach and the social contracts theory. The contextualist approach stresses that the sources of ethical concerns for marketers come from the interests of different stakeholders and affect the evaluation of the ethical justifiability of a particular marketing activity.

According to the social contracts theory, ethical concerns arise when one community's legitimate norms (e.g., those of marketers) conflict with those of another community (e.g., consumers or the larger society). Therefore, a theory that considers different stakeholder interests and distinguishes various marketing scenarios and their ethical evaluations would be the most fruitful.

One of the theoretical approaches well suited to analyzing complex interactions among various dimensions of a phenomenon is contingency theory. Rooted in organizational behaviour research by Herbert Simon, contingency theory deals with the effect of interactions among various organizational and environmental factors on performance outcomes. According to Zeithaml, Varadarajan, and Zeithaml, contingency theory emphasizes the importance of situational influences on the management of organizations and questions the existence of a single best way to manage. Contingency theory contributes to practical management by encouraging managers to:

- Identify important contingency variables that distinguish between contexts,
- Group similar contexts based on the variables, and
- Determine the most effective solution for each group.

The contingency approach is particularly helpful in analyzing the ethics of marketing activities. Based on contingency theory, we reject the possibility that a single set of criteria can determine marketing ethics in all circumstances.

Instead, we examine the interactions between the contextual variables and emphasize the analysis of the ethical implications of specific scenarios. As the most frequent ethical conflict that faces marketing managers involves attempting to balance corporate interests against those of consumers, a useful framework should first examine how a marketer's perception of marketing ethics interacts with that of the consumer, who is as an integral and indispensable party to and a key stakeholder of the marketing exchange process.

Marketing is often considered as an exchange between marketers and consumers that aims to satisfy consumer needs and maximize the return on investment for shareholders. Thus, there is an inevitable and omnipresent tension between marketers' interests and those of consumers. This conflict forms the basis for different positions on the ethics continuum of marketing practices.

However, placing consumers' interests against those of marketers on the ethics continuum may be too simplistic, because it may imply that marketing is a zero-sum game and reject the possibility of a win-win outcome. Both marketers and consumers may form their perceptions of the ethics of specific marketing scenarios according to ethical principles such as rights, justice, fairness, and equity. In many cases, marketers and consumers agree on the ethical evaluations of certain marketing scenarios and raise no ethical concerns. For instance, both groups agree in principle that providing beneficial products to consumers is ethical as well as desirable and responsible.

However, existing research has documented significant gaps between marketers and consumers in their ethical philosophies as well as ethical evaluations of specific marketing practices. From time to time, a marketer's perception may conflict with that of the public, which results in ethical concerns and, perhaps, disapproving behaviour by the public such as protests and boycotts.

For instance, consumers may believe that reduced pricing for medications such as AZT for the critically ill is ethical and laudable, but manufacturers may consider it unacceptable and unethical based on their obligations to shareholders. In other cases, while consumers perceive targeting harmful products at vulnerable consumers as unethical and exploitative, some marketers consider any restriction of marketing as an infringement of their legal right to free speech under the First Amendment. Thus, consumers' ethical evaluations of a particular marketing situation may be negative, while the marketer's perceptions are based on different moral priorities.

Given such complexities, this research integrates previous studies, applies contingency theory to analyse the ethical implications of the marketing exchange, and explains how ethical concerns arise in various marketing situations based on the agreement of lack thereof in the perceptions of ethics between marketers and consumers. Several recent studies have used two-dimensional frameworks and focused on the targeting of harmful products at vulnerable consumers.

In our three-dimensional model, we include three concepts as the contextual variables, i.e., the nature of the product, consumer characteristics, and market selection. Furthermore, we examine three categories in each variable. In the following sections, we define each of the three contingency variables and discuss how interactions among these dimensions distinguish between various contexts, and how ethical conflicts or dilemmas may arise under certain circumstances.

NATURE OF THE PRODUCT

The nature of a product is an important contingency

variable that affects the ethical impacts of marketing practices. Although there is a continuum of product benefits and harms, products can generally be classified as beneficial, harmful due to abuse/misuse, of inherently harmful. Many products, such as wholesome food and medications, provide a variety of benefits to consumers, including physical, functional, emotional, and social benefits.

On the other hand, products such as cigarettes and other tobacco products are inherently harmful, and it is unethical to market such products. Moreover, some products are benign to sophisticated consumers but may be harmful to others due to abuse of misuse. Alcoholic beverages, for instance, may be beneficial or benign for mature adults who use them responsibly, but are harmful to under-aged youths. The greater the harm of a product, the harsher will be the criticism of marketing practices promoting the product.

Although a physical product itself may be beneficial, the nature of a product's marketing correlates may be unethical. Besides bodily harm, consumers may suffer from economic harm such as the loss of benefits due to deceptive pricing, and psychological harm such as disrespect, humiliation, and a sense of powerlessness that is caused by fraudulent and irresponsible marketing practices such as product defects and deceptive investment schemes.

In addition to consumer discontent and social censure, awareness of the economic impact and psychological effects of unethical marketing practices on consumers has become more important, given the penalties for both economic and psychological damages under the current corporate sentencing guidelines.

CONSUMER CHARACTERISTICS

Existing studies suggest that consumer capability is the most salient factor in ethical evaluations of marketing practices. Clearly, consumer capability/vulnerability is multifaceted. Consumers need mental, physical, and economic abilities to effectively execute a marketing exchange. At times, however, some consumers may lack one or another type of ability to the extent that they can not make informed decisions about a product or benefit from it. Lack of such capabilities may lead to some degree of vulnerability.

In general, a consumer's ability falls on a continuum that runs from being sophisticated to being vulnerable. Here, we group consumers into three categories: sophisticated, at-risk, and vulnerable. Many consumers may be sophisticated due to maturity, education, prior experience, or professional background. Some consumers are considered at-risk when they are prone to addiction or compulsion even though they may possess basic skills and capabilities. These consumers also include those who are socio-economically disadvantaged. For instance, some consumers may be at greater risk if they already suffer from a disproportionate occurrence of harmful behaviour patterns, including those who may not be able to control their own behaviour, such as alcoholics, smokers, or other drug addicts. Moreover, some consumers may be vulnerable due to personal characteristics such as age, education, and physical and mental health.

MARKET SELECTION

With respect to any consumer group, a marketer basically has the following options: to target the group with a unique marketing mix, to market to the group via integrated mass marketing, or to exclude the group from marketing programs. While integrated mass marketing remains a popular strategy for many products, targeted marketing is considered more effective for companies to gain competitive advantages.

When a product has universal benefits, market selection involves decisions about the inclusion of one group of consumers or the exclusion of another, and may be perceived as unequal or unfair. When a company's marketing programs exclude certain consumers inadvertently or by design, consumers may have limited choice or incur higher switching costs of going elsewhere.

According to the contingency approach, each of the dimensions discussed above is important in ethical evaluations of marketing activities. However, none of the dimensions alone can determine the ethicality of a marketing situation. The degree of negative or positive ethical evaluation depends on the interaction among the three dimensions. To inform marketing practice and provide ethical guidelines, a normative framework of marketing ethics should enable decision-makers to make better moral judgments that are applicable to specific and often complex situations. Thus, analyzing the specific contingencies of a given marketing activity would be more helpful for assessing the ethical evaluations of marketing than would offering a limited set of general prescriptions.

CONTINGENCIES AND ETHICAL IMPLICATIONS

They have different ethical implications due to differences in perceptions between marketers and the public based on the universal principles of equality, fairness, and justice. Each block provides a unique interaction of the three factors. The white block indicates positive or non-negative ethical evaluation. Black indicates negative ethical evaluation that marketers should avoid.

These two areas often represent situations of universal agreement about ethical practice. The gray block suggests caution due to potential ethical concerns and represents the area in which there are different ethical perceptions and hence disagreement on the ethicality of marketing practices. Based on contingency theory, we describe the following seven common marketing practices and discuss their ethical implications.

Scenario 1. Mainstream Marketing

First, companies may market beneficial products to sophisticated and at-risk consumers through targeted marketing or mass marketing, as in the blocks from A1B1C1 to A2B1C2. In these cases, companies will receive positive evaluations from consumers and should proceed. Ringold suggests that marketing transactions with equal participants (i.e., capable and informed consumers) are typically regarded as fair and ethically sound. While many consumers are sophisticated and will not be considered at-risk or vulnerable under normal circumstances, this is not to say that unethical practices would not occur in these situations. Unethical practices may affect capable consumers (who do have bounded rationality and are sometimes vulnerable to unscrupulous marketing) as evidenced by numerous fraudulent investment schemes. As well, in the case of silicone breast implants, many sophisticated consumers fell victim to unethical practices.

Scenario 2. Positive Targeting and Social Marketing

Second, targeting and integrated marketing to vulnerable consumers is positive as long as the products are beneficial, and may be meaningful in some product categories (blocks A1B1C3 and A2B1C3). Children, due to their body size and stage of mental development, are often targeted with beneficial products and features such as specially formulated medications, safety caps for medication containers, and educational toys.

Targeting beneficial products at vulnerable consumers mostly receives positive ethical evaluation. Based on the concept of social responsibility, many businesses provide beneficial products to vulnerable and disadvantaged consumers, such as charitable donations to those who are weak and poor. Social marketing programs also target beneficial products at these consumers, such as free vaccinations for the children of poor families, and low interest rate mortgages for households with limited income. Marketers should receive positive evaluations from the public for these goodwill practices that contribute to consumer well being.

Scenario 3. Marketing Potentially Harmful Products

Third, the gray areas are the most challenging for marketing organizations and merit caution (blocks A1B2C1 and A2B2C2 are coded gray). Targeting products that are harmful due to abuse/misuse at any consumers is generally a questionable practice. The marketing of such products to consumers who are already at risk and disadvantaged is even more problematic. For instance, targeted marketing of malt liquor of higher alcohol content to inner-city minorities by some companies led to severe criticism and consumer boycotts due to the disproportionate consumption of such products and more frequent alcohol-related health problems among these groups. Therefore, when marketing products that are potentially harmful due to abuse or misuse, it is important that marketers examine the characteristics of their target markets and use extreme caution to avoid marketing such products to consumers at risk or a disadvantage.

Scenario 4. Predatory Marketing

Fourth, marketing of harmful products to any consumer group is unethical, as indicated by blocks from A1B3C1 to A1B3C3, which are coded black. Targeted marketing is appropriately met with intense public scrutiny and even consumer boycotts when products are detrimental to consumer well being and lead to health and social problems. For this reason, the marketing of cigarettes has been curtailed in many countries.

Negative ethical evaluations are even stronger when harmful or potentially harmful products are targeted at vulnerable consumers, because companies are considered to be preying on the weaknesses of such consumers (A1B2C3 and A2B2C3). Because cigarettes and other nicotine products are detrimental to consumer health, it is even more problematic when they are targeted towards the vulnerable (e.g., young children).

Scenario 5. Discrimination and Redlining

Fifth, the exclusion of certain consumer groups, particularly vulnerable and disadvantaged consumers, from access to beneficial products is unethical because such actions limit consumer choices. It is also illegal to exclude any consumer groups from marketing programs specified under U.S. laws such as the Fair Lending Act and the Fair Housing Act. However, segmentation and targeted marketing often mean the inclusion of some groups and exclusion of others, which results in inadvertent redlining. For instance, when marketers launch new products or expand into new geographical markets, they often select business locations based on criteria such as demographic statistics, the cost of doing business, and crime rates. Naturally, companies choose areas where consumers are affluent and the cost of doing business and crime rates are low, thus bypassing poor communities.

Hence, the conflict between consumer interest and corporate objectives poses an ethical dilemma. A number of banks, insurance underwriters, and mortgage companies, such as American Family Insurance and Chevy Chase Bank, faced lawsuits by minority consumers for alleged discrimination and redlining under the Fair Lending Act and the Fair Housing Act.

Although the companies admitted no wrongdoing in the consent decrees, it is the effect, not the intent, of these marketing practices that causes cries of "redlining" from those experiencing the lack of equity and fairness. In such cases, marketers need to ensure that their market selection and marketing activities are based solely on valid business criteria and consumer characteristics that are not directly related to factors such as age, gender, or ethnicity.

Scenario 6. Demarketing

However, not all exclusive marketing practices are unethical. Some exclusion is not only positive but also necessary to protect consumers (blocks A3B3C1 to A3B2C3). Many social marketing programs are designed to dissuade consumers from adopting harmful of potentially harmful products, such as alcoholic beverages, cigarettes, and other addictive drugs.

In addition to efforts by government agencies and civic organizations, many corporations also sponsor and participate in these programs. To encourage responsible consumption of alcohol products and to prevent drunk driving, Anheuser Busch Company, for instance, sponsored a consumer education programme that included advertising, designated drivers, and free taxi rides. These demarketing efforts play a critical role in educating and protecting consumers and minimizing the potential harm to them.

Scenario 7. Reverse Discrimination

Finally, targeting beneficial products at vulnerable and disadvantaged consumers is not entirely without controversies, especially when other groups are not included in these programs. While marketers may face discontent from disadvantaged consumers—who are the traditional targets of discrimination—lawsuits also come from the non-target segments.

For instance, long distance telephone carriers and airlines have designed special promotions for certain nationality groups who make more calls or travel more often to certain destinations. These and other affinity programs give the target consumers special rates or discounted fare. Members of other ethnic groups, who are automatically disqualified, may cry discrimination for exactly the same reasons as traditional victims of discrimination.

Although most reverse discrimination cases have to do with employment-related issues, some are directly related to social marketing programs that are designed to assist the disadvantaged. In a number of cases, white entrepreneurs have charged. Small Business Administration with reverse discrimination, in that these non-members of protected groups have been discriminated against precisely due to their ethnic background.

Thus, marketers need to pay attention to the perceptions and responses of non-target groups, who may derive different meanings from such marketing efforts. Any targeted marketing programme should be fair and sensitive to non-target consumer segments.

ETHICAL IMPLICATIONS ASSESSMENT

A society has many avenues to ensure that marketing will benefit rather than harm consumers. Consumer activism, legislative activity, and government enforcement help to guard against unethical conduct by corporations. While"obey the law" and legal clearance of marketing programs by companies may be necessary for ethical conduct, they are apparently not sufficient.

Ethical decision-making for businesses requires companies to act in"enlightened self-interest" to ensure the integrity of their marketing programs. Today, many marketing organizations have adopted the consumer-centreed business philosophy, making"customer satisfaction" their number one priority. If marketers truly subscribe to that mission, then consumers' interests should be given more weight in resolving potential ethical conflicts in marketing decisions.

To fully respect consumer sovereignty and uphold the principles of fairness and justice, we recommend that marketers conduct an"ethical implications assessment" of their marketing programs. Companies could establish a Marketing Ethics Committee, which includes consumer voices, to conduct such exercises and make the decisions about marketing practices for a given product. Companies can take the following steps using the contingency framework that we have outlined.

First, prior to the launch of products or marketing programs, companies need to study the perceptions of consumers, including those of non-target segments, in terms of consumer capability, nature of the product, and marketing strategies. In the second stage, the above dimensions should be examined simultaneously to determine the type of contingencies that the company may be facing and whether"ethical clearance" should be given to the proposed marketing programme.

If the marketing programme lands in the black zone, the committee should recommend stopping or aborting the programme. The committee can endorse a marketing programme only if it appears in the white zone. If the results point to the gray zone, the committee should recommend further revisions to avoid potential pitfalls. Finally, only when all negative or questionable contingencies are cleared should the committee give the final seal of approval. By so doing, marketers have a better chance of ensuring that their marketing programs will benefit consumers, thereby creating benefits as well for the company in a win-win situation.

COMPARISONS WITH OTHER THEORIES

Normative theories of marketing ethics provide a basis for moral deliberation by practitioners and others of the many complex and often troubling ethical issues in marketing. As researchers and practitioners search for meaningful guidelines amidst complex interactions, the contingency approach provides a plausible framework for analyzing the ethics of the marketing exchange and can help sound decision-making in marketing and public policy. The contingency framework considers the parties to and objects of the exchange, and related marketing strategies. Thus, it is comprehensive and enables systematic analyses of the ethical implications of marketing across multiple dimensions and various scenarios. Analyzing the specific contingencies can help generate concrete guidelines for ethical decision-making.

Compared with the general normative theories of marketing ethics, the contingency approach is more flexible in analyzing the ethical implications of various situations based on the three contextual variables. Meanwhile, unlike ethical or moral relativism, the contingency approach stresses the universal principles of equity, justice, and fairness in analyzing specific scenarios, hence remains truthful to a normative theory.

Because the framework considers different products and consumers with different levels of capability as well as the differential impact of marketing on consumers, the perspective of justice provides the most compelling basis for the ethical evaluations of marketing practices. In a sense, the contingency framework serves as a bridge between the principled approach and the utilitarian perspective of marketing ethics, which seem to be incommensurable with each other.

The framework can be expanded in greater detail and applied to other consumer characteristics such as age, income, and education. Products may range from economic models to premium models with enhanced features. The ethical implications of other components of a marketing mix, i.e., distribution, promotion, and price, should be explored. Distribution strategies, for instance, may range from exclusive to selective of intensive distribution.

These marketing practices, when interacting with consumer characteristics and product categories, may lead to ethical concerns. Given the increasing efforts by marketers to target various consumer segments with unique marketing mix strategies, the ethical implications of a marketing campaign based on market segmentation and differentiated marketing warrants systematic and rigorous examination before implementation.

Several practical implications of this approach can be derived. First, to encourage ethical behaviour, companies and industry organizations have established codes of ethics of relied on self-regulation, consumer ombudsmen, or external audits. However, these efforts alone are not enough to eliminate unethical conduct.

Many companies have been relatively passive in examining their positions in marketing ethics and are still operating according to traditional business models and processes that do not consider consumer interests and the ethical implications of their actions as critical issues. The ethical implications of marketing activities often remain afterthoughts, and are yet to be systematically incorporated into management decision-making. The contingency framework can facilitate this preemptive approach to ethical decision-making.

To integrate ethics into a firm's planning and strategy formulation processes, marketers should study consumers' ethical evaluation of their marketing programs. An"ethical implications assessment" is necessary before the implementation of a marketing programme. In addition to financial, market, and competitive objectives, marketers should include consumers' interest and ethical integrity as important criteria for management decision-making.

Furthermore, ethics must be coordinated throughout the marketing planning process from product development, market selection, advertising and promotion to implementation and evaluation. Given the competing priorities facing companies in their decisions, finding an ethically sound synergy among product types, consumer characteristics, and marketing strategies is as complicated as solving a crossword puzzle--it has to make sense in all dimensions.

The contingency approach can also serve as a framework for public policy makers to analyse the ethical implications of marketing activities. While public policy makers can take the initiative to protect consumers and promote good corporate citizenship, they also face tremendous challenges and complex dilemmas when making critical decisions, such as restricting certain types of advertising or the availability of some products. For instance, should the legislature make marijuana and similar drugs legal for distribution because they may benefit one group of people?

Regulators need to consider the benefit accruable to one group of consumers as well as the potential harm to another. As Laczniak and Murphy put it,"weighing the concerns of multiple stakeholder groups ... becomes the essence of appropriate ethical decision-making ... [and] the root of the complexity of such decision-making". While public policy makers should certainly protect the rights of marketers in a free market economy, they must also consider the interests of consumers, particularly those with various degrees of vulnerability, such as children and the elderly.

Future studies of marketers' and consumers' ethical evaluations of the various marketing contexts would help to validate the contingency approach. How consumers form their perceptions of marketers' intentions and make ethical evaluations of marketing will be a fruitful avenue for future research. Researchers may focus on specific situations that would raise ethical concerns for marketers, especially variations in consumers' ethical evaluations of marketing practices (e.g., advertising and distribution) for different market segments (e.g., children and the elderly). In addition to consumer capability, information and choice are two important criteria to determine marketing ethics under the principle of consumer sovereignty. Thus, how companies present information about their products, and how they handle potentially damaging information, may help to shed some light on the ethical decision-making of marketers.

The increasing diversity of the marketplace in the U.S. has significant and complex implications for marketing practices. As more companies are concentrating their resources on the most desirable and profitable segments of consumers, they inevitably exclude other groups.

Consumer and marketing research should use more representative samples of diverse groups to examine consumer responses to marketing programs, including the responses of non-target markets. In the foreseeable future, the United States will be a marketplace in which all Americans are minorities, and that will pose special challenges and opportunities for both private companies and public organizations. Determining when segmentation and differentiation may lead to perceptions of discrimination or reverse discrimination will continue to be a focal issue for future research.

This research focuses on marketing and consumers in the United States. Cross-country and cross-cultural research would help to understand marketing ethics in a broader context. In the past, multinational corporations experienced difficulties with their marketing strategies in other countries, as in the case of Nestle's baby formula. Despite adverse public attitudes at times, multinationals and local companies used a variety of techniques and media to promote their products to consumers in developing countries without close scrutiny of the consumer perceptions of such practices.

In light of increasing globalization, more companies are crossing national boundaries to produce and market their products in other countries. Thus, how the local communities of the global marketplace evaluate the marketing practices of multinational corporations has become an important subject of investigation.

Chapter 6

Resource Management

Over many centuries India has absorbed managerial ideas and practices from around the world. Early records of trade, from 4500 B.C. to 300 B.C., not only indicate international economic and political links, but also the ideas of social and public administration.

The world's first management book, titled 'Arlhashastra', written three millennium before Christ, codified many aspects of human resource practices in Ancient India. This treatise presented notions of the financial administration of the state, guiding principles for trade and commerce, as well as the management of people.

These ideas were to be embedded in organisational thinking for centuries. Increasing trade, that included engagement with the Romans, led to widespread and systematic governance methods by 250 A.D.

During the next 300 years, the first Indian empire, the Gupta Dynasty, encouraged the establishment of rules and regulations for managerial systems, and later from about 1000 A.D. Islam influenced many areas of trade and commerce. A further powerful effect on the managerial history of India was to be provided by the British system of corporate organisation for 200 years.

Clearly, the socio cultural roots of Indian heritage are diverse and have been drawn from multiple sources including ideas brought from other parts of the old world. Interestingly, these ideas were essentially secular even when they originated from religious bases. In the contemporary context, the Indian management mindscape continues to be influenced by the residual traces of ancient wisdom as it faces the complexities of global realities.

One stream of holistic wisdom, identified as the Vedantic philosophy, pervades managerial behaviour at all levels of work organisations. This philosophical tradition has its roots in sacred texts from 2000 B.C. and it holds that human nature has a capacity for self transformation and attaining spiritual high ground while facing realities of day to day challenges. Such cultural based tradition and heritage can have a substantial impact on current managerial mindsets in terms of family bonding and mutuality of obligations.

The caste system, which was recorded in the writings of the Greek Ambassador Megasthenes in the third century B.C., is another significant feature of Indian social heritage that for centuries had impacted organisational architecture and managerial practices, and has now become the focus of critical attention in the social, political and legal agenda of the nation.

One of the most significant areas of values and cultural practices has been the caste system. Traditionally, the caste system maintained social or organisational balance. Brahmins (priests and teachers) were at the apex, Kshatriya (rulers and warriors), Vaishya (merchants and managers) and Shwdra (artisans and workers) occupied the lower levels. Those outside the caste hierarchy were called 'untouchables'.

Even decades ago, a typical public enterprise department could be dominated by people belonging to a particular caste. Feelings associated with caste affairs influenced managers in areas like recruitment, promotion and work allocation. Indian institutions codified a list of lower castes and tribal communities called 'scheduled castes and scheduled tribes'.

A strict quota system called, 'reservation' in achieving affirmative equity of castes, has been the eye of political storm in India in recent years. The central government has decreed 15 per cent of recruitment is to be reserved for scheduled castes, and a further seven and half per cent for scheduled tribes. In addition, a further 27 per cent has been decreed for other backward castes.

However, the liberalisation of markets and global linkages

has created transformation of attitudes towards human resource (HR) policies and practices. Faced with the challenge of responding to the rationale of Western ideas of organisation in the changing social and economic scenario of Indian organisation, practitioners are increasingly taking a broader and reflective perspective of human resource management (HRM) in India. This manuscript has three main parts. In the first part is provided an overview of important historical events and activity that has influenced contemporary managerial tenets, the second part of the manuscript describes the emerging contemporary Indian HRM practices and indicates some interesting challenges. The concluding section, the third part of the manuscript, succinctly integrates the two preceding parts.

VALUE OF CONTEXT

The managerial ideologies in Indian dates back at least four centuries. Arthashastra written by the celebrated Indian scholar-practitioner Chanakya had three key areas of exploration, 1) public policy, 2) administration and utilisation of people, and 3) taxation and accounting principles. Parallel to such pragmatic formulations, a deep rooted value system, drawn from the early Aryan thinking, called vedanta, deeply influenced the societal and institutional values in India.

Overall, Indian collective culture had an interesting individualistic core while the civilisational values of duty to family, group and society was always very important while vedantic ideas nurtured an inner private sphere of individualism.

There has been considerable interest in the notion that managerial values are a function of the behaviours of managers. England, Dhingra and Agarwal were early scholars who contended that managerial values were critical forces that shape organisational architecture. The relevance of managerial values in shaping modern organisational life is reflected in scholarly literature linking them to corporate culture, organisational commitment and job satisfaction, as well as institutional governance.

Thus, understanding the source of these values and in particular societal work values (which link the macro-micro relationships and in turn organisational practices) had become a popular line of enquiry, and a great deal of evidence has been presented to support the importance of national culture in shaping managerial values.

One of the most widely read formulations of this literature is the seminal work of Hofstede who popularised the notion of clustering culture in generic dimensions such as power distribution, structuring, social orientation, and time horizons. In turn, these dimensions could be employed to explain relevant work attitudes, job incumbent behaviours and the working arrangements within organisational structures. Two of these dimensions were individualism and collectivism.

The traditional social ethos from the ancient roots, which was developed over centuries, underwent profound transformation during the British rule. Consequently, in the contemporary context multiple layers of values (core traditional values, individual managerial values, and situational values) have emerged. Though the societal values largely remain very much anchored in the ancient traditions they are increasingly reflecting corporate priorities and values of global linkages.

But in the arena of globalisation where priorities of consumerism, technological education, mass media, foreign investment and trade union culture predominate, newer tensions are becoming evident. For instance, contemporary Indian multi national companies and global firms in India have started shifting their emphasis to human resources with their knowledge and experience as the central area of attention in extending new performance boundaries. Considerable research evidence attests to this trend with particular relevance to greenfield organisations with little or no historical baggages in their organisational culture.

Within Indian traditions the choice of individualistic or collectivistic behaviour depends on a number of culturally defined variables. The dynamics of these variables are underpinned through three key elements guiding Indian managerial mindscapes. These three constructs are Desh (the location), Kaal (the timing), and Patra (the specific personalities involved). Sinha and Kunungo claim that the interaction of these three variables determines the guidelines for decisional cues.

This managing or nurturing of the outer layer of collectivism in an inner private sphere of individualism is expressed which demonstrates the behavioural anchors in Indian organisational life. According to Sharma, this culture based framework, which has three types of gunas (attraction), is being increasingly used in employee assessment and organisational team building strategies. The contention is that each guna is a separate contribution to the core of human personalities.

The Sattava (or truth orientation) is the sentiment of exalted values in people, organisations or society. Alternatively, the Tamasik guna depicts a negative orientation which can be expressed behaviourally as ignorance, greed or corruption. Those individuals with a Rajasik guna are inherently driven by a desire to make a worthwhile contribution to their surroundings.

Collectively, these spiritual orientations, which manifest as Sattava, Tamas or Rajas gunas, articulate as positive or negative HRM functions such as leadership, motivation or other institutional behavioural activity. The culture of Sradha (upward loyalty) and Sneha (mentoring with affection) outline the behavioural anchors derived from the civilisational roots.

The acceptance of 'Sradha' by youngers and the display of 'Sneha' by the seniors have been the root of sustainability of all types of Indian oragnisations. This has a striking similarity to the concepts of 'oyabun' and 'kobun' in the Japanese cultural context.

CONTEMPORARY INDIA

In a recent survey of Indian CEO's, it was suggested that Indian managerial leaders were less dependent on their personal charisma, but they emphasised logical and step by step implementation processes. Indian leaders focused on empowerment and accountability in cases of critical turnaround challenges, innovative challenges, innovative technology, product planning and marketing or when other similar challenges were encountered. These social scientists contend.

Leaders in other countries often tell about why they chose a peculiar person for a certain role per task, detailing the personal characteristics that made that person right for that situation. They may also consider, in detail, how an assignment would help someone grow and develop their abilities.

In general, Indian leaders simply did not discuss how they matched particular people to certain roles or tasks, nor did they usually consider in detail how the personal characteristics of individuals might shape or inform the best way to influence that person.

INDIAN HRM IN TRANSITION

One of the noteworthy features of the Indian workplace is demographic uniqueness. It is estimated that both China and India will have a population of 1.45 billion people by 2030, however, India will have a larger workforce than China. Indeed, it is likely India will have 986 million people of working age in 2030, which well probably be about 300 million more than in 2007.

And by 2050, it is expected India will have 230 million more workers than China and about 500 million more than the United States of America (U.S.). It may be noted that half of India's current population of 1.1 billion people are under of 25 years of age. While this fact is a demographic dividend for the economy, it is also a danger sign for the country's ability to create new jobs at an unprecedented rate. As has been pointed out by Meredith.

When India's young demographic bubble begins to reach working age, India will need far more jobs than currently exist to keep living standards from declining. India today doesn't have enough good jobs for its existing workers, much less for millions of new ones. If it cannot better educate its children and create jobs for then once they reach working age, India faces a population time bomb: The nation will grow poorer and not richer, with hundred of millions of people stuck in poverty. With the retirement age being 55 to 58 years of age in most public sector organisations, Indian workplaces are dominated by youth. Increasing the retirement age in critical areas like universities, schools, hospitals, research institutions and public service is a topic of considerable current debate and agenda of political parties.

The divergent view, that each society has an unique set of national nuances, which guide particular managerial beliefs and actions, is being challenged in Indian society. An emerging dominant perspective is the influence of globalisation on technological advancements, business management, education and communication infrastructures is leading to a converging effect on managerial mindsets and business behaviours.

And when India embraced liberalisation and economic reform in the early 1990s, dramatic changes were set in motion in terms of corporate mindsets and HRM practices as a result of global imperatives and accompanying changes in societal priorities.

Indeed, the onset of a burgeoning competitive service sector compelled a demographic shift in worker educational status and heightened the demand for job relevant skills as well as regional diversity. Expectedly, there has been a marked shift towards valuing human resources (HR) in Indian organisations as they become increasingly strategy driven as opposed to the culture of the status quo. Accordingly, competitive advantage in industries like software services, pharmaceuticals, and biotechnology (where India is seeking to assert global dominance), the significance of HRs is being emphasised.

These relativities were demonstrated in a recent study of three global Indian companies with (235 managers) when evidence was presented that positively linked the HRM practices with organisational performance. In spite of this trend of convergence, a deep sense of locality exists creating more robust 'cross vergence' in the conceptual as well as practical domain.

The intellectual sphere, which emphasises the mindset transaction in work organisations, has been significantly impacted by the forces of globalisation. Indeed, Chatterjee and Pearson (2000) argued, with supporting empirical evidence from 421 senior level Indian managers, that many of the traditional Indian values (respect for seniority, status and group affiliation) have been complemented by newer areas of attention that are more usually linked to globalisation, such as work quality, customer service and innovation.

The most important work related attribute of the study was the opportunity to learn new things at work. Such cross verging trends need to be understood more widely as practitioners face a new reality of human resource development of post industrial economic organisations. The other three spheres, namely the emotional, the socio cultural and the managerial domains are undergoing, similar profound changes. For instance, the socio cultural sphere confronts the dialects of the national macro level reform agenda as well as the challenge of innovating by addressing the hygiene and motivational features of the work place.

Consequently, this sphere, which is underpinned by the anchors of Sradha and Sneha, has the opportunity to leverage work setting creativity in dimensions of autonomy, empowerment, multiskilling and various types of job design. And the emotional sphere, which focuses on creativity and innovation to encapsulate the notions of workplace commitment and collaboration as well as favourable teamwork, brings desirable behavioural elements of transparency and integrity into organisational procedures and practices. The managerial sphere provides the mechanisms for shifting mindsets, for in Indian organisations HRM is viewed to be closely aligned with managerial technical competency.

Thus, understanding of the relativity of HRM to strategic intended organisational performance is less well articulated in Indian firms. The current emphasis of reconfiguring cadres (voluntary and nonvoluntary redundancy schemes), downsizing, delayering and similar arrangements will become less relevant as holistic perspectives gain ground.

Chapter 7

Auditing and Planning

Both public sector and not-for-profit organizations continue to wrestle with the challenges of defining and managing organizational effectiveness. Human resource management teams are drawn increasingly into new strategic and operational initiatives proceeding under a variety of labels, e.g., downsizing, reinvention and business process improvement. Over the past ten years, a significant number of HR executives joined their organizations' strategic planning teams. Twisting between the realities of fewer resources and expanded accountability, HRM strategic planning often flounders. This is due to the lack of simple, yet compelling management tools for demonstrating how HRM services contribute to the accomplishment of broader organizational objectives.

The author offers a proven model, the HRM Effectiveness Audit, as a guide for establishing a measurement-based, value-added service improvement system. Through partnering and training, the author has helped implement HRM reviews in a variety of organizations, including the U.S. Patent and Trademark Office, Virginia Department of Social Services, and South Carolina Budget and Control Board — Office of Human Resources.

As we move into the 21st century, public sector and not-for-profit organizations continue to wrestle with the challenges of defining and managing their effectiveness. On the federal level, initiatives have been largely driven by Congressional oversight arising from the Government Performance and Results Act of 1993 (GPRA). GPRA requires federal agencies to demonstrate contributions to organizational results through performance measurements and strategic planning.

In 1998, the Office of Personnel Management published the HRM Accountability System Development Guide to provide guidelines to human resource management (HRM) teams. On the state level, executive and legislative mandates to downsize and reduce operating costs continue to force HRM teams to re-examine their internal business methods.

Not-for-profits also face strong pressures. For example, to qualify for Medicare payments, health care systems are subject to regular reviews by the Joint Commission on Accreditation of Health Care Organizations (JCAHCO). HRM teams in these organizations must demonstrate their contribution to enhancing the quality of organization-wide services. Yet, with all these initiatives, HRM teams continue to struggle with the challenge of how best to maneuver in the new arena of higher accountability and expectations. In some organizations, the power of the customer has been harnessed. HRM teams take "a partnership approach" with the agencies they serve..

There is a cry for new tools to equip the HRM adequately to participate as a "strategic business partner." This chapter offers a practical procedural model for auditing, measuring and improving HRM services. The generic model springs from Ray Borbidge's The HRM Effectiveness Audit written during Borbidge's association with the author.

Over time, this model has been shaped and refined as the result of numerous audits conducted in a variety of public and private sector organizations.

The audit unfolds through four phases:

- *Phase I*: Ranking Importance of the HRM Service Portfolio
- *Phase II*: HRM Team Self-Evaluation
- *Phase III*: Measuring Current Service Levels
- *Phase IV*: Developing Action Plans

CORE PRINCIPLE

The audit pivots around the core principle of high

participation of internal customers. Many business improvement efforts fail by neglecting to involve customers in the definition of what "effectiveness" means for delivery of a product or service.

Private sector organizations learned this lesson years ago. In particular, the automotive industry improved its competitive position by more actively engaging customers in product design. Consequently, the industry now effectively challenges international competitors who previously cut deeply into their market share.

In recent years, governmental agencies and not-for-profits also have enlisted their customers to improve organizational effectiveness. The Internal Revenue Service is a prime example. HRM teams within these organizations ask their customers to be partners in improving internal business processes.

The audit model described in this chapter provides a means for engaging customers of HRM services. The various HRM functions (employment, employee relations, training, etc.) are treated as interrelated processes with three specific elements: inputs, outputs, and customers. This systems model keeps people focused on customer satisfaction.

To illustrate, inputs for the employment function can be defined in terms of the knowledge and skills of the employment staff, capital resources, and budgetary capabilities. Newly hired employees are the outputs. And, the primary customers are those who request the service and ultimately receive the output. In this case, the primary customers are the hiring managers.

Throughout the audit, internal customers are heavily involved in driving the process. In Phase I, internal customers rank the relative importance of the HRM service portfolio. In Phase III, they participate in focus groups to define effectiveness metrics for each HRM service area.

And finally, in Phase III they also provide regular feedback on service levels when they complete their satisfaction surveys. The audit team receives benefits from high customer participation leading to a well-executed review that radiates credibility.

PRE-AUDIT ISSUES

The naming issue: The word "audit" suggests a comprehensive review of practices, procedures and results. Audits are associated frequently with financial reviews and may create a sense of apprehension. Each organization undertaking an audit must decide the appropriate name to fit its culture. Alternative names invoking less emotional impact include: "review," "assessment" or "service improvement system." For simplicity, here, we will use the "audit" label throughout.

The sampling issue: Teams initiating the audit process ask the question: How widely throughout the organization should we collect data? The answer depends on organizational size. The prime consideration is: How many managers are there in the midlevel and one level higher? If the task of engaging the entire target population is logistically not feasible, then a sampling plan should be considered.

Here's a real case example of how a sampling plan can work. In an audit with a 10,000-employee health care organization, there were approximately 600 midlevel managers across five business units and three management levels (supervisor, manager, director).

The audit team decided to use a stratified random sampling plan to select 120 participants. The 600 managers were placed into a five-by-three matrix. Then, every fifth manager was selected from an alphabetical list of names within each cell of the matrix. This plan ensured representative participation across the organization. Groups were scheduled for 75-minute meetings over a two-day period.

The demographic issue: Audit teams must also determine what demographic characteristics are most important. Surveys normally start with a profile of demographic data. Typical characteristics might include: business unit, functional group, management level, and location. The team must anticipate the various ways for "cutting and slicing" the data to identify unique needs of various subgroups.

The baseline issue: The first time an audit is performed, a few extra steps are necessary. Specifically, the team must investigate what is most important to measure. Through focus groups, managers articulate their criteria for measuring HRM effectiveness.

From these measurements, the audit team creates a valid customer satisfaction survey. In a first-year audit, such focus groups provide the data necessary for completing Phase I and the first part of Phase III of the audit. With these caveats about sampling, demographics, and baselining, let's walk through the four phases of the audit process.

PORTFOLIO

The purpose of Phase I of the audit is to establish the relative importance of the various HRM services in relation to the accomplishment of organizational objectives. As internal customers, midlevel line and staff managers rank a list of HRM services according to the importance of each service toward meeting their business objectives over the coming year.

Each HRM management team decides the appropriate comprehensive list that reflects the scope of HRM services. The eleven service categories span the range of work done by most HRM departments. The first category on the list, HR Department Organization, draws special attention. Although not a direct service per se, HRM department organization does affect how all employees interface with the personnel function.

For example, do managers have a single point of contact, or is the department decentralized by specialization? Note that the way the department is organized can dramatically affect how internal customers view the effectiveness of HRM services.

Typical HRM Service Portfolio:

- HR Department Organization
- HR Planning/Organizational Development
- Recruitment and Selection
- Compensation Administration
- Employee Benefits Administration
- Employee Relations and Communications
- Personnel Policies and Workplace Rules
- EEO/AA and Other Regulatory Compliance

- Training and Development
- Labour Relations
- Safety, Health and Wellness

The work product from Phase I is a spreadsheet that leads to a rank order of importance for all HRM services. To create the spreadsheet, eleven functions are listed down the sheet. Names of participating managers are listed across the top columns. Each column of data represents the rankings of the eleven services.

A mean score is calculated for each of the eleven. Finally, the aggregate rank order of importance for the entire portfolio emerges. At this point, an important decision must be made: How deeply down the rank of important HRM services does the audit team wish to explore?

With first-year audits, the author recommends selection of the top four or five ranked HRM services. Through this decision, the audit team limits the scope of its assessment to the most critical. Accordingly, a more narrowly defined focus emerges. Now, the stage is set for Phases II and III.

PHASE II: HRM TEAM SELF-EVALUATION

The purpose of the self-evaluation phase is to stimulate discussion and challenge the status quo. This phase can be completed anytime before the analysis of survey results in Phase III. Each specialized group completes a "best practices" questionnaire. The best source for this is How to Conduct a Human Resources Effectiveness Audit with questionnaires for all of the eleven service areas.

Each of the questionnaires contains 25-40 items. Groups completing the questionnaire compare current practices with a set of standards based on reputable sources, including the Baldridge Quality Award criteria.

Each HRM group completes their section of the questionnaire. Through the last two items in each section, the HRM functional subgroup develops two consensus ratings: one that reflects the group's own perspective about how well their service is delivered, and one that speculates on how the customers of the service will later rate it in the customer satisfaction survey. The consensus ratings are scaled on a five- or seven-point continuum with the midpoint representing a rating of "adequate." Of the two ratings for each category, the speculative responses carry the most weight. When compared to the "overall" satisfaction survey mean for a particular HRM service, the speculative ratings show how closely attuned the HRM subgroup is to the needs of its customers. An illustration will illumine this point later. Concurrently, with the implementation of Phase II, the audit team can begin Phase III.

PHASE III: MEASURING CURRENT SERVICE LEVELS

The purpose of Phase III of the audit is to develop performance metrics for the various HRM services and to measure current satisfaction levels.

In the first year of an Audit, the baselining portion of Phase III is part of the focus group activities. Focus groups move from rating the HRM portfolio to defining what effectiveness means for the top four or five services. An open dialogue ensues from the facilitating question, "In your quiet moments, you evaluate the recruitment and selection (e.g.) services provided to you. What are the criteria you use to evaluate how well these services are provided?"

For recruitment and selection, customers may cite a variety of factors: elapsed time from posting position to delivery of the candidate certification list, the quality of candidates, or recruiter response time for communications with hiring managers. There are many possibilities. The demographic portion has been omitted. Notice that respondents are asked to comment on all items rated below "adequate." Such comments provide a wealth of feedback for process improvement work.

When the data is entered into a spreadsheet, not only are the seven-point ratings recorded, but also the comments are categorized. Thus, one quickly gets an overview of the range of comments, rich fuel for subsequent improvement efforts. In the second year audit and beyond, focus groups verify the validity of the survey before it is circulated again. Does it continue to address the major performance issues for that HRM service?

If so, then the survey is distributed to collect another set of data points. With a new set of data points, the audit team gauges its progress toward closing performance gaps. Imagine the power of a report that can make statements like this: "The recruitment and selection team reduced the average time to fill vacancies by 24 per cent and boosted its customer satisfaction rating from 3.5 to 5.0 within one year."

PHASE IV: DEVELOPING ACTION PLANS

The purpose of Phase IV of the audit is to develop an HRM business plan based on the priorities emerging from the audit. In this example, the audit focused only on the top four most important HRM services: recruitment and selection, employee relations, compensation, and training and development. The grid has been sorted in ascending order according to the arithmetical mean of the "overall" satisfaction rating.

For example, if the recruitment and selection data in the Phase III column came from survey, then the "3.2" shown in the grid represents the calculated average of all responses to Question No. 11. A "3.2" rating indicates that the majority of respondents are dissatisfied with the service level. Note: Even a mean slightly above "adequate" should generate some concern, because it suggests that a significant number of managers are dissatisfied.

The audit team also pays special attention to comparisons of the second and third columns, which indicate how attuned the HRM team is to the needs and expectations of their internal customers. In the example, the recruitment and selection category offers a striking comparison. The recruitment team expected an above-adequate "5" rating. Instead, the internal customers rated this service at "3.2," which is significantly below adequate. The question remains, "Why did the recruitment team not know about the pervasive dissatisfaction?" The gap between expectations and reality suggests a need for improved feedback mechanisms.

The grid leads the way for exploration. When the audit

team wants to dig deeper, it can isolate the specific issues within the survey, i.e., the underlying source of broader dissatisfaction. The audit team drills down to uncover the sources of overall performance problems. They examine the pattern of responses to the underlying questions within each section. Then, they drill deeper by reviewing the comment categories associated with unsatisfactory ratings.

The beauty of the audit blossoms from the story told by internal customers. Rather than being armed with only anecdotes, the audit team has the ammunition from a powerful round of data collection. On this foundation, the HRM team crafts a persuasive plan of attack for improving its services. Encouragements and Pitfalls every audit team confronts controversial issues such as: group apprehension, backsliding, and report positioning.

GROUP APPREHENSIONS

At first, HRM teams may reluctantly embrace the audit procedure. Concerns about negative feedback and job security are typical. HRM team leaders should lay the foundation for positive collaboration by explaining the positive benefits of the audit.

Here are two likely benefits that show how the entire HRM team benefits. First, the audit identifies "low-hanging fruit," i.e., easily implemented, low-cost improvements that can dramatically enhance satisfaction ratings. Second, by engaging internal customers throughout the process, many people throughout the organization see the HRM department as responsive, attentive, and business-focused. These points begin to paint the upside picture in favour of the audit.

BACKSLIDING

Maximum value of the audit comes from periodic repetition. With the second and third data points, trends begin to emerge. Performance gaps begin to close. Some widen. New issues arise. Priorities are refocused. The second-year hump is the biggest obstacle.

If the audit is forgotten or deliberately avoided in the

second year, a golden opportunity passes. And there is a penalty, too. All the goodwill generated by the first-year audit is squandered. Internal customers become jaded thinking that the first-year exercise was mere lip service.

REPORT POSITIONING

Float a draft of the final report to upper management before organization-wide release. This assures that the proposed HRM action plans conform to broader strategic directions. Feedback alters tactics and priorities for service improvements.

To illustrate, assume midlevel managers do not rate "regulatory compliance" as a high priority for meeting their business goals. However, if regulatory agencies are threatening their own audit reviews, top management may insist that this area become a top priority.

Regularly administered, the HRM Effectiveness Audit places the HRM team firmly at the table with other strategic business partners. The resulting business plan demonstrates how the HRM team will meet the business needs of its internal customers. The entire process effectively engages customers in a dialogue defining a measurement system for tracking progress in HRM service improvement. If public sector HRM teams expect to clearly show that they deserve the label of a strategic business partner, they will need to adopt methodologies similar to those described herein.

Planning

The phenomenon of contingent employment has been on the rise in most industrialized countries since the late 1970s. Contingent arrangements no longer function solely as stopgap measures; indeed, in many firms they have become an integral feature of human resource management. While temporary workers have always been used to cover for holiday and sick leave, there is some evidence to suggest that they are now providing employers with a buffer against market uncertainty.

Scholars and practitioners have defined contingent workers in various ways. In his study, Meager defined temporary workers as "those whose employment at the organization in question is recognized by both sides to be on a temporary basis, irrespective of whether the individuals are employees of the organization (they may be self-employed, or employees of an employment business-that is, a type of employment agency that employs and hires out temporary workers)."

A somewhat broader definition, provided by Polivka and Nardon, considers contingent employment as "any job in which the individual does not have an explicit or implicit contract for long-term employment or one in which the minimum hours of work can vary in a nonsystematic way."

The contingent workforce can take different forms, depending on corporate needs and strategies. *The most common types are*:

- Temporary employees, who can be recruited from outside temporary agencies, directly hired by companies to be temporary employees, or assigned from a company temporary labour pool.
- Contract employees, who can work either ' on- or off-site.
- Subcontractors, who can take many different forms in which independent contractors are responsible for planning and managing their own work.
- Consultants, who are not on the employer's regular payroll, and who are being used by employers increasingly in new and creative ways.
- Leased employees, a form of contingent work in which an employee leasing firm leases workers to a client company. Although the leased employees work in the client company's facility and perform jobs for the client company, they are employees of the leasing firm. An employee leasing firm differs from a temporary agency in that the leasing company provides the client company with an entire workforce, or a high percentage of its workforce, making employee leasing a variation of the traditional permanent workforce.

Economic conditions have increased the variability and uncertainty of product demand, expanded and internationalized the scope of markets, and decreased firm market shares.

The new realities of competition have pressured firms to cut labour costs, achieve greater flexibility in the quantity and skills of their workforce, and alter firm boundaries by shifting the costs and risks of production onto subcontractors and other forms of contingent employment.

A number of demand-side variables have significantly influenced the growth of temporary employment:

- A rise in the level of demand for output above its long-term trend
- The intensification of international cost competition
- The growth of fixed, non-wage labour costs relative to wage costs
- The availability of paid time off for the regular workforce
- The need to adjust the work week of the regular workforce
- The expansion in skill requirements within a firm requiring the use of temporary employees until permanent workers are hired

Companies that use contingent worker systems tend to fall into two groups in terms of labour costs. The first group uses them because they realise direct short-run labour cost savings. based on empirical studies, it is estimated that employing contingent workers produces 20% to 40% savings compared to the use of core workers who perform similar jobs.

These lower contingent worker costs are the result of several factors:

- Contingent employees often have lower employee benefit levels compared to core workers. Firms can hire contingent workers without increasing the cost of health insurance, employer-funded pension plans, or unemployment insurance.
- Contingent employees are often paid at a lower rate compared to core workers.

- Contingent employees are often paid only for the actual work required by the employer.
- Contingent employees provide management with an excellent opportunity to identify suitable employees for permanent core jobs.

The second group of companies uses contingent worker systems because of the importance of long-run labour cost issues.

Among these issues are:

- The use of contingent workers to decrease union power over existing employees. Contingent workers may be used to remind permanent workers that alternative sources of labour are readily available to replace those who use unions, or other means, to express dissatisfaction with the workplace.
- Downsizing. Meager found that employers considered the advantages of being able to adjust the number of employees quickly to shifting work loads, without incurring major severance costs, was a strong benefit of using temporary workers-even more significant than any advantages due to lower wage and non-wage costs of using temporary employees. In addition, contingent workers are typically hired with the explicit understanding that their employment will be for a limited duration. Therefore, they can easily be added to or dropped from the workforce without tarnishing a firm's image or jeopardizing the organization's ability to hire new employees in the future.
- Non-labour costs, such as expensive equipment. Such equipment is more efficiently operated by expert contingent employees, thus reducing long-term usage of expensive equipment by core employees.

Case studies have also shown that companies would not necessarily use more core workers if they did not use contingent workers. Instead, without a more flexible human resource system, a company might have had to end its activities in a specific area.

In his book, Belous summarized the major labour market costs and benefits of increased human resource flexibility.

He lists the main benefits as follows:

- The potential for employers to lower their labour costs and increase productivity;
- The potential for employers to increase their competitiveness in a product market as a result of reduced labour costs;
- The increased job security of remaining core workers and the increased job opportunities for contingent workers;
- The ability of the national economy to sustain economic growth and not ignite a high level of inflation;
- The increased ability of many workers to be active in the world of work, which traditional full-time employment may block; and
- The increased ability of workers to find re-employment if they become unemployed.

The major costs of increased human resource flexibility are:

- The high level of economic insecurity for many contingent workers due to fewer opportunities to obtain employee benefits, such as health insurance and pension coverage;
- Lower wages for many contingent workers than for core workers who are doing similar jobs; 3) the potential for an increase in the level and rate of unemployment in a recession;
- The potential unwillingness of some employers to make the same investments in human capital development (e.g., training, skill development, and education) for contingent workers as for core workers; and
- The potential for affirmative action consequences arising from the growth of contingent workforces.

According to various estimates made by Belous, there is a strong basis for asserting that:

- The contingent workforce in the U.S. is growing considerably faster than the entire labour force.
- Nearly one-fourth or more of the American labour force in the 1980s was in the contingent work force.
- A significant number of the jobs generated in the 1980s were for contingent workers.
- The growth rate of temporary employment has remained strong well into the 1990s.
- Although the majority of temporary workers still fill positions on the lower end of the job ladder, a growing number of temporary workers are now filling professional positions.
- Although temporary work has had the image of unskilled labour, in the microelectronic revolution, the temporary service industry has become a key source of training and human resource development.
- Temporary employment has become a major part of corporate efforts to create just-in-time workforces.

Many studies have shown that the use of contingent workers is a growing and significant phenomenon, not only in the U.S., but in other countries as well. A large number of Japanese corporations, for example, are using some of the same strategies that American companies have adopted, including more subcontracting and greater use of part-timers and temporary employees.

OBJECTIVES, PROCESS AND IMPORTANCE

Even many lifetime employers in Japan have recognized that a healthy core workforce requires the use of a significant number of contingent workers. In his exhaustive study of the contingent economy, Belous asserts that in most cases, the growth of the contingent workforce was an ad hoc response to dramatic shifts in the business conditions experienced by companies. Managing a contingent human resource system is quite different from directing a traditional core workforce.

A different set of managerial talents and sensitivities is needed, and an employer must alter numerous wage and benefit policies and work assignments within a company's human resource system. In most cases, the decision to employ contingent workers was made at the line manager or division manager level, and seldom at the corporate level. There was usually no coherent policy, and when such a decision was made, it was not made using any analytical tools.

When it comes to physical capital, such as plant and equipment, organizations have good systems on which to base a decision to "make or buy." However, in terms of human resources (workers, managers, and their skills), organizations seldom use cost-benefit analysis or other analytical tools that could assist them in determining when to use core or contingent workers.

This chapter presents an analytical tool to assist managers in their decision-making process. Our model is by no means the first to investigate human resource issues through the use of a quantitative model. Conference proceedings dating as early as 1970 show the early activity of researchers applying quantitative models to human resource planning.

Indeed, this activity appeared as early as the 1960s and continued through the 1970s. Of course the activity did not stop there, but continues today as well. These investigations have used such tools as linear programming, integer programming, goal programming, dynamic programming, and steady state flow analysis.

Even though these and other tools are used repeatedly, the most notable tool employed has been Markov chain analysis. The closest line of research to ours is the work applying cost-benefit analysis to human resource planning problems. Our contribution to quantitative approaches to human resource planning is to apply inventory theory models to human resource planning problems in general and to determining the size of the temporary workforce in particular.

Our work can be viewed as a quantitative explanation of the observations of Meager mentioned above - i.e., that temporary workers can be viewed as a buffer against market uncertainty. Before we actually need to perform the required tasks, we generally do not know exactly how much work we will have; as a result, we generally do not know exactly how many workers we will need until the time to do the work is at hand. However, we can estimate how likely it is that we will have a certain amount of work; this can be converted into a probability distribution of the number of workers required. In order to complete all of the work one could hire enough workers to cover every possible eventuality, but this is an unnecessarily expensive option.

A more economical course of action would be to hire fewer workers, and in the event that this turns out to be insufficient, we can call in agency temporary workers. This work contributes a quantitative method for identifying the tradeoffs involved between the likelihood and cost of having too many workers and the likelihood and cost of have too few workers. Because these tradeoffs are closely related to those found in problems in inventory theory, using it we are able to identify what the level of the core workforce should be.

The human resource planning problem closely approximates a single period inventory problem, often termed the newsboy problem, so we look to it to help solve our problem. The newsboy problem can be found in any introductory inventory management book.

The newsboy problem investigates how much of an item to order when faced with a replenishment decision for the single period problem with stochastic demand. Below we review the five stages of the newsboy problem, giving a brief description of each and introducing notations where appropriate.

- Review inventory levels. For the item being considered, one measures the current inventory level; the amount of inventory is represented by the variable I.
- Place an order/or not. After reviewing the inventory level, we may wish to buy more of the item in expectation of future demand. The quantity ordered is called Q. The cost of an order is divided into two parts; the per item cost c and the fixed cost A.
- Receive delivery. The items we ordered are delivered before we need to satisfy the demand.

- Experience and satisfy demand. Customers come in and request the item. If the item is in stock, then we make a successful sale; if not, then the customer leaves unsatisfied. Demand is represented by the random variable D, its density is represented by f(D), and its cumulative distribution function by F(D).
- Pay end-of-period costs. If we predicted demand perfectly - i.e., the amount we ordered was exactly equal to the actual demand - then there are no end-of-period costs. In general, we will either have some inventory left over or have some customers we were unable to satisfy.

For each item that is left, we represent the cost of having it at the end of the period (its holding cost) by h. Typically, the item will have some value; this case is represented by a negative holding cost (h [less than] 0). For each customer that we were unable to satisfy (because we did not have enough items), we need to pay an end-of-period shortage cost. This cost is represented by [Pi].

APPLICATION OF THE INVENTORY MODEL TO HIRING TEMPORARY EMPLOYEES

What should be the size of the workforce of an organization? The optimal hiring decision will balance the cost of having too many workers against the cost of not having enough workers.

Clearly we do not hire enough people for every eventuality because this would be just too expensive. Thus, we might decide to hire less workers, and when the need arises we hire temporary workers. As we will show below, the inventory model described in the previous section could help in this decision.

We will divide our discussion into four human resource planning problems:

- Single period problem, without fixed cost.
- Single period problem, with fixed cost.
- Multi-period problem.
- Multi-location problem.

Whereas the first situation is the least realistic one, it serves as the basis by which we can explain the others.

JOB ANALYSIS

SINGLE PERIOD PROBLEM WITHOUT FIXED COST

Consider the example problem of a small restaurant located near a major league ballpark obtaining the human resources necessary to place flyers on the windshields of cars at an upcoming baseball game. We, as manager, have decided to offer all of its regular employees (i.e., core employees) overtime to hand out the flyers. College students from a local university can also be hired ahead of time (i.e., directly hired temporary employees) if the need for extra help is anticipated. On the day of the game, if there are not enough employees (core and directly hired temporary) to put the flyers on each car, a local temporary agency will be contacted to supply the extra workers (i.e., agency temporary employees).

RELATIONSHIP TO THE INVENTORY PROBLEM

We identify a unit of inventory with a person who is available to do the job. In our example we consider each person who is to distribute the flyers as an item regardless of whether they are core employees, directly hired temporary employees, or agency temporary employees.

We now return to the five stages of the inventory problem, and relate them to the human resource planning problem.

- Review inventory levels. We check to see how many core employees we have. The restaurant in our example problem has 50 employees, but only 15 have agreed to take on the extra work. Thus I = 15.
- Place an order/or not. After noting the number of our core employees, we must decide whether to hire direct temporary workers for the job that is to be done.

The per-person hiring cost, c, would not only include the worker's wages, but the cost of recruiting and other employment processing costs as well. In our example, this would involve hiring college students for the day to distribute the flyers. In order to hire the college students we would have to put up announcements at the local university.

The number of announcements that need to be posted is proportional to the number of college students that we wish to hire, with the cost per person that we wish to hire being \$.50. In addition, when students apply for the job we need to process them and have them fill out the appropriate governmental forms. Combining the time of the contact person and bookkeeper, the cost per college student hired is \$5.00. The largest cost is the actual payroll cost. Each student will be working three hours. Because this is temporary work and we can hire young college students (under the age of 20) we can pay them the training wage of \$4.25 an hour.

Note that we differentiate these college students from agency temporary workers because one is hired before demand is known and the other after. Note also that at this point, we still do not know the number of employees that we need. We will have this information the morning of the game when the amount of tickets sold is announced. From past experience, however, we know that the number of employees we need is normally distributed with a mean of 40 and a standard deviation of 6.

- Receive delivery. The workers we decided to hire are signed up. In our example, this means that we have decided on which college students to hire; they have committed to come and hand out the flyers, and we have committed to paying them.
- Experience and satisfy demand. The time to do the work arrives and we see how many workers we need. Now, we can determine how many extra workers we have, or alternatively, we can determine how many workers we are short. This means that the day of the game has arrived and ticket sales have been announced. Thus, we now know how many workers we need to hand out the flyers. By comparing this number to the number of core and direct temporary

workers we have hired, we also know how many spare workers we have, or alternatively, how many more workers we are short.

- Pay end-of-period costs. At this time, we have to decide what to do with extra workers, and what to do if we do not have enough workers. If we have too many workers, we can let all of them come to work and thus incur no penalty for, nor have any extra benefit from, the extra workers (h = 0). Alternatively, we may be able to have the workers do another job, which even though it would benefit us, would not justify us hiring workers specifically for that job. The benefit from the extra workers corresponds to a salvage value in the inventory theory literature, i.e., h [less than] 0.

Incorporating the fact that it is not justified to hire the worker specifically for this job, we have -c [less than] h [less than] 0. In other cases we may be able to arrange with the workers that they not come to work at all. However, since we have promised them work, we can not recover all of the money we planned to pay them.

On the other hand, in return for not having to come to work they may be willing to accept partial pay (this may even be built into their original work agreement). This means that -h is the amount of wages we are able to save. In this case, we again have a benefit for having too many workers (the cost of hiring the workers is properly considered a sunk cost), and again we have -c [less than] h [less than] 0.

In our example problem, if we have too many workers, then we can have the extra workers hand out flyers to fans arriving at the game by bus. Although this would benefit us, it would do so to a lesser extent because, since these fans do not have cars immediately available to them, they are less likely to be coming to our restaurant after the game. We would have been willing to pay $20.00 for this service, thus h = -$20.00.

If we do not have enough workers to meet the demand, we can call in temporary workers from an agency. Even though these workers can be assumed to be always available, they have a higher cost than directly hired temporary workers ([Pi] [greater than] c). This means that when game day arrives, if we discover that we need more workers, being too late to hire more college students, we will call a temporary agency, which would send us exactly the number of additional workers we need.

For many reasons, not the least of which is that the temporary agency would collect its fee, the workers hired through the agency would cost us more than the college students. Note that we have used the minimum wage here as the hourly wage and not the training wage because these employees are regular employees of the temporary agency and thus do not receive the training wage. Further note that since we do not process these workers, we do not incur this cost nor the cost of announcing the job opportunity.

An obvious alternative to temporary workers is overtime - that is, letting our core workforce work longer hours so as to meet all the demand. However, this alternative is sometimes not available. In our example, when game day arrives it is not a viable option either for the core workers or the directly hired temporary workers to work additional hours because each worker is hired for the length of the game; it would do us no good to put flyers on car windshields after the fans (and their cars) have left.

In addition, many researchers have observed that the direct cost of overtime is often higher than the cost of temporary workers. Even when the direct cost of overtime is lower than the cost of temporary workers, there are often hidden costs that can cause the true cost of overtime to be larger than the cost of temporary workers.

Take as another example the staffing of keyboard operators. Whereas a keyboard operator can work overtime, it is likely that his typing speed will go down and his error rate will go up. Furthermore, the extra hours would undoubtedly affect his work for the next few days as well. While the hidden costs for typists might be quite low, for other, more dangerous work (e.g., construction work), the cost of mistakes is much greater. In fact, in some industries, these hidden costs are so great that legal limits are put on overtime (e.g., pilots and truck drivers).

DESCRIPTION AND SPECIFICATION

THE OPTIMAL POLICY

The only decision to be made is how many direct temporary workers we should hire (Q). The initial inventory I is not determined at this point in time, but is given. In addition, the cost data (c, h, and [Pi]) are given. From the similarity of this problem to the inventory problem, we know that we should hire enough direct temporary workers so that the number of workers after hiring is R, the preferred workforce size.

R can be calculated using the following formula:

Equation (1):

$$F(R) = [Pi] - c/ [Pi] + h$$

Equation (1) can also be interpreted as saying that the preferred workforce level is the one that balances the marginal cost and marginal benefit of hiring an additional worker.

Note from Equation:

- That as h grows more positive, the value of R decreases. This means that our model predicts that the employer will reduce his workforce. This issue has been widely argued in the discussion over the impact of the level of minimum wages on employment in the U.S.

Along with the optimal hiring decision we can also obtain the following quantities from the relationship of the human resource problem to inventory theory:

- Probability of having extra workers
- Expected number of extra workers
- Expected cost of extra workers
- Probability of hiring agency temporary workers
- Expected number of agency temporary workers hired
- Expected cost of agency temporary workers

Returning to our example problem we see that:

$$F(R) = 28.12 – 22.08/ 28.12 + (–20.00) = .7438.$$

Using normal tables, we see that the optimal decision is to have a workforce size of R = 44 workers. Since we already have 15 workers then we should hire Q = R - I = 44 - 1 5 = 29 workers. Furthermore, we calculate the following quantities for our example problem:

- Probability of having extra workers: 74%
- Expected number of extra workers: 4.91
- Expected cost of extra workers: -$98.13
- Probability of hiring agency temporary workers: 26%
- Expected number of agency temporary workers hired: .91
- Expected cost of agency temporary workers: $25.50

NOT HIRING CONTRACTED WORKERS

In some situations the pool of core workers is so large that we would like to reduce the workforce level instead of hiring more workers. But since we have committed ourselves to the core workers to provide them with overtime in this project we can't just decide not to provide them with this opportunity.

We may decide to do nothing, thus when the time to do the job arrives we will simply have more workers than needed (this was discussed above). However, sometimes there may be a better alternative. Perhaps, if we let the core workers know ahead of time that they will not be needed they will be willing to take a nominal sum to not show up for work. Since we have promised them work we save the worker's full wages c less the sum we give him to stay home; we call the amount we save c[prime].

Again, from the relationship of our problem to inventory theory, we know that if "incentives" are to be given then the new preferred workforce size is given by the following formula:

Equation (2):

F(R[prime]) = [Pi] - c[prime]/ [Pi] + h

Note that because of the stochastic nature of the demand and the fact that we would have to pay this "incentive" to the core workers before we know what the actual demand is, there might be a situation (when demand is relatively large) that we both give "incentives" to core workers not to come to work and (later in time) have to hire agency temporary workers.

Modifying our example problem slightly let us assume that all 50 of our core workers have decided to take on the overtime work. Clearly, this is more than the preferred workforce level of 44 calculated above. Further assume that the hourly wage of our core workers is $7.76. Note that their hourly wage is actually much less; this figure reflects what they make with tips.

Even though these workers are more costly to employ than the college students, a policy decision was made by management to offer employment to all these workers. These workers would be willing to accept an hour of pay without working rather than the three hours of pay for putting flyers on the car windshields. This means that it is best of us not to give incentives and for all of our core workers to come to the ballpark on the day of the game.

SINGLE PERIOD PROBLEM, WITH FIXED COST

The description of the single period model with fixed cost is almost identical to the description above; in fact, we use the same example. The fixed cost represents all hiring costs, which are independent of the number of people hired. This may be the cost of setting up a training programme, assuming that both the core workforce and the agency temporary workers are not already trained.

The optimal hiring policy is similar to the one discussed for the single period problem without fixed cost. When we decide to hire at least one direct temporary worker, then we consider the fixed cost a sunk cost, thus the preferred number of workers as given in Equation (1) remains unchanged. The change in the optimal hiring policy comes when we have to make the decision of whether to hire or not.

If the initial workforce size is close to - say one less than - the preferred workforce level, it would be worthwhile to hire one worker if all we have to pay is c. But we would be unwilling to pay the fixed cost A in addition to c just to get one more worker.

To define the optimal policy we now define two workforce levels, r and R. R is, as before, the preferred workforce size. r is called the hiring point and is defined as the workforce level less than R whose cost differs from R by A.

The optimal policy is to hire direct temporary workers to bring the workforce level up to its preferred level if the present workforce level is less than the hiring point (Q = R - I if I [less than] r), and not to hire if the present workforce level is greater than or equal to the hiring point (Q = 0 if I [less than or equal to] R). In our example, this fixed cost is the cost of hiring a bus to bring the students from the university and to take them back after the game.

The cost of the bus is independent of the number of people we need because no matter how many we decide to hire they will all fit on one bus. The bus is needed only if we hire the college students because our core workers can walk from the restaurant (a short 10-minute walk to the ballpark) and the temporary agency is responsible for getting its workers to the ballpark.

MULTI-PERIOD PROBLEM

When modeling the multi-period version of the human resource problem, one has to be very careful with the analogy to the inventory problem. When examining the single period problem we related items to workers.

This analogy needs to be modified for the multi-period version of the problem; whereas when inventoried items are demanded they are gone and need to be replaced by orders for more items, when core workers are demanded they are still available for the next period. This difference means that the multi-period human resource problem is properly viewed as a series of single period problems.

Thus, when modeling the multi-period version of the problem we do not use the multi-period version of the inventory problem; rather, we still use the single period version as described below. The first thing we note is that since all periods are identical there is no mason to change the workforce level from period to period.

This means that we will not use directly hired temporary workers. If the core workforce is insufficient, then we will him more core workers. This means that we will hire workers only once (at the beginning) and will use temporary workers as needed. Our objective is still to minimize costs, and since all periods are identical the objectives of minimizing the per-period cost, minimizing the long-run average cost, and minimizing the total discounted cost are all equivalent.

Consider the staffing levels at a hospital emergency room Friday night. We need to determine how many nurses we need as core employees in order to minimize costs. Since all periods are alike in terms of demand for human resources and costs, the core workforce size is determined at the outset, and there is no reason to change it over time. As the demand fluctuates from period to period we can adjust the workforce level by hiring agency temporary workers.

We now explain each of the stages in this new context, focusing on the differences between this model and the single period version described.

- Review inventory levels. In our example, this would mean examining the number of nurses that we have already committed to hire each Friday night. Let us assume that we presently have 30 nurses that work each Friday night, I = 30.
- Place an order/or not. As discussed above, we do not consider hiring direct temporary workers each period; rather, we consider hiring additional core workers at the beginning. Therefore, the value c no longer includes the cost of recruiting; it now solely represents the wages, benefits, and all other costs of having a permanent employee.

The cost of recruiting is a one-time cost. If we are dealing with the infinite horizon version of the problem, one-time costs are irrelevant. On the other hand, if we are dealing with a finite horizon or if one expects to have to replace workers during the planning horizon, the recruiting and training costs can be incorporated into c by spreading it over the expected employment time of a worker.

We also have to estimate how the need for workers is distributed on a typical Friday night. In our example, this means that when we are setting our staffing levels we need to decide how many core workers will work each Friday night. The cost of employing a nurse on a Friday night (including benefits, etc.) is c = $118.30. To calculate this cost we took the average weekly salary of $455, divided it by five (number of working days in a week), and multiplied by a 30% factor. In our hospital the need for nurses is normally distributed with a mean of 30 and a standard deviation of 7.

- Receive delivery. The workers that we decided to hire in the previous stage are ready to work.
- Experience and satisfy demand. In our example, the demand is the number of nurses we need for any particular Friday night.
- Pay end-of-period costs. For each nurse we have working Friday night that we do not actually need, we have to pay a penalty of h. Normally, h will be less than zero, indicating that this "penalty" is really a benefit. Using one of the explanations found in Section 3.1, we may be able to call up some of the nurses and offer them partial pay and the day off. In this way, we are able to save 51% of their wages, h = -.51 * $118.30 = -$60.33. For each additional worker (above the core workforce) that we need we must pay a penalty of [Pi]. Again, this will generally come from the need to hire an agency temporary worker.

In our example, we can get an agency temporary worker to work Friday night at a cost of [Pi] = $191.10. We took the wage figure of $525, divided it by five and multiplied by a 30% factor and a 40% premium for the temporary agency. The optimal human resource level is again determined by Equation (1), and for our example is 31. This means that we should hire one more nurse to work each Friday night.

MULTI-LOCATION PROBLEMS

Each of the problems considered above can be extended to a problem of a company with two or more locations, the costs for each of the locations being as described above. Linking these locations is the ability to use workers from one location at another location of the same company. The decision of whether this should be done is made after the workload at each location is known.

Extending our earlier flyer example, the situation is now that we plan to distribute flyers at two locations, the ballpark and a major shopping mall located nearby. If we find that we need more people at the ballpark and we have too many people at the shopping mall, we can send some of the shopping mall workers over to the ballpark by means of public transportation. The cost of doing this is simply the bus fare, \$2.00. This transfer of a worker is referred to in inventory theory as a transshipment.

Similarly, the problem of different kinds of workers working at a single location can be modeled as a multi-location problem. Returning to our example of staffing nurses at a hospital, assume that the hospital hires two types of nurses: regular registered nurses and nurses who have received special training to work in the intensive care unit. Because of their special training the workers who work in the intensive care unit get a higher wage.

In addition, these nurses are qualified not only to work in the intensive care unit, but in place of regular registered nurses as well (a transshipment with zero cost). However, the nurses who are not specially trained can not work in the intensive care unit (no transshipments allowed).

Using the same argument we gave above when we related the various single location versions of the human resource planning problem to the single period, single location inventory problem, we can relate both the single period and multi-period versions of the multi-location human resource planning problem to the single period multi-location inventory problem.

The single period, multilocation inventory problems have been examined as follows. Robinson solves two cases: multiple identical locations and general two locations. Herer and Rashit solve the two-location problem with fixed ordering costs. In this chapter we have used techniques from inventory control to aid human resource planners in developing hiring strategies. We have taken both a traditional and a new inventory model and have shown that each can be used for human resource planning.

Having developed this relationship, we used it to quantitatively explain to what extent an organization should plan to use agency temporary workers. All organizations have peaks and valleys in their demand for employees. One way to handle this is to hire and fire workers according to the erratic demand.

Obviously, it is not economical to do so. Good economies demand that the decision of whether or not to hire a worker should be based on the tradeoff between the cost of hiring an extra worker and the cost of not hiring enough workers.

Not having enough workers might imply the cost of not being able to complete the work at hand or, more likely, having to pay an extra premium to acquire an employee from a temporary agency. Our model provides planners with the tools to deal with these strategic issues related to human resource planning.

RECRUITMENT, SELECTION, PLACEMENT AND INDUCTION PROCESS

THE BASIC SCENARIO

We know from the inventory model to which our human resource problem is related that there exists a "preferred" workforce size that we represent by R. If our core workforce size is smaller than the preferred size, then we will hire enough direct temporary workers to bring the workforce to the preferred size (Q = R - i). If our core workforce size is too big (1 [greater than or equal to] R), then we will not hire any direct temporary workers (Q = 0). Thus the only question that remains is what the preferred workforce size is. Again from inventory theory we know that

Equation (3):

$$F(R) = [Pi] - c/ [Pi] + h$$

First we note that since F is a cumulative distribution function it is always between zero and one. Hence, to be able to solve Equation (3) for R, the right-hand side should also be between zero and one. This is guaranteed by the two relations discussed above, [Pi] [greater than] c and -c [less than] h. The left-hand side of Equation (3), F(R), is the probability that the demand for workers is less than or equal to R.

This can be interpreted as the probability of not needing to hire agency temporary workers-in other words, the probability that we will have extra workers (ignoring the essentially impossible situation that we have hired exactly the number of workers we need). Along this line of reasoning, 1 - F(R) can be interpreted as the probability of needing to hire temporary workers. Rearranging Equation (3), we obtain

Equation (4):

c + hF(R) = [Pi](1 - F(R)).

Examining the optimal hiring decision in this way we see that the preferred workforce level is the one that balances the marginal cost and marginal benefit of hiring an additional worker.

The cost of hiring the worker is the left-hand side of Equation (4); the c is the direct cost of hiring the worker and hF(R) is the cost of having an extra worker (normally negative) multiplied by the probability that the worker will not be needed. On the other hand (the right-hand-side of Equation (4)), if we have an extra worker we might need to hire one less temporary worker.

Thus the benefit of hiring an extra worker is the cost of a temporary worker multiplied by the probability that we would have needed to hire temporary workers.

In today's challenging economic environment, local governments across the United States are experiencing decreased revenue collections that are translating into hiring freezes, job eliminations, and programme cuts. Needless to say, city and county employees are by no means ignorant of these facts, which leads to uncertainties and insecurities about their continued employment, pensions, and future employment.

Such anxieties have the propensity to create an unstable

information environment, leading to decreased morale, decreased productivity, and decreased confidence on the part of the citizenry in their local government. It is during times of crisis—commonly defined as any situation that threatens the integrity or reputation of your entity—of the kind we are currently facing that the public manager cannot afford to fail.

This is not the time to refuse to act or to take the wrong kind of action when communicating with insecure employees, public officials, and residents. A well thought out, transparent communication strategy can serve to assuage the jitters experienced by all who have a stake in, and depend on, the essential services your local government provides.

CRISIS COMMUNICATION PLAN

Experience continually reminds us that crises can happen anywhere, at any time, and often occur when they are least expected. When a crisis does occur, events usually unfold rapidly, leaving little time for planning. Although some crises can be predicted and prevented, those that cannot be avoided or anticipated can be minimized if handled properly through advance preparation. Enter the crisis communication plan. Effective crisis communication calls for putting the necessary organizational structure, processes, and tools in place before a crisis hits. Consequently, if your organization does not have a viable communication plan in place, I recommend you develop and implement one as soon as possible.

In addition, choose communication channels thoughtfully: the manner in which and the forum from which you are communicating can be every bit as crucial as what you are attempting to communicate. During a period of fiscal uncertainty, scrutiny of local government communications is higher than ever as employees, citizens, elected officials, and the media clamor for information.

While a viable, effective communication plan can boost a local government's reputation, poor communication strategies or tactics expose it to ridicule from within and without, regardless of how well intended. A communication plan should be easy to read, simple to implement, and designed in such a manner that it can be modified as scenarios change and adapt to local culture. Finally, such a plan should emphasize the manager's personal visibility, accessibility, goals, and objectives.

IMPLEMENTING THE PLAN

Those who are charged with implementing the crisis communication plan should:

- Clarify the manager's strategy and vision for dealing with the economic uncertainty. Developing a strategy and vision will help communicate goals and priorities to employees who look to leadership in times of crisis. It will also improve managers' and employees' abilities to make the right decisions in their day-to-day work.
- Reinforce your strategy and vision in every employee meeting as well as when you address your elected officials. Everyone—from the manager's office to rank-and-file employees—makes decisions every day. They'll align their priorities with the organization's strategy only if they're as clear about it as you are.
- Establish a website where employees can learn what your organization is doing—and what your competitors are doing—to manage the crisis. Transparency is always preferred by employees, but now it's critical. To build trust, ensure that the workforce has easy access to the knowledge it needs to deal with the current situation.
- Send a weekly e-mail update with successes and challenges. Employees respect leadership that is candid. By regularly communicating with them, you'll help them gain confidence in the organization's future.
- Meet with groups of employees to listen to their concerns and solicit their suggestions. It is imperative that employees who are involved in addressing challenges know that their organization values their concerns and opinions and recognizes that each

department consists of unique individuals, duties, and goals.

- Ask department and division directors to develop their own plans for improving quality, serving citizens more effectively, and reducing costs. Harness your employees' energy and act on appropriate suggestions. Send a clear signal: employees' ideas are always valued, regardless of the economic environment.
- Realign performance goals to account for reduced revenue. If you're forced to reprioritize the manner in which services are provided, let employees know their goals may need to change, too. Articulate the new strategy and explain why flexibility is important.
- Make sure people know how the decreased revenues will affect salaries and benefits and possibly their jobs. Tell employees as soon as possible whether their salary or their benefit and retirement package, or both, will be changing. Your workforce would rather know what to expect, even if the news is less than desirable. No one likes surprises.
- Challenge people to cross-train and learn new jobs. Employees can add value—for themselves and the organization—by acquiring new skills. Those who adapt may fare better during a restructuring and will appreciate the opportunity to expand their skills.
- Share key performance indicators with each employee. This is especially important if your key measures have changed to battle the economic crisis. Communicating this information will also help people understand how their role contributes to the organizational goals.

COMMUNICATING WITH EMPLOYEES

In a crisis, employees invariably have a high demand for updated information as well as the desire to provide continuous feedback. Before communicating with employees, here are questions the public manager should consider:

- Who will initiate the communication?
- Which groups of employees will receive the communication?
- How or where will the communication happen?
- When will the communication take place?

COMMUNICATING WITH ELECTED OFFICIALS

Despite the advances in information technology and the increasing use of message boards, e-mail, blogs, Twitter, and other social media, when it comes to communicating with your elected officials, low tech rules. The manager should consistently make time for face-to-face communication. In these stressful, uncertain times, rumors and disinformation abound. These are not the times for the manager to be perceived as scarce or unavailable.

Elected officials consistently expect good and bad news to come directly from the manager There is nothing more damaging to a manager's reputation than the failure to communicate vital information that makes its way into the newspaper or other media outlet, leaving elected officials with the impression that they are the last ones to know. Such a scenario diminishes managers' credibility with their constituents as well as managers' reputations with persons within and without the organization.

COMMUNICATING WITH THE PUBLIC

During times of economic crisis, residents also become insecure. Their insecurity is partly fueled by fears that those public sector services they depend on may be reduced or eliminated outright. Obviously, not all people are concerned about the same projects or services. Some may be concerned about reductions in indigent health care or law enforcement or EMS services, while others may focus on the arts or parks and recreation services.

I suggest that you provide a simplified copy of the current and projected budget (based on reduced revenues) to the public in an easily read and understood format. Rather than attempting to assuage fears, it's best to concede the looming problems, explain why they exist (such as reduced building permit or business tax revenues), and identify actions already taken and plans for future actions to mitigate or correct the problem. Town hall meetings are often helpful, as are notices placed on the local government's Web page.

A WORD ABOUT THE MEDIA

In our era of blogs, e-mail, personal Web pages, and related social media, many individuals in your organization have access to news outlets and special interest groups. During times of crisis, such access could prove detrimental to your organization's reputation as well as thwart your communication efforts. This is especially true when the media are flooded with many statements from many sources that don't seem to jibe.

In these situations, it is best if only appropriately trained and, more important, designated employees communicate with the media. Such a practice ensures that rumor and innuendo are eliminated and a consistent, cogent message is transmitted to all. Further, the savvy manager should always presume that when speaking with a reporter for a print story or recorded interview, the discussion is "on the record" at all times. Finally, if bad news exists, the manager should be the one to report it, up front, with candor.

By clearly and consistently communicating your plan and keeping everyone—department directors, division directors, employees, elected officials, and residents—informed during times of economic uncertainty, the public manager can go a long way toward keeping employees' productivity levels high while implementing the necessary strategic changes to ensure the local government's long-term success.

Chapter 8

Development Programme

EMPLOYEE TRAINING

Empirical research supports common sense—leadership matters to an organization's effectiveness. Leadership skills can be learned; although learning on the job is too haphazard a way to ensure an organization's viability. A leadership development programme (LDP) requires nine overlapping tasks, which should be managed by HR professionals.

Each task answers a basic question:

- What kind of candidates is the organization looking for?
- What does it take to be a good leader in the organization?
- How does one become a programme participant?
- How does the participant stack up as a leader right now?
- What specific actions should the participant take to become a better leader?
- In what ways is the LDP reinforced by other HR systems?
- How can the participant's work group be part of the developmental process?
- Is there a leadership succession plan?
- Is the LDP giving a satisfactory return on investment?

It is axiomatic that superior organizations have superior leaders. Yet, broadly skilled leaders are in short supply. The time-honoured way of learning one's technical specialty, and then somehow transitioning into supervision is not a reliable method for producing adequately trained staff. Most organizations need a vigourous and deliberate way to improve the skills of supervisors, managers, and executives. They need a leadership development programme (LDP). Although costly, an LDP is a wise investment for a compelling reason— well-led organizations tend to attract quality applicants, produce satisfied employees, incur less unwanted turnover, engender loyal customers, and yield impressive financial returns.

However, it is fair to raise a basic policy question in deciding how to ensure the organization is leadership ready: buy or build. Under the "buy" approach, the organization relies upon recruiting and selecting talented leaders from outside. This is a fast way to get skilled personnel with fresh ideas and obviates the need for erecting an expensive internal development programme.

The major disadvantages of not developing from within are a likely decrease in morale for those bypassed and temporary dips in productivity while new leaders "learn the ropes." In addition, unionized organizations may encounter additional resistance.

The prime advantage of building leadership talent, besides eliminating the disadvantages of going outside, is twofold. First, the organization gets to groom the next generation in line with its culture and strategic agenda. Second, the organization has greater control over the supply of leaders with the requisite skills, making strategic implementation faster. The need for talented leaders exists, and on balance, it appears the benefits outweigh the costs of creating an LDP within the organization. The following plan provides an overview and detailed outline of the nine essential tasks for creating a leadership development programme to help current and future leaders reach their potential in the service of organizational goals.

CORE PROGRAMME PREMISES

Two premises, based on ample evidence, are at the program's foundation. First, leadership matters to an organization's performance. Hence, an organization should concentrate resources on securing, developing, and keeping good leaders. Second, it is possible to develop leaders. Leaders may be born, but they are also made.

Several other premises guide this plan:

- LDP develops the whole person, not only one's skills at work. Many people can benefit from some aspects of the programme. (In this respect, leadership development can be viewed as an organization-wide initiative, "operationalized" through the widespread use of individual development plans.)
- Most organizational members have opportunities to lead at work. Many people can benefit from some aspects of an LDP.
- Leadership is fundamentally a relationship between leaders and followers; the context in which the leader resides must be considered in creating developmental activities.
- Valid assessment and measurement of progress are necessary.
- Growth entails motivation, substantial effort, challenge, and a willingness to accept risk and setbacks.
- People learn best in a nurturing environment.
- Certain traits—enduring personality characteristics—correlate with leadership effectiveness. Careful selection improves the odds of developing the most promising candidates. Selection, versus open enrollment, should be part of the programme.
- Developing leaders requires considerable effort and expense. Measuring overall success allows us to make the programme more effective and efficient. We must evaluate the programme, and to do this we must have clear goals.

Each premise suggests a value. Build these values into the programme if they agree with the current or ideal culture of your organization. If not, adjust the programme accordingly. Little is more dispiriting to participants than for the organization to create an unrealistic "cultural island," only to thrust graduates back into an environment that does not support, and may even punish, different ways of leading. In this respect, leadership development is a product and a shaper of the organization's culture.

EXECUTIVE DEVELOPMENT

OVERALL APPROACH

A comprehensive LDP requires careful selection of participants from the applicant pool, adequate funding, and dedicated administrators and development staff. Beyond that, the symbolic aspects of leadership need attention (e.g., awards ceremonies, distinguished leaders speakers' series, etc). Create or use existing methods to visibly reward current and aspiring leaders for behaving in accord with officially designated competencies.

Equally important, the organization should show its commitment to the programme by intolerance of poor leaders. Ineffective programme participants and current leaders who are incapable or unwilling to improve despite organizational support should be removed. Dramatic acts demonstrate real versus espoused values around leadership. Next, give potential leaders challenging opportunities early in their careers, ideally in their twenties and thirties. They should be nurtured and have enough responsibility to make an impact and significant mistakes. Noble failures are not punished.

Indeed, the wise organization tries to accelerate its mistakes, thereby increasing its learning. Mistakes are tolerated, provided they are in service to the organization, and participants learn from those mistakes. Young leaders receive targeted training and development based on individual needs. Older leaders receive broadening experiences and educational opportunities. Finally, the organization rewards the developers of the next generation of leaders. Mentors are highly valued and rewarded.

Task 1. Create Programme Selection Criteria

"What kind of candidates is the organization looking for?"

Define criteria for programme selection. Each strategic business unit (SBU) and support office may answer this question slightly differently, based on unit-specific strategy, goals, and current and future leadership needs. General selection criteria can be established beyond specific SBU needs. Find a good match between immediate and future role demands and the applicant's personality.

Admittedly, this is easier said than done, owing to inconsistent findings over decades of earnest research. Still, despite situational contingencies that determine the traits necessary to lead in a particular circumstance, several traits appear to correlate with leadership effectiveness in most situations.

The following list of traits is not exhaustive, but can be used as one part of the selection criteria. Alternatively, it can be used as a starting point for discussion within the organization. If not these, then what leadership traits does the organization consider fundamental? What traits, upon entering the programme, are likely to accelerate skill acquisition?

Desire—wants to lead; wants to get things done through other people; wants to have an impact (perhaps the most heavily weighted variable).

- *Purposeful*: Has vision and goals; wants to achieve something, to accomplish things.
- *Confident*: Believes she or he can make a difference, but isn't grandiose.
- *Assertive*: Is willing to assert self and to compete, without becoming unduly upset.
- *Psychological fitness*: Has insight and comfort with self; is empathic towards others and open to feedback.
- *Centreed*: Has sufficient impulse control; stays focused under pressure.
- *Energy*: Has physical stamina to do lots of things and work long hours.

General intelligence—possesses average or slightly above average general intelligence (e.g., logical, linguistic, mathematical, spatial, relative to subordinates, and sufficient for the occupation). General intelligence and other characteristics are necessary but not sufficient characteristics to guarantee leadership success. Context and technical skills matter, to say nothing of motivation. Still, the applicant who possesses these eight traits has met one threshold test to become a leader. A summary argument for the importance of traits might by found in the following quote:

"Regardless of whether leaders are born or made or some combination, it's clear leaders are not like other people. They need the "right stuff," and it is not equally present in all people. Leadership is demanding. It is a disservice to leaders to suggest that they are ordinary people who happened to be in the right place at the right time. Maybe place matters, but it takes a special kind of person to master the challenges of opportunity."

Other programme selection criteria might include: * Strategic directions—Where is the organization going and what type of skills does it need to get there? For example, a marketing unit may need staff with an aesthetic sense. This might suggest recruiting and selecting candidates for the programme from nonbusiness backgrounds.

- *Demographic diversity goals*: Many organizations see this as a real need, in that women and minorities tend to be concentrated in lower salary levels.
- *Technical skills*: What are some basic, foundational skills of a technical nature that are required to be a good leader within the organization? Some organizations insist that the candidate must first possess solid technical expertise before earning the right to manage others. Performance appraisal data might aid assessment.

Task 2. Define Leadership Competencies

"What does it take to be a good leader in the organization?"

Identifying the critical leadership competencies that correlate with organizational effectiveness tells us what leadership skills are needed. Some organizations use generic leadership competencies found in theory; others build their own competencies; and some derive competencies from the organization's mission statement and core values. The exact competency set may vary by level—supervisor, manager, or executive—and organizational unit. However, most organizations find foundational competencies apply in many situations, and, therefore, can be used in the same developmental activities.

Researchers are offering fresh ideas of what makes a good leader. As a distinct competency, moral leadership at work is attracting attention. Why? Organizations are better off if they behave ethically. Most employees come to the organization with some understanding of ethical values, and some attraction to these values.

The aspiring and current leader should be taught how to use all five bases of his or her power to reinforce ethical values. We should recognize leaders have a degree of influence over their employees, and they should use it to create a better society. Moral leadership is not foreign in many organizations. It aligns with many mission statements and core values such as integrity, human growth at work, and stewardship.

A degree of realism is needed here. Although it is possible for a leader to influence the ethical development of her or his employees, we should not expect significant change. Advancing the most abstract values will avoid cultural bias and organizational irrelevancy. A moral leadership competency might include the following values and behaviours.

- Compassion.
- Willingness to help others.
- Truthfulness, including not lying by omission.
- Avoiding gossip and political behaviour designed to advance a personal agenda. Also, not attempting to gain an unfair advantage over one's coworkers that does little, if anything, to further legitimate organizational goals.
- Fairness. Leadership that promotes equality between races, genders, and hierarchical and occupational levels.
- Repudiation of destructive competition.

- Tolerance for diverse views.

Task 3. Establish an Application Process

"How can I become a participant in the programme?"

The programme application procedures should be simple, fair, and accurate.

It is a three-step process:

(a) Advertise the programme,
(b) Evaluate applicants' suitability,
(c) Inform them of the decision.

A. Advertise programme. Some policy questions the organization needs to address in creating general selection criteria follow.

- Length of service, status, and standing—For example, longer than 24 months as a regular, full-time employee and acceptable performance appraisal ratings.
- Occupations—Where are the predicted shortages, due, for example, to resignations and retirements over the next few years?
- Grade-level categories—For example, those at or under a certain grade level enter a first-line supervisor track; those at the highest-grade levels enter an upper management track.
- Location—Where does the programme reside? Perhaps the organization could have a regional and headquarters programme.
- Specific experience requirements—For example, 2 years as a brand manager assistant.
- Specific educational requirements—For example, 12 semester hours of management credit.
- Implementation of leadership skills—Likelihood of having an opportunity to lead in a reasonable time after graduating from the programme, given the organization's workforce trends and strategic directions.
- Commitment to the organization—For example, requirements to remain for a given length of

time, or willingness to relocate at the organization's discretion to fill a management position.

B. Assess applicants. Use the leadership traits noted above and any other traits or criteria assumed to correlate with leadership ability to develop an assessment protocol for programme applicants. This protocol could involve:
   - A limited number of essay questions based on the eight traits.
   - A limited number of essay questions concerning previous, verifiable leadership experiences. This is possibly the best predictor of success.
   - Standardized tests based on the (eight) traits.
   - Leader, peer, and subordinate, if any, ratings of applicant's potential. For existing leaders, a 360-degree leadership survey can be a piece of the application. Leader aspirants could use the same survey.
   - Technical knowledge usually gleaned from performance appraisals, within one's occupation. If the individual wishes to lead in an area outside of her or his current occupation, these criteria may be waived.
   - A concise biographical information blank; e.g., work history, formal education, and training.
   - Personal interview—open-ended, structured questions based on results of the above data collection.

C. Notify applicants. A crucial but often overlooked job. Prompt notification is one way applicants judge the quality of an organization; don't jeopardize your standing with the people who are interested in working with you.

Task 4. Assess Current Leadership Skills

"How do I stack up as a leader right now?"

Craft valid, reliable, and efficient ways of measuring

participants' current leadership style tied to competency criteria. A 360-degree leadership survey and performance appraisals are good sources of data. The assessment data collected during application may also be used. For example, the individual's and others' assessment of his or her leadership traits could provide insight into the participant's style and motivation. Assessment data is analysed and packaged by an LDP staff member, and fed back to the participant. These data provide targeted information to assist the participant in creating an action plan, and aggregated results help to create development activities for all participants.

Assessment centres are a popular way of providing participants with a multifaceted portrait of their leadership style and potential. Despite considerable cost, they are in use in thousands of private and public sector organizations. The typical centre puts candidates through 2 or more days of intensive activities that evaluate their planning, organizing, decision-making, and leadership ability. Trained observers rate performance on these simulations and exercises. Assessment centres provide a valid measure of leadership, providing a nuanced picture of the participants' styles.

Larger organizations usually favour assessment centres where, due to the high volume of participation, per-unit cost declines. Still, a smaller organization could have an abbreviated version targeting a few critical competencies. Allowing the organization's executives to help design exercises and assess others will enhance their own leadership style. Owing to its intensity, the assessment centre provides accuracy, depth of understanding, and participant commitment to the action plan. An assessment centre makes a powerful statement about the organization's intention to build an excellent organization through its leaders.

Task 5. Provide Developmental Activities

"What specific things do I need to do to become a better leader?"

Offer a set of measurable, challenging, and time-bounded developmental activities for participants. The LDP assumes that (almost) all motivated participants can become effective leaders within 3 to 5 years. This requires accurate assessment of skill needs, focused development, and consistent organizational support. Using the survey and other assessment data, participants prepare a detailed individual development plan (IDP) and review it with an LDP administrator, their supervisor, and organizational mentor.

IDPs capture participants' specific strengths and areas of needed improvement. The participant develops a plan that focuses on greatest needs, while capitalizing on strengths. A 1-to-3 year time frame allows plenty of small, deliberate steps that add up. Each IDP details any number of time-bounded activities, for example, classroom training, rotational assignments, committee work, and directed readings.

Each participant takes primary responsibility for his or her own learning. An IDP is a practical way for this to happen. The IDP is checked frequently and revised, as needed, with input from the programme administrator, supervisor, and mentor. At various intervals formal evaluation occurs, usually by readministering the 360-degree leadership survey and performance appraisals. Resurveying every 6 to 12 months yields useful data to affirm growth and revise action plans.

Leadership development typically occurs in three related areas: technical, conceptual, and interpersonal.

Technical

Technical training enhances skills to perform the work unit's tasks, and/or to oversee the work of others. Technical skills are most important at the lower levels of leadership, where leaders are closest to the work. It is the easiest developmental task to accomplish, and usually involves a combination of traditional classroom training—more frequently just-in-time and OJT.

Conceptual

Here the focus is on teaching the leader how to think in a more abstract and critical fashion. It is harder to do than technical training, but possible. Conceptual leadership competencies that might be used for assessment include creativity, strategic thinking, decisiveness. Of course, these competencies are not immediately relevant for all occupations and levels of leadership.

The developmental method for conceptual skills may target specific areas or be more general in nature. Nevertheless, every participant should ensure that her or his skill needs receive sufficient attention.

Some common methods include business games; college or graduate courses; certificate and degree programs; simulations; critical thinking training; directed readings; writing articles for publication; making presentations at professional conferences; rotational assignments; task force assignments; seminars and workshops; focused meetings with consultants and other subject matter experts; being mentored; mentoring others; and shadowing executives.

Interpersonal

The ability to work effectively with people is the essential determinant of leadership success. Developing interpersonal skills is, however, the most challenging of the three leadership categories. Still, it is possible. Most developmental methods involve experiential learning, i.e., learning by doing. The learning is reinforced with cognitive understanding of theory.

Common methods include:

- Role playing with observer feedback.
- Role playing with video feedback and observer feedback.
- Participating in organization development (OD) projects with goals related to the participant's specific skill needs.
- Receiving coaching and counseling from an OD consultant.
- Engaging in case analyses with other programme participants.
- Job rotation through managerial tasks, with frequent feedback.
- Being mentored.

- Receiving special assignments that require high levels of interpersonal interaction.
- Shadowing executives.
- Using an assessment centre as an observer of others.
- Attending interpersonal skill workshops, for example, at the National Training Laboratory's Human Interaction or the federal government's Federal Executive Institute or Management Development Centres under the direction of the U.S. Office of Personnel Management.
- Maintaining a learning journal.
- Providing coaching and counseling to peers within the programme.
- Attending "interpersonal forums" with other programme participants to discuss progress and problems.
- Attending feedback-intensive programs, for example the Centre for Creative Leadership's Leadership Development Programme.

Task 6. Align Structures to Reinforce Programme

"In what ways is the LDP reinforced by other HR systems?" Successful LDP programs find ways to tie desired leader behaviour to the organization's formal personnel systems.

These include:

- Writing position descriptions that capture required leader behaviour as a critical success factor.
- Designing selection systems that heavily weight past leadership successes and clear potential for leadership in the hiring decision.
- Including leadership as the key element of the leader's performance appraisal.
- Providing balanced feedback on a routine basis.
- Creating meaningful reward programs for the effective leader.
- Providing frequent and timely reinforcement of desired behaviour.

- Withholding rewards from and removing leaders who are not performing and demonstrating little motivation.

Many organizations, such as American Express, AT and T, Eastman Kodak, and Honeywell require their top leaders to engage in a 360-degree feedback process and use the results to sharpen their skills.

Moreover, all four firms use the survey findings—and trend lines from administration to administration—in making decisions about salary, bonuses, succession planning, selection, placement and, in some cases, termination of employment. Thus, leadership development is linked to other HR structures.

Other HR systems should be audited to determine their congruence with the LDP's goals. At AT and T, for example, executives in some divisions get feedback early in the rating period as to what their bonus will be, assuming the leader's performance continues along the projected path.

This HR system serves as an "early warning device" that leadership matters, thereby reflecting the corporation's values in an administratively feasible way. The same format described for executives could be adopted at the supervisory and managerial levels within an organization.

Task 7. Develop Leaders in Context

"Can the groups I lead be part of the developmental process?"

As much as possible, leadership development should occur on the job, not away from the job. Leaders get things done through others. Leadership is essentially a transaction between a leader and followers. It makes sense to create developmental programs that attend to the transactional context within which the leader resides.

For instance, empowered groups such as self-directed work teams distribute the leadership function rather than relying on one formally designated person. Increasingly, teams are held accountable to each other via performance appraisal and customer satisfaction surveys of each other's timeliness, quality, and so forth.

The mature team recognizes it is responsible for its reputation, along with the leader. We can increase the developmental yield by helping the leader Team-based leadership development reflects modern thinking about leadership.

This model downplays the ancient understanding of leadership as dominance of one over many. We step away from teaching leaders how to make decisions by themselves, towards developing the capacity of people to maintain themselves within a social setting and achieve group goals. The leader alone is not responsible for creating an effective organization.

The development must occur within the group because the view of the leader as the person with all the answers is challenged by the reality of having individual team members at all levels making continuous decisions. Further, in a multicultural world it is logical that any one leader cannot have all the answers. Even the most cosmopolitan and seasoned person has limits to her/his ability to know other groups, other cultures and other markets.

Education and training within the group is practical, being immediately applied within the leader's setting. For instance, he/she does not deal with difficult people in the abstract, but deals with a specific difficult member of his/her current team. In this respect, group-based development is a practical experiential method of learning. How might an organization conduct leader and group development? Team building is a powerful method.

Team building is widely used to improve the work group's effectiveness and job satisfaction, whereby the team examines its current performance in several areas. The leader plays an important role in the process, as he or she is often the principal, although by no means the only, actor in the group.

During a team building intervention, members, with the help of an outside facilitator, examine their functioning compared to the ideal, high-performing team. The goal is to replace ineffective behaviour with more productive methods of working together.

Considerable research finds high-performing teams share certain elements, including:

- Interdependence and commitment to goals.
- Effective communication of ideas and feelings.
- Quality decision making and problem solving.
- Relevant technical expertise.
- The ability to manage conflicts with a minimal amount of tension.
- An optimal level of social cohesion.
- Challenging performance norms.
- Active participation and distribution of leadership.
- A supportive leader who uses power appropriately.

In each area, the group reviews its behaviour and often finds more effective ways of working. One could argue that the leader's first responsibility is to create a high-performing team because teams are fundamental units having critical leverage points for improving the enterprise.

Like individual development, team building is most effective when carried out over a period of time, say, one session per month for 12 months. One-time team building interventions are usually not effective, given the tendency of groups to revert to type soon after the initial enthusiasm wanes.

However, because the group often concentrates on real business issues, we tend not to see productivity slippage because of time away from the job. Real work gets accomplished within the team building session itself. The investment produces fast returns. In addition to team building with a leader and her or his intact work group as described above, the organization may also wish to conduct many other of the developmental activities described in task 5 with the leader and intact team.

In many instances, the activities lend themselves better to work with the intact team than the leader "going it alone." Conceptual skills such as thinking strategically and being entrepreneurial can be directed at the work team, especially when implementation becomes the real test of utility for learning something new. Interpersonal skills such as resolving differences and effective communications are most effectively taught in groups.

Finally, although not working with the intact team, peer team-building interventions are a useful developmental activity. Peer groups could tackle special, organization-wide projects, with a facilitator assisting them to enhance their leadership and team member skills while they solve business problems. Moreover, the cohesion generated from this type of learning makes it easier for the leaders to collaborate on any number of initiatives and projects that go beyond their immediate relationship. In this way, peer team-building has a substantial, albeit indirect, impact on organizational effectiveness.

Task 8. Plan for the Next Generation of Leaders

"How can we ensure we have the right mix of leaders today and tomorrow?"

Assuming the organization chooses to build its talent pool, the leadership succession plan becomes a central part of the development process. In a sense, LDP and leadership succession planning are synonymous.

One distinguishing feature is viewing LDP as a specific programme for developing individual leaders, whereby succession planning accounts for the aggregation of leadership development needs, activities to address those needs, and measurement of leadership readiness across the organization. Succession planning takes a broad, longer-range view of future managerial needs and resources. The LDP should fit within the organization's strategic goals—organizational directions determine current and future leadership needs. The succession plan ensures an adequate supply of capable leaders is available to carry out strategic intent throughout the organization.

The succession planning process has several steps designed to develop leadership talent.

These steps involve the following:

- Assessment of LDP applicants or participants' current leadership potential and skills—Includes range of biographical data (for instance, career progress, education, interests, and realistic career aspirations).

- Appraisal of leadership behaviour from formal appraisal systems and surveys—Answers the question, in the aggregate, "How well led is this organization?"
- Determination of future management and leadership needs through forecasting and strategic planning.
- Definition of leadership requirements in the near future, expressed in qualitative terms for various organizational levels—The executive committee must review this document carefully and reach an agreement on the numbers and types of leaders needed.
- Specification of actions for training and developing categories of LDP participants (methods noted in task 5)—Specification usually involves a discussion about the wisdom of "fast tracking" participants. Every organization must weigh the costs and benefits of such an approach.
- Creation of a measurement system for summarizing developmental progress and overall organizational leadership readiness.
- Act to meet immediate needs for leaders.
- Modify the programme to manage surpluses of leaders.

Ultimately, assessment of leadership potential and readiness remains a line management responsibility. The succession-planning process must be directed by the organization's leaders, not the HR staff. Staff may, however, administer the plan under the line's direction.

Task 9. Evaluate the Leadership Development Programme

"Are we getting a good return on our investment?"

The organization's executives and programme designers should define the exact nature and scope of the evaluation, based on programme goals. Furthermore, because evaluation requires a degree of time and expertise, the decision to conduct an evaluation at any level should be based on resource availability.

Answering the question "How well is the programme working?" requires clear programme goals. Without clear goals the programme is unlikely to succeed and impossible to measure. From clear goals derive the potential to evaluate the LDP at five levels: reaction (Level 1), knowledge and skill transfer (Level 2), on-site behavioural change (Level 3), business impact (Level 4), and monetary return on investment (Level 5.)

Data needed at each level influences the kinds of programme activities one conducts. A well-planned evaluation minimizes the burden by building in practical and unobtrusive ways of gathering data. Evaluation begins at the very beginning of the programme design, not at the end.

Generally, each succeeding level of evaluation increases rigor and cost. It is financially prudent, therefore, to consider the program's success criteria. For example, if success is primarily measured by satisfied participants who assert their intention to apply what they have learned, a Level-1 evaluation suffices.

Conversely, if the programme must pay its way to stay alive, you should determine return on investment by tabulating and subtracting programme costs from bottom-line indicators such as revenue enhancement or cost savings. Following are some general suggestions for evaluating the LDP. Make the evaluation robust, given the importance and cost of an LDP. As each level builds upon the one below it, you should collect data on level one through four. Information on participant reactions, knowledge and skill acquired, on-site application, and business impact helps us to understand and explain level five, monetary return on investment.

State goals and intended audience for each developmental activity clearly. Measuring return on investment (ROI) revolves around two goals, reducing costs and increasing desired impact. For this purpose, leadership development goals should map back to one or both of these primary objectives. In addition, you can cite non-monetary outcomes such as increased job satisfaction from pre-post climate surveys and fewer grievances or less unwanted turnover by tracking personnel records.

Gather baseline data for participants and comparison groups. Although it is tempting to forego compiling baseline data, you should resist the temptation. The ability to show before-and-after change is a powerful argument that training has made a difference, especially when you have a control group that did not receive the training.

Use a control group and, if possible, randomly assign people to training or no-training conditions. To avoid being accused of turning the organization into a laboratory, refer to the control group as the comparison group. Comparison groups may, at some point, become participants in the programme.

If so, the study can be explained to the organization as a "lagged participation" evaluation. In the ideal situation, the organization could randomly assign leaders to the participant and comparison groups to avoid the danger of biasing the results by choosing "winners." In the "real world" choosing the most qualified candidates might make perfect sense.

Use judgement rather than random assignment to determine who is in the initial participant and comparison conditions, if you so desire.

This may be especially important to ensure that an adequate number of women and minorities are included in the programme. Gather a sufficient sample size and attempt to get representative participants for the study to permit organizational generalization; at least to the strata included in the study. Initially, the organization may identify three levels—supervisors, midmanagers, and upper-managers.

PERFORMANCE APPRAISAL

Calculate costs and benefits over the shelf life of the programme. That is, estimate how many times the programme will run and subtract this cost from the projected future benefit. Some organizations include an inflation factor to enhance precision. Consider using trend-line data to isolate the effects of training. Use past data to predict future trends, then compare that to the posttraining actual performance.

Note the gap in the two trend lines, and attribute this gap to the effects of training. It is an inexpensive and intuitive method. Be careful. It may be inaccurate attribution because posttraining changes may be caused by something other than training. Past is not always a good predictor of future. However, as one indication of the program's effectiveness, it is a reasonable method to use.

Use regression analysis—a statistical method that shows the relationship between two or more variables. To use this technique one specifies all of the potential independent and dependent variables that are likely to influence the desired outcome. Examples of independent variables include amount of budget, supervisory style, and skill level of workers. Dependent variables, i.e., those that are acted upon, might include: sales, revenue, profit, scrap rate, cost savings, and turnover.

We are looking for a correlation between the independent and dependent variables. For example, assume leaders are taught how to improve quality. We later find that scrap rate declines. We can begin to build a case that training made the difference. Especially if we do not see a similar downward movement in scrap rate within the comparison group that did not receive the training. Measure quality with a customer satisfaction index. Record the difference in customer satisfaction before and after training for participants and comparison groups. Next, correlate customer satisfaction to sales.

Customer satisfaction is hard data in the sense that it is part of the unit-profit contribution. Customer satisfaction data is a good metric in organizations that use a standardized, valid instrument such as the American Customer Satisfaction Index Rating, Gallup and Schulman, Roncas, Bucuvalas, Inc. (SRBI). These may be useful, assuming we can isolate the participants' contribution to these indices. This is another reason to use a comparison group.

Consider employee grievances. Assume leaders are

trained in how to diffuse conflict. After training, have managers and HR staff calculate average cost of a grievance award plus the labour cost of time spent by the organization processing the claim, plus external legal fees to arrive at the unit cost of one grievance. Then calculate before-and-after changes in number of grievances filed and annualize the difference to arrive at ROI, minus cost of training itself, of course.

A final thought on evaluating an LDP: Don't forget intangible benefits from training. By intangible, we mean important indicators that do not tie directly to monetary outcomes such as increased job satisfaction, improved communication and teamwork, and fewer complaints. Calculating these benefits can be a challenge; nonetheless, even here the organization may be able to measure financial returns.

It is often noted that a firm's only distinctive competence is its employees. But, coordinated effort is needed to convert employee potential into positive outcomes. Leadership at every level is the necessary catalyst. High performing organizations are led by technically, conceptually, and interpersonally skilled individuals who have the ability to empower and guide employee behaviour. Leadership is a teachable skill, albeit difficult and time consuming. Also, an internally built and administered LDP is a large undertaking, especially when the programme comprises the nine steps described here. However, the organizational benefits can be substantial, far outweighing the costs. Systematic leadership development is a strategic choice, representing a long-term investment in the organization's future and that of its employees.

Chapter 9

Job Compensation

JOB EVALUATION

The concept of pay equity is important not only from the standpoint of employee morale, commitment, and performance, but for compliance with equal employment opportunity laws such as the Equal Pay Act of 1963 and the Civil Rights Act of 1964. Recently, job evaluation has received considerable attention as part of the continuing concern for sex-based pay equity.

In the 1981 Supreme Court ruling, Gunther v. County of Washington, the court held that female dominated jobs were not required to be identical in content (i.e., duties) to jobs held primarily by males in order for federal courts to hear testimony of possible wage discrimination. Subsequently, job evaluation methodology and results have become prominent issues in sex-related discrimination cases, as well as a focal point of pay equity legislation being passed by local and state governments.

In addition to legal considerations, important reasons for the use of job evaluation in compensation management are:

- Having a rational and communicable basis for explaining different wage rates,
- Maintaining job satisfaction and minimizing grievances,
- Having a flexible basis for revising pay rates and establishing rates for new jobs
- Containing the administrative costs of employee compensation. Recently a number of measurement problems cited in a National Academy of Sciences

study by Treiman and Hartmann have been addressed in the personnel literature.

For example, research has focused upon such psychometric properties of job evaluation plans as reliability, sex-biasing, and validity. However, an important methodological issue that has received scant attention in the literature is that of job evaluation factor weighting.

WEIGHTING IN JOB EVALUATION

Most formal job evaluation plans entail the measurement of job worth by ranking or rating jobs on a set of "compensable" factors. Attributes of job worth measured by these factors typically fall into the categories of skill, responsibility, effort, and working conditions. When combining the separate factor scores to form a composite, or when using the individual factors as variables in a prediction model, a decision must be made concerning the weighting of each factor.

The determination of job evaluation factor weights is usually done in one of three ways:

- A priori weights may be chosen and applied to the factors reflecting a subjective notion about worth;
- Weights may be derived empirically, from a statistical regression analysis of the relationship between job evaluation scores and criterion wage rates;
- Job evaluation factors may be deemed equivalent in value and thus receive "equal" weights.

It has been suggested that many job evaluation systems used today could have weighting schemes that reflect a bias against female dominated jobs, although supportive evidence in this regard is incomplete. Studies have not been published, for example, that compared the sex-related effects of alternative weighting methods.

Weighting bias could occur in a number of ways. First, if a judgmental (a priori) weighting scheme is used, higher weights may be attached to factors that favour male dominated jobs. Second, female jobs may be underpriced when the job evaluation plan is used as a "policy-capturing" technique. That is, if female dominated jobs are adversely affected by systematic pay discrimination in the labour market, the use of a job evaluation system to predict (through statistical correlation) existing pay structures would tend to incorporate the wage bias from the market.

Finally, weighting bias would occur if job evaluation factors that favoured male dominated work tended to correlate highest with the criterion wages. One strategy used to prevent this kind of bias is to select a diverse set of factors for the job evaluation instrument. Another important consideration in choosing among different weighting approaches is the interpretability of the resulting wage structure; that is, the face validity of the structure in terms of participant understanding and acceptance.

With regard to the issue of acceptance, job evaluation consultants and researchers have noted a trend toward increasing employee demands for participation in compensation design and for greater communication about the technical aspects of compensation methodology, such as job evaluation and market surveying. As discussed earlier, very little information is available in the job evaluation literature about the comparability of different weighting methods in terms of:

- Sex-related pay equity,
- Criterion validity,
- Pay classification structures.

There is also a lack of discussion about the psychometric properties of job evaluation systems that might contribute to differences among weighting models.

Therefore, the present research had two primary objectives: First, to review and discuss some of the psychometric parametres that could help to explain how and when different weighting methods might produce divergent results, and second, to empirically examine the effects of different weighting methods in a field study.

Comparisons of different weighting methods were made within the framework of policy-capturing (i.e., wage prediction) because of the predominant use of this approach in job evaluation.

PSYCHOMETRIC CONSIDERATIONS IN WEIGHTING

In discussing the manner in which psychometric characteristics of a measurement instrument may influence different weighting models, the concept of nominal versus effective weights should be clarified. When combining the separate scores of a set of variables into a total score (for each subject or case), the separate variables tend to contribute unequally to this composite.

That is, the variables will have different effective (i.e., "true") weights. In job evaluation, for example, if jobs have very similar ratings on a particular factor (i.e., the factor has low variance) and the factor is highly correlated with other factors (i.e., it measures the same aspects of worth), this factor would obviously contribute very little to the differences among jobs in their total scores. Therefore, the factor would have a low effective weight.

WAGE AND SALARY ADMINISTRATION

The term "nominal" weighting refers to the transformation of scores for each variable through multiplication by a chosen numerical value (i.e., weight). In job evaluation, the process is variously called a priori or "committee" weighting, depending on how the weights are chosen. However, the important point to understand is that nominal weights will influence but not ultimately determine the effective weights of variables in a composite.

Certainly, with regard to the goal of communicating methodological nuances to organizational members, differences in the effects on compensation plans of nominal versus effective weights could be important. Little evidence is available in the job evaluation literature regarding the differential effects of alternative weighting methods on pay plans, or the psychometric properties of job evaluation systems that may underlie different weighting outcomes.

Recently, an extensive review of the psychometric and statistical literature by the present authors (Davis and Sauser, in press) identified four parametres that would affect the relative predictive power of different weighting methods within the policy-capturing framework.

The first important psychometric consideration in choosing among weighting methods is the ratio of sample size (subjects/cases) to the number of predictors employed, or the n to p ratio. Generally, multiple regression weighting will require a larger sample size than other methods because it capitalizes on a larger number of predictors and because the statistical weights (i.e., beta weights) are optimized in the developmental sample.

In addition, when predictor-criterion correlations are high, it is possible to use smaller sample sizes to obtain optimal statistical weights in multiple regression. Therefore, statistical approaches to weighting may be feasible even for small organizations with limited job samples.

A third property of importance related to weighting is the degree of interrelatedness (i.e., multicollinearity) among the predictors. In multiple regression models, as intercorrelations among the predictors increase, errors of estimating each regression weight will increase causing the weights to fluctuate across different samples. This means that weights developed in one sample (the benchmark sample) may not give high prediction in another sample. In job evaluation, the issue of cross-validity is important when the benchmark job sample constitutes a small percentage of the total jobs to which the plan will be applied.

A fourth and final parametre related to weighting is the degree of heterogeneity of the measurement instrument. Research by Laughlin, Pruzek and Frederick, and Darlington found that as "validity concentration" in a set of predictors increased, the less advantage multiple regression weighting had over nonstatistical methods. Validity concentration refers to the degree to which predictive power in a set of predictors is concentrated in a relatively few underlying dimensions.

In summary, we have identified and discussed the

potential impact on weighting methods of four relevant psychometric properties.

These were:

- The n-to-p ratio,
- The level between predictors and criterion,
- The degree of multicollinearity among predictors, and
- The degree of validity concentration in the predictor set.

In the present study, four different weighting methods were applied in a policy-capturing approach to job evaluation.

They were:

- an unweighted summation of "raw" job evaluation scores,
- Unit weighting (weights of 1),
- A priori committee weights, and
- Multiple regression weighting.

The intention of our research was to determine if the different weighting methods employed had any differential effects when applied to job evaluation data collected in a public sector organization. In addition, we attempted to explain the results in relation to the underlying psychometric parametres previously discussed.

JOB EVALUATION INSTRUMENT AND COMMITTEE PROCESS

An 8-factor job evaluation instrument was developed by two compensation consultants (the authors). Factors chosen for the instrument were intended to cover a wide range of jobs that are characteristic of municipal employment (e.g., administrative, technical, professional, and a variety of skilled to semi-skilled work such as equipment operation, maintenance, and clerical- office work).

In addition, the factors were chosen to cover the four criteria specified in the Equal Pay Act of 1963 (i.e., Skill, Effort, Responsibility, and Work Conditions). The factors were named as follows:

- Accountability (i.e., impact of decisions and errors);

- Job Scope (i.e., standardization of duties and closeness of supervision received);
- Communication Exchange (i.e., frequency, importance, and complexity of interpersonal communication);
- Job Preparation (i.e., education, training and/or experience required);
- Task Variety (i.e., diversity of duties performed);
- Task Complexity (i.e., technical complexity and uncertainty);
- Work Conditions (i.e., noise, temperature, lighting, and exertion);
- Job Pressure (i.e., time pacing, deadlines, and hazards.

A job evaluation committee was trained and given the task of evaluating 52 full-time jobs in a small municipality. The committee included two department supervisors, a clerical employee, a department manager, and two citizens from the community.

The members were asked to develop an a priori weighting model for the eight job evaluation factors, with each weight reflecting the relative importance of that factor to the organization. These numerical weights were expressed as a per cent of 100 points. Detailed and current descriptions of each job were distributed to the committee members and after independently rating each job, the members discussed the ratings and anonymously re-rated every job.

A final evaluation score for each job was secured by averaging across the scores of the six evaluators. Three months after the original job evaluation, a random sample of 10 jobs was selected and reevaluated by the committee using the procedure described above. The test-retest reliability coefficient for the ten jobs was .987.

In order to compare the criterion validity (i.e., policy-capturing) of different factor weighting schemes, a published wage survey of fourteen similarly-sized cities was obtained from the state association of municipalities. A "going wage" for each of the 52 jobs was obtained by computing the median wage rate from the sample. Psychometric characteristics of the job evaluation instrument were examined by computing intercorrelation coefficients between the factors (based on the job evaluation ratings) and by computing a principal components analysis of the factor ratings.

Using the different weighting methods previously described (i.e., unweighted, unit, judgmental, and multiple regression), four separate regression equations were calculated between the market wage rates and the job evaluation ratings (n = 52 jobs). Differences between the weighting models were examined in three ways.

First, significant differences between values and cross-valid values were tested using a formula presented in Cohen and Cohen for dependency among predictors (i.e., where the prediction equations share the same criterion). In job evaluation, where the benchmark job sample is a small subset of the total jobs to which the pay policy formula will be applied, cross-validity will be more relevant as an index of predictive power.

On the other hand, when the benchmark sample of jobs constitutes a majority of total jobs (as sometimes occurs in small organizations), predictive accuracy in the sample is more important. Second, the weighting models were compared in terms of their effects on male and female dominated jobs. To complete this analysis, we re-computed the prediction equations using only male jobs, which represented a discrimination-free sample.

Third, we computed intercorrelations between the predicted wage rates (policy rates) of all weighting models and calculated the rates of agreement in classification between all of the models. The predicted wages from each model were transformed into classification systems by establishing a minimum wage class ($6869 annually) and sequentially specifying higher class salaries with 10% intervals.

For each weighting model, the 52 jobs were placed into the classes by comparing the class salaries with the predicted policy salaries. Agreement rates between models were based on the number of jobs that "fit" into the same class.

CHARACTERISTICS OF THE INSTRUMENT

The average intercorrelation in ratings among the 8 job evaluation factors was r = .59. A factor analysis of the data revealed 2 underlying principal components that accounted for 91.1% of the variance in job ratings. The first principal component accounted for 76.9% of the score variance and was labelled "Skill-Responsibility." Six of the eight job evaluation factors had correlations of .89 or above with this component. The second principal component accounted for 14.2% of the variance and was highly correlated to the factors of Working Conditions (r = .98) and Job Pressure (r = .42).

These analyses indicated a great deal of multicollinearity and validity concentration in the set of factors used to evaluate the 52 municipal jobs, which is not uncommon in point-factor job evaluation systems. Based upon these results, it might be logical to hypothesize that very small differences among the alternative weighting methods would be expected.

POLICY-CAPTURING ACCURACY

When the 8 female dominated jobs were removed from the regression analyses, the predictive accuracy of all models improved. This occurred because most of the female jobs had market rates substantially below their predicted equitable salary, given the level of job evaluation ratings assigned.

We used a formula recommended by Cohen and Cohen to test for significant differences between the R-coefficients and estimated cross-validities of the weighting models. In the combined male-female job sample, the estimated cross-validity of multiple regression weighting was significantly lower than that for all three of the other weighting methods. No significant differences in sample coefficients were found among the models. When only male dominated jobs were used, the R-coefficient for multiple regression was significantly higher than that for the other models. However, no significant differences were found among the estimated cross-validity coefficients of the different models.

COMPARABILITY OF MODELS

Intercorrelations in predicted policy salaries among the 4

weighting models ranged from .95 to .99; in other words, the different policy-capturing models produced very similar pay hierarchies. In this study, salaries ranged from approximately $9,500 to $32,000. Given this large a range, it was not surprising that the weighting methods were able to achieve a highly similar ordering of salaries. However, less agreement occurred among the methods in the placement of jobs into discrete salary classes (with 10% intervals). Agreement rates among the weighting models ranged from 59% to 94%, with the largest difference occurring between multiple regression and the other three models (mean agreement of 64%).

Another relevant finding was that higher classification similarity occurred between the "equal" weighting methods (unweighted factors and unit weighting) and between the "differential" weighting methods (committee and regression weighting) than between the equal weighting versus differential weighting models.

For example, 94 per cent agreement was found between the unweighted and unit weighted systems, and 82 per cent agreement was found between committee and regression weighting. In contrast, the mean agreement rate between the equal weighting and differential weighting models was 71%.

INCENTIVE PLANS AND FRINGE BENEFITS

EFFECTS ON FEMALE AND MALE JOBS

We calculated the predicted salaries and classifications for 8 female jobs and 12 male jobs that had similar job evaluation ratings. All of these jobs had average total ratings between 3.75 and 4.88 (less than one standard deviation apart). An examination will reveal the following: First, market rates for female jobs were below those for male jobs, which implied possible wage discrimination in the market. Incidentally, predicted salaries for both male and female jobs were lower when the 8 female jobs were included in the regression sample.

Second, the differential weighting schemes (i.e., committee and multiple regression) produced higher average salaries for the female jobs but lower average salaries for male jobs. A plausible explanation for this result is found in the factor score patterns for male versus female jobs in relation to the specific weights applied. The female jobs had relatively higher ratings on the factors of Communication, Task Variety, and Task Complexity. These factors received comparatively high positive weights under both the committee and multiple regression weighting schemes. On the other hand, the male jobs tended to have lower ratings on these factors but higher ratings on factors such as Job Preparation and Working Conditions, factors which had smaller and sometimes negative weights.

A third finding was the tendency for certain kinds of jobs across the male-female categorization to benefit from different weighting methods. For example, management-oriented jobs (e.g., Senior Citizens Director, Head Mechanic, Animal Control Officer, Parts Manager, and Planning/Codes Assistant) had lower salaries and classifications under the multiple regression model.

This was also true of other administrative positions not displayed. In contrast, the lower rated jobs in both male and female categories (e.g., most of the clerical jobs and vehicle-equipment operators) tended to fair better under the multiple regression scheme. In multiple regression, multicollinearity (that is, "redundancy") among predictors is handled by computing partial regression coefficients for each predictor.

Where there are a number of highly intercorrelated predictors, some of the individual beta weights will be small, or even negative, as the redundant variance is partialled-out. In the present study, administrative positions received comparatively high ratings on the skill-responsibility group of factors (e.g., Accountability, Job Scope, Communication, and Job Preparation); however, because of the high interrelationships among these factors, some of them received small beta weights.

In contrast, many of the non-managerial positions had their highest ratings on job evaluation factors with higher beta weights, such as Task Variety, Task Complexity, and Job

Pressure. A fourth finding of importance was related to the interpretability of the different pay plans. From this perspective, it would appear that the nonstatistical methods provided more explainable and defensible results. For example, under multiple regression, the highest rated female job (i.e., Senior Citizens Director) would fall into the same class with the Secretary-Receptionist and below the positions of Mayor's Secretary and Administrative Assistant. In summary, our data indicated that multiple regression weighting produced a rather idiosyncratic pay structure that could be awkward to explain and justify to employees.

IMPLICATIONS FOR PRACTICE

Results from our analyses indicated high levels of predictive accuracy for all four weighting methods, although multiple regression weighting had a slightly higher sample than the other models. There were no significant differences among the models in estimated cross-validity. Still, given the small sample size used in the study and high multicollinearity among the job evaluation factors, these findings suggest that multiple regression analysis may be a viable weighting procedure even for small organizations, such as many city and county governments.

With respect to comparability of wage structures, the different weighting models produced similar rank orders of the jobs from high to low, as reflected in the high intercorrelations among the models. However, as the results indicated, differences occurred in the placement of jobs into discrete pay classes and in terms of the relative impact on male and female dominated jobs.

Particularly, the multiple regression model tended to benefit female jobs and non-managerial jobs relative to male jobs and managerial positions. As previously discussed, multiple regression analysis derives predictor weights in a manner that considers redundancy (i.e., intercorrelations) among the variables.

Therefore, in job evaluation the beta weights may take on rather unique and often dispersed values that are not directly related to the under lying organizational contributions made by the compensable factors. This kind of weighting scheme tends to incorporate the idiosyncratic score patterns of different jobs more than other models. Consequently, the compensatioh manager's task of explaining the weighting scheme and interpreting the results for employees may be more complicated.

At the present time in the development and application of point-factor job evaluation plans, no definitive solution has been suggested for dealing with the problem of multicollinearity among job evaluation factors. Past research has consistently reported high factor intercorrelations and has found that most of the variance in ratings can be accounted for by 2 to 3 underlying dimensions.

One answer to the problem might be to evaluate jobs on fewer dimensions; however, this approach has been resisted for a number of reasons. First, employees may not understand or accept abbreviated factor plans that cover only a portion of the many job characteristics that are logically associated with job worth.

Second, an abbreviated factor system may not meet the requirements of the Equal Pay Act which specifies that "equal work" among different jobs should be measured in terms of four primary dimensions (i.e., skill, responsibility, effort, and working conditions). A third concern has to do with the need to achieve reliability of measurement, which past psycho metric research has shown to be related to instrument length.

We suggest two possible strategies for handling the multicollinearity problem. One solution is simply to avoid multiple regression weighting when the resulting pay hierarchy appears too complicated to explain and defend. A second approach might be to conduct a factor analysis of the job evaluation scales and compute scores for each principal component.

Following this procedure, the principle components could be weighted using multiple regression analysis. This approach allows the use of all of the original factors, but eliminates the problem of applying a set of idiosyncratic beta weights.

To illustrate its potential effects, we computed factor scores for the 2 underlying dimensions found through a factor analysis of the present data. As discussed earlier, the two components were labeled "Skill-Responsibility" and "Working Conditions." Applying multiple regression, the two components had beta weights of .863 and .115, respectively.

The pay classification hierarchy for this model exhibited greater similarity to the plans under unit and committee weighting than to the multiple regression system. Rates of agreement in salary classification between the principal components method and the other models were 83% with committee, 85% with unit, and 67% with multiple regression. The present research and findings are mainly relevant within the context of a policy-capturing approach to job evaluation.

Milkovich and Newman have discussed the relationship of job evaluation methodology to a broader range of organizational concerns, including climate and culture, labour relations, and employee participation and acceptance. These issues may at times have higher priorities in the overall job evaluation process than policy-capturing.

Overall, our findings indicated that differences in pay structures can result from the application of alternative weighting approaches. The findings were somewhat surprising in view of the high multicollinearity and validity concentration that characterized the 8-factor job evaluation system used here. We would expect and predict even greater divergence between different weighting methods under the following conditions:

- A larger and more diverse sample of benchmark jobs,
- A more heterogeneous job evaluation instrument, and
- Lower multicollinearity in the predictor set.

The important implication for compensation managers is that it would probably be wise to analyse the effects of a number of different weighting schemes before selecting a final plan. One encouraging finding from this study was the fact that a job evaluation committee comprised of supervisors and non-supervisory employees was able to develop a weighting scheme that performed about as well as unit weighting and multiple regression. Whether or not other committee weighting plans will do as well based on the use of other job evaluation instruments is a relevant question for future research. Within the framework of the present research, the following recommendations are offered to compensation managers concerning a weighting strategy:

- Develop and examine a number of different weighting schemes.
- Avoid commitment to an a priori weighting model until alternative weighting methods have been explored.
- Inform committee members about weighting methodology.
- Inform committee members about potential differences in outcomes.
- Establish a set of criteria, or objectives, for assessing the alternative models (e.g., predictive power, gender effects, and interpretability).
- Select a final weighting model based on the established objectives.

While past research concerning the "tools and techniques" of job evaluation has had merit, there has been too little focus upon the purpose of pay as an outcome and job evaluation as a measure related to that outcome. The comparable worth debate has further "muddied the water" with regard to first determining, and then operationalizing, a basis for conducting valid job evaluation.

This chapter asserts that job evaluation is valid to the extent it results in adequate and equitable pay in organizations. This assertion is based upon the premise that pay adequacy and pay equity facilitate employee productivity—a primary purpose for compensating people in the first place.

"Job evaluation" has been defined as a generic term to describe a set of procedures which create a hierarchy of jobs based upon their worth to an organization. Job evaluation has become important as a means of implementing comparable worth statutes, particularly in the public sector. At present, at least 14 states now have some form of legislation prohibiting gender inequality in compensating jobs of comparable worth.

Unfortunately, there are currently no clear standards for assessing the validity of job evaluation. No consistent approach for resolving this problem is apparent either in current practice or in rationalizations of practice.

SEEKING A COMMON GROUND

Several threats to the validity of job evaluation exist. The training of raters and the selection of factors and factor weights all have a bearing on the validity of job evaluation outcomes. Subjectivity on the part of raters, for example, is an often cited problem. The selection and weighting of compensable factors also has significant bearing upon the validity of job evaluation outcomes. Misuse (or misinterpretation) of statistical procedures is also problematic.

Research emphasizing the "tools and techniques" of job evaluation—training of raters, selection of factors, and determination of factor weights and quantitative measurement of job content—is important and merits continuing investigation. However, empirical research on job evaluation and comparable worth has been compromised because concern with "tools and techniques" overshadows more basic methodological problems, such as establishing a theoretical basis for defining job worth. The parametres of a research domain need to be outlined before it can be effectively explored.

Of primary importance at present is determination of a theoretical basis for confirming (or disconfirming) the validity of pay (the outcome) resulting from job evaluation (the measure). Considering job pricing and job evaluation together departs from the usual view that job evaluation and pricing are separate. However, systems theory suggests that job evaluation and pricing should be considered parts of an organized, unitary compensation system.

Moreover, job evaluation as it is usually practiced merely reflects external exchange rates and does not adequately define job worth apart from external rates. The validity of the job evaluation process by itself (i.e. "tools and techniques") is a necessary, but insufficient, delineation of the parametres of job evaluation validity. Ultimately, the worth of jobs is determined not only by the number of job evaluation points awarded a position, but also by what an employer is willing to pay a position. This chapter, consequently, considers job pricing as an outcome of job evaluation.

Before proceeding further, it should be acknowledged that "pay" is only one of a large number of variables affecting work behaviour in organizations. Also, "compensation" is a broader term than "pay" encompassing rewards aside from financial remuneration, such as benefits and "psychic income". The reader should keep in mind that this chapter is concerned with pay rather than with the broader concept of compensation.

In this regard, while it is limiting to view man as "homo economicus, money-oriented man geared solely to the satisfaction of his limited economic self-interest," pay by itself is an important topic—worthy of independent treatment, particularly in light of controversy stemming from the current comparable worth debate.

THE COMPARABLE WORTH DEBATE

Comparable worth proponents believe that pricing jobs on the basis of purportedly objective (and sex-blind) job evaluation is more valid than reliance upon an external labour market which discriminates against female dominated positions. Comparable worth supporters believe that job evaluation should be used to adjust the pay for lower paying, typically female dominated positions upward so that wages are "internally consistent" throughout organizations.

When plotted, an "internally consistent" salary policy line is represented by a straight line depicting a linear relationship between job evaluation points and pay by position. Comparable worth opponents support a "market approach" as being the most valid approach to job pricing. The "market approach" is a traditional perspective. Prior to the comparable worth controversy, the validity of job pricing was defined in terms of the congruity of fit between an organizational salary policy line resulting from the job evaluation process, and going rates for key jobs in the external market.

When plotted, the traditional approach for aligning job evaluation points with pay usually causes "doglegs" (bends) in organizational policy lines where job evaluation points for some positions are "devalued" (or, depending upon one's perspective, "overvalued") relative to points awarded to other positions.

A third party appraisal of the role of job evaluation in job pricing was conducted by a committee of the National Academy of Science at the request of the Equal Employment Opportunity Commission (EEOC). This committee did not adopt or otherwise accept a criterion for assessing the validity of job evaluation.

A CASE STUDY

Salary policy lines A and B in this figure were plotted using the same job evaluation data set, only the criteria for aligning job evaluation points with pay differed. Salary policy line A represents the actual 1979 recommendation made by Willis and Associates for 44 administrative positions in Washington Community College District V. This consulting firm employs a "point-factor" job evaluation method much like the Hay System commonly used in comparable worth studies. As can be seen, salary policy line A has a bend which means that job evaluation points for nine positions below 362 points were devalued relative to points awarded to 35 positions above 362 points. Salary policy line A represents a traditional "market approach" view of job pricing.

This recommended salary policy line was plotted judgementally by the consultant using external market data as its basis, and reflects the fact that the market discriminates. The rationale for plotting salary policy line B came from another Willis study—the landmark 1974 comparable worth study of Washington State civil service jobs. In this study, which used "internal consistency" as the validity criterion for pricing jobs, Willis used regression analysis (in his words," computer developed lines of best fit") as an alternative to market driven "sight methods" for developing salary policy lines.

As can be seen, there is considerable disparity between salary policy lines A and B (both reflecting "recommended pay") even though a validity coefficient for the job evaluation points used in plotting these salary policy lines would be a perfect +1.0! In summary, there has been a tendency in the comparable worth debate to focus upon methodology (e.g. "tools and techniques") without due consideration of the purpose of pay. This has contributed to the lack of a common ground, as illustrated in the District V case study where two different salary policy lines were justified, based upon industry practice, using the same job evaluation data set.

The balance of this chapter articulates a purpose for pay which includes rationalization of validity criteria based upon that purpose, then discusses the internal and external validity of job evaluation, and finally returns to the District V case study where a salary policy line is plotted based upon validity criteria rationalized earlier.

THE PURPOSE OF PAY: A PSYCHOLOGICAL PERSPECTIVE

In considering the purpose of pay, it is not practical to take a purely economic perspective—for example, contending that pay's purpose within a given company, industry, and geographical location is to maintain equilibrium between labour supply and employer demand.

It is argued here that "employee satisfaction" is the primary purpose of pay, because satisfaction with pay leads to desirable employee behaviours. In this regard, employer satisfaction is necessary but should be viewed as a by-product of a satisfied workforce, rather than as a purpose per se. Increasing the value of reward outcomes for employees through compensation increases employee effort and reduces employee avoidance behaviours such as absenteeism and turnover. Increased employee productivity, through increased effort, reduced absenteeism and turnover, benefits the employer.

Dissatisfied employers can resort to "breaking unions" to obviate organized labor's "monopoly effect" upon wages, can change incentive systems (e.g. by implementing pay for performance compensation systems), or can simply replace employees.

Ultimately, however, employees must be satisfied with pay if management's goals of using pay to attract, retain, and motivate employees are to be served. An exception to this premise includes economic substitution on management's part through automation of work processes. Worker satisfaction with pay is not an issue if there are no workers. (Even here, though, the machines must be "satisfied" through maintenance and capital improvement if management's production goals are to be realised.) Also, employee dissatisfaction with pay could be balanced by satisfaction with overall compensation which, as noted, includes psychic income and benefits.

Given relationships between pay, satisfaction, and benefit accruing to employee and employer, it follows that employee satisfaction should be considered the underlying variable determining the validity of job evaluation (or any other approach taken to establish and maintain pay). Satisfaction occurs to the extent pay is perceived to be equitable when internal and external pay comparisons are made by adequately paid employees.

Employee satisfaction resulting from pay adequacy and equity serves as an effective proxy for the job worth construct. Such "satisfaction" indicates that the worth of the job has been tapped (at least from the employee's perspective). Looking at "job worth" from the standpoint of the employee may seem a radical departure from standard practice. However, from the employer's perspective, if the "true worth" of a job is not tapped by job evaluation (and reflected in pay) then, barring mitigating circumstances mentioned previously, resulting employee dissatisfaction will compromise the attraction, retention, and motivation of employees—important purposes of pay.

Elaboration regarding job evaluation's role in establishing and maintaining pay adequacy and equity follows. Pattern summarizes the practical difficulty of an economic emphasis when he notes that: Labour market economics theory is not very useful to the compensation planner and administrator. It is concerned basically with the "behaviour" (i.e. movement) of wages rather than with the behaviour of people, despite much speculation about what causes the supply and demand of labour to be what it is in given circumstances. As a result, we must turn to the behavioural sciences, and away from normative views of economists—to obtain information vital to compensation planners and administrators.

PAY ADEQUACY, PAY EQUITY, AND JOB EVALUATION

Thomas Patten's excellent discussion of the metagoals of compensation addresses "pay adequacy" in terms of a "floor" (such as the minimum wage), and a "ceiling" (such as pay resulting from the collective bargaining power of a union). Patten took a managerial perspective in developing his definition of pay adequacy.

Using this definition of adequacy, however, pay could still be inadequate for employees. (The minimum wage, for example, may be inadequate for most employees from the standpoint of meeting living expenses.) Resulting dissatisfaction, in turn, could compromise the objectives of compensation pertaining to attracting, retaining, and motivating employees.

Consequently, this chapter defines pay adequacy in terms of minimum tangible compensation required to meet employee physiological and security needs (primary needs). A wide variety of socioeconomic, psychological, and physiological factors influence individual determination of whether pay is adequate. A labour pool comprised of physicians and one comprised of unskilled labourers, for example, might have very different pay adequacy boundaries.

Pay adequacy precedes pay equity as a satisfier. Primary needs of employees must first be met before pay equity can have much potency as a satisfier. If an organization does not offer adequate pay, the role of job evaluation in maintaining equitable pay becomes moot because, barring a mitigating adjustment in overall compensation, employees will be dissatisfied and attracted to other job opportunities in other organizations, regardless of pay equity.

The question of pay adequacy is essentially one of "how much pay is enough" to cover primary needs. Pay equity, on the other hand, is concerned with the fairness of pay. Equity theory states that employees are satisfied to the extent inputs to job equal outputs (such as pay) when comparisons are made with the perceived inputs and outputs of others. Many, if not most, employees in the North American workplace have met primary needs through employment or other resources.

This suggests that pay equity may be more potent as a satisfier across most organizations than is pay adequacy. This view is supported by Lawler's observation that studies of the importance of pay as a motivator find employees rating fair pay as more important than high pay. In making this observation, Lawler separated pay adequacy and pay equity constructs. Unfortunately, these constructs are often contaminated in the conduct of research.

"Adequacy" has primacy as a satisfier for new entrants to a labour market whose primary needs are not being met through resources other than pay, or for inadequately paid job incumbents who must meet primary needs through pay. "Equity" has primacy as a satisfier for those who have met primary needs either through pay or from other resources.

Employees, or entrants to a labour market who have met primary needs through resources other than pay, are motivated to avoid either current or prospective positions if pay is perceived to be inequitable. This avoidance behaviour may take the form of a search for a position where pay will be equitable, and may also contribute to other avoidance behaviours such as excessive absenteeism.

Inadequately paid employees or unemployed individuals who must depend upon pay, on the other hand, are attracted to new employment opportunities as a means of meeting unmet primary needs. To summarize, job evaluation can play an important role in establishing and maintaining pay adequacy and equity which, in turn, facilitates employee productivity—an important purpose of pay. With pay adequacy and equity as validity criteria, it now becomes possible to examine the internal and external validity of job evaluation in a meaningful way.

INTERNAL AND EXTERNAL VALIDITY

This model presumes that pay adequacy requirements (as defined) have been satisfied. Campbell and Stanley's classic definitions of internal and external validity are integrated in this figure with Wallace and Fay's descriptions of employee demands pertaining to internal and external equity.

When compared across organizational jobs, if pay is perceived by adequately paid employees to be equitable then "job evaluation" meets conditions of internal validity. When pay is perceived by adequately paid employees to be equitable when compared to jobs outside of the organization, then "job evaluation" meets conditions of external validity.

Internal and external dimensions of validity are included in the model because equity theory pertains to external as well as internal comparisons of pay among employees. To be valid, job evaluation should result in pay which is perceived to be equitable when comparisons are made by adequately paid employees with pay for jobs both inside and outside the organization.

THREATS TO VALIDITY

This suggests that internal equity should not be achieved by reducing pay for more highly paid positions downward to make pay for these positions compatible with "underpaid" positions. Put another way, it would be invalid to achieve internal equity at the expense of external equity.

Salary policy line, for example, while "internally consistent" (when compared to "market approach" salary policy line A) would have resulted in pay reductions for 29 of 44 positions evaluated. Accordingly, implementation of salary policy line B would have compromised the external equity (and validity) of job evaluation for 29 positions.

Conversely, implementing salary policy line A (representing the "market approach" to job pricing) would have compromised internal equity (and validity) because this line contains a dogleg, meaning that job evaluation points for nine positions below 362 points have been devalued relative to points for 35 positions above 362 points.

In the past, employees were inclined to accept the fairness of a market based job pricing criterion. Today, many employees—particularly those employed in public sector female dominated positions—would regard the placement of their position on such a dogleg to be inequitable. The comparable worth controversy has led to changes in employee perceptions regarding standards of fairness, particularly with regard to internal equity.

This line was derived by fitting the "internally consistent" and "market approach" salary policy lines indicated at the highest point indicated in either line, and then correcting in order to return internal equity to the job pricing structure. The method used in plotting salary policy line C offers one approach for using the job evaluation process to achieve a valid salary policy line. First, job evaluation should be conducted and jobs priced based upon market data. This would create an externally equitable salary policy line which could include several doglegs.

Secondly, the same job evaluation data should be analysed and a new line plotted using linear regression formulas to ensure internal consistency. The two salary policy lines should then be fit together; positions should be adjusted upward at the highest point in either salary policy line. When curve fitting is completed, the adjusted line should be corrected ("smoothed") in order to reestablish internal equity. This can be done either using the "sight method" or, better yet, algebraically using the point-point form of a linear equation. This means that positions at the same point on the salary policy line would be paid the same, and job evaluation points would be valued equally for all positions within the job family. The only exception to this would be pay differentials based upon seniority, merit, quantity or quality of work, or any other factor other than sex (differentials based upon the Bennett Amendment to Title VII of the 1964 Civil Rights Act).

VARIABLE COMPENSATION INDIVIDUAL AND GROUP

EXTERNALLY EQUITABLE

All positions would be paid on an "equal to or greater than" basis with the external market. Also, no positions would be paid less, to resolve pay inequities elsewhere in the organization. Salary policy line C, however, would not be possible without additional financial resources.

Some of the dogleg positions in the District V study would have required 30% pay increases beyond the consultant's original recommendations to be congruent with salary policy line C. How much in additional resources would be required in other organizations would depend upon the existing organizational pay structure, including the number of "underpaid" positions and the extent of discrepancies in pay.

Salary policy line C represents in theory what some states and municipalities are working toward in practice. A tendency has been to use job evaluation in order to phase in pay increases for earmarked," underpaid" positions while maintaining pay for other positions. The Minnesota state legislature, for example, granted pay equity adjustments during 1983 to 8225 employees representing 151 job classifications. The Washington state legislature recently took the same action.

On the face, this chapter provides theoretical justification for using job evaluation to remedy pay inequity, supporting a basic position of comparable worth proponents. It should be noted, however, that salary policy line C represents only one approach for using job evaluation to achieve valid pay (as defined).

Job evaluation could be used instead to reduce employee inputs relative to pay. Using the Willis job evaluation method as an example, this could mean reducing the mental demands, knowledge and skills, accountability and/or working conditions requirements of "underpaid" positions to bring job evaluation points down in line with actual pay.

The literature is silent with regard to this use of job

evaluation. Nevertheless, given that pay meets employee adequacy requirements, this is a theoretically valid option because feelings of equity are based upon relative not absolute comparisons. The notion of using job evaluation to improve equity by reducing relative inputs, rather than by increasing relative outputs (such as pay), may seem intuitively unappealing. The job enrichment literature suggests that jobs need to be made more (not less) interesting, requiring an increase in inputs such as responsibility.

However, the satisfaction inherent in having more interesting work could be contradicted by dissatisfaction due to inequitable pay. The intrinsic nature of work is only one factor among many that affects worker satisfaction, and the influence of intrinsic factors is often subordinate to other factors such as pay. In closing, this chapter did not cover economic or ideological issues pertaining to how an organization would or should cover pay increases suggested as one possibility for achieving valid job pricing practices. Other possibilities exist, such as decreasing position inputs.

Also, as emphasized throughout, this chapter focused only upon the effect of pay on employee satisfaction. Equity theory, and compensation theory in general, provide for other outputs in the form of intangible rewards (i.e. "psychic income") and potential rewards which also affect employee satisfaction. Other dimensions of equity, such as individual equity, based upon individual contributions also need to be explored. Research is needed for the purpose of validating the models presented in this chapter. Future research should be directed at better understanding employee perceptions of equity, and the role job evaluation can play in affecting those perceptions.

The pay adequacy/equity boundary, in particular, also needs to be better understood. To conclude, while past research concerning the "tools and techniques" of job evaluation has had merit, there has been too little focus upon the purpose of pay as an outcome and job evaluation as a measure related to that outcome. This chapter examined the internal and external validity of job evaluation only after defining "employee satisfaction" from pay adequacy and pay equity as validity criteria.

Chapter 10

Promotions, Demotions, Transfers, Separation, Absenteeism and Turnover

Employed persons include:

- All those who worked for pay any time during the week which includes the 12th day of the month or who worked unpaid for 15 hours or more in a family-operated enterprise
- Those who were temporarily absent from their regular jobs because of illness, vacation, industrial dispute, or similar reasons.

A person working at more than one job is counted only in the job at which he or she worked the greatest number of hours. Unemployed persons are those who did not work during the survey week, but were available for work except for temporary illness and had looked for jobs within the preceding 4 weeks.

Persons who did not look for work because they were on layoff are also counted among the unemployed. The unemployment rate represents the number unemployed as a per cent of the civilian labour force. The civilian labour force consists of all employed or unemployed persons in the civilian noninstitutional population.

Persons not in the labour force are those not classified as employed or unemployed. This group includes discouraged workers, defined as persons who want and are available for a job and who have looked for work sometime in the past 12 months (or since the end of their last job if they held one within the past 12 months), but are not currently looking, because they believe there are no jobs available or there are none for which they would qualify. The civilian noninstitutional population comprises all persons 16 years of age and older who are not inmates of penal or mental institutions, sanitariums, or homes for the aged, infirm, or needy.

The civilian labour force participation rate is the proportion of the civilian noninstitutional population that is in the labour force. The employment-population ratio is employment as a per cent of the civilian noninstitutional population. From time to time, and especially after a decennial census, adjustments are made in the Current Population Survey figures to correct for estimating errors during the intercensal years. These adjustments affect the comparability of historical data. Effective in January 2003, BLS began using the X-12 ARIMA seasonal adjustment programme to seasonally adjust national labour force data.

This programme replaced the x-11 ARIMA programme which had been used since January 1980. At the beginning of each calendar year, historical seasonally adjusted data usually are revised, and projected seasonal adjustment factors are calculated for use during the January-June period.

The historical seasonally adjusted data usually are revised for only the most recent 5 years. In July, new seasonal adjustment factors, which incorporate the experience through June, are produced for the July-December period, but no revisions are made in the historical data.

DESCRIPTION OF THE SERIES

Employment, hours, and earnings data in this section are compiled from payroll records reported monthly on a voluntary basis to the Bureau of Labour Statistics and its cooperating State agencies by about 160,000 businesses and government agencies, which represent approximately 400,000 individual worksites and represent all industries except agriculture. The active CES sample covers approximately one-third of all nonfarm payroll workers.

In most industries, the sampling probabilities are based on the size of the establishment; most large establishments are therefore in the sample. (An establishment is not necessarily a firm; it may be a branch plant, for example, or warehouse.) Self-employed persons and others not on a regular civilian payroll are outside the scope of the survey because they are excluded from establishment records. This largely accounts for the difference in employment figures between the household and establishment surveys.

An establishment is an economic unit which produces goods or services (such as a factory or store) at a single location and is engaged in one type of economic activity. Employed persons are all persons who received pay (including holiday and sick pay) for any part of the payroll period including the 12th day of the month. Persons holding more than one job (about 5 per cent of all persons in the labour force) are counted in each establishment which reports them. Production workers in the goods-producing industries cover employees, up through the level of working supervisors, who engage directly in the manufacture or construction of the establishment's product. In private service-providing industries, data are collected for nonsupervisory workers, which include most employees except those in executive, managerial, and supervisory positions.

Those workers include production workers in manufacturing and natural resources and mining; construction workers in construction; and nonsupervisory workers in all private service-providing industries. Production and nonsupervisory workers account for about four-fifths of the total employment on private nonagricultural payrolls.

Earnings are the payments production or nonsupervi-sory workers receive during the survey period, including premium pay for overtime or late-shift work but excluding irregular bonuses and other special payments. Real earnings are earnings adjusted to reflect the effects of changes in consumer prices. The deflator for this series is derived from the Consumer Price Index for Urban Wage Earners and Clerical Workers (CPI-W).

Hours represent the average weekly hours of production or nonsupervisory workers for which pay was received, and are different from standard or scheduled hours. Overtime hours represent the portion of average weekly hours which was in excess of regular hours and for which overtime premiums were paid.

The Diffusion Index represents the per cent of industries in which employment was rising over the indicated period, plus one-half of the industries with unchanged employment; 50 per cent indicates an equal balance between industries with increasing and decreasing employment. In line with Bureau practice, data for the 1-, 3-, and 6-month spans are seasonally adjusted, while those for the 12-month span are unadjusted. These indexes are useful for measuring the dispersion of economic gains or losses and are also economic indicators.

DESCRIPTION OF THE SERIES

Employment, wage, and establishment data in this section are derived from the quarterly tax reports submitted to State employment security agencies by private and State and local government employers subject to State unemployment insurance (UI) laws and from Federal, agencies subject to the Unemployment Compensation for Federal Employees (UCFE) programme. Each quarter, State agencies edit and process the data and send the information to the Bureau of Labour Statistics.

The Quarterly Census of Employment and Wages (QCEW) data, also referred as ES202 data, are the most complete enumeration of employment and wage information by industry at the national, State, metropolitan area, and county levels. They have broad economic significance in evaluating labour market trends and major industry developments.

In general, the Quarterly Census of Employment and Wages monthly employment data represent the number of covered workers who worked during, or received pay for, the pay period that included the 12th day of the month. Covered private industry employment includes most corporate officials, executives, supervisory personnel, professionals, clerical workers, wage earners, piece workers, and part-time workers. It excludes proprietors, the unincorporated self-employed, unpaid family members, and certain farm and domestic workers. Certain types of nonprofit employers, such as religious organizations, are given a choice of coverage or exclusion in a number of States. Workers in these organizations are, therefore, reported to a limited degree.

Persons on paid sick leave, paid holiday, paid vacation, and the like, are included. Persons on the payroll of more than one firm during the period are counted by each UI-subject employer if they meet the employment definition noted earlier. The employment count excludes workers who earned no wages during the entire applicable pay period because of work stoppages, temporary layoffs, illness, or unpaid vacations.

Federal employment data are based on reports of monthly employment and quarterly wages submitted each quarter to State agencies for all Federal installations with employees covered by the Unemployment Compensation for Federal Employees (UCFE) programme, except for certain national security agencies, which are omitted for security reasons. Employment for all Federal agencies for any given month is based on the number of persons who worked during or received pay for the pay period that included the 12th of the month.

An establishment is an economic unit, such as a farm, mine, factory, or store, that produces goods or provides services. It is typically at a single physical location and engaged in one, or predominantly one, type of economic activity for which a single industrial classification may be applied. Occasionally, a single physical location encompasses two or more distinct and significant activities. Each activity should be reported as a separate establishment if separate records are kept and the various activities are classified under different NAICS industries.

Most employers have only one establishment; thus, the establishment is the predominant reporting unit or statistical entity for reporting employment and wages data. Most employers, including State and local governments who operate more than one establishment in a State, file a Multiple Worksite Report each quarter, in addition to their quarterly UI report. The Multiple Worksite Report is used to collect separate employment and wage data for each of the employer's establishments, which are not detailed on the UI report. Some very small multi-establishment employers do not file a Multiple Worksite Report.

When the total employment in an employer's secondary establishments (all establishments other than the largest) is 10 or fewer, the employer generally will file a consolidated report for all establishments. Also, some employers either cannot or will not report at the establishment level and thus aggregate establishments into one consolidated unit, or possibly several units, though not at the establishment level.

For the Federal Government, the reporting unit is the installation: a single location at which a department, agency, or other government body has civilian employees. Federal agencies follow slightly different criteria than do private employers when breaking down their reports by installation. They are permitted to combine as a single statewide unit: 1) all installations with 10 or fewer workers, and 2) all installations that have a combined total in the State of fewer than 50 workers.

Also, when there are fewer than 25 workers in all secondary installations in a State, the secondary installations may be combined and reported with the major installation. Last, if a Federal agency has fewer than five employees in a State, the agency headquarters office (regional office, district office) serving each State may consolidate the employment and wages data for that State with the data reported to the State in which the headquarters is located. As a result of these reporting rules, the number of reporting units is always larger than the number of employers (or government agencies) but smaller than the number of actual establishments (or installations).

Data reported for the first quarter are tabulated into size categories ranging from worksites of very small size to those with 1,000 employees or more. The size category is determined by the establishment's March employment level. It is important to note that each establishment of a multi-establishment firm is tabulated separately into the appropriate size category. The total employment level of the reporting multi-establishment firm is not used in the size tabulation.

Covered employers in most States report total wages paid during the calendar quarter, regardless of when the services were performed. A few State laws, however, specify that wages be reported for, or based on the period during which services are performed rather than the period during which compensation is paid. Under most State laws or regulations, wages include bonuses, stock options, the cash value of meals and lodging, tips and other gratuities, and, in some States, employer contributions to certain deferred compensation plans such as 401(k) plans.

Covered employer contributions for old-age, survivors, and disability insurance (OASDI), health insurance, unemployment insurance, workers' compensation, and private pension and welfare funds are not reported as wages. Employee contributions for the same purposes, however, as well as money withheld for income taxes, union dues, and so forth, are reported even though they are deducted from the worker's gross pay.

Wages of covered Federal workers represent the gross amount of all payrolls for all pay periods ending within the quarter. This includes cash allowances, the cash equivalent of any type of remuneration, severance pay, withholding taxes, and retirement deductions. Federal employee remuneration generally covers the same types of services as for workers in private industry.

Average annual wage per employee for any given industry are computed by dividing total annual wages by annual average employment. A further division by 52 yields average weekly wages per employee. Annual pay data only approximate annual earnings because an individual may not be employed by the same employer all year or may work for more than one employer at a time.

Average weekly or annual wage is affected by the ratio of full-time to part-time workers as well as the number of individuals in high-paying and low-paying occupations. When average pay levels between States and industries are compared, these factors should be taken into consideration. For example, industries characterized by high proportions of part-time workers will show average wage levels appreciably less than the weekly pay levels of regular fulltime employees in these industries.

The opposite effect characterizes industries with low proportions of part-time workers, or industries that typically schedule heavy weekend and overtime work. Average wage data also may be influenced by work stoppages, labour turnover rates, retroactive payments, seasonal factors, bonus payments, and so on.

Beginning with the release of data for 2001, publications presenting data from the Covered Employment and Wages programme have switched to the 2002 version of the North American Industry Classification System (NAICS) as the basis for the assignment and tabulation of economic data by industry. NAICS is the product of a cooperative effort on the part of the statistical agencies of the United States, Canada, and Mexico. Due to difference in NAICS and Standard Industrial Classification (sic) structures, industry data for 2001 is not comparable to the sic-based data for earlier years.

Effective January 2001, the programme began assigning Indian Tribal Councils and related establishments to local government ownership. This BLS action was in response to a change in Federal law dealing with the way Indian Tribes are treated under the Federal Unemployment Tax Act. This law requires federally recognized Indian Tribes to be treated similarly to State and local governments. In the past, the Covered Employment and Wage (CEW) programme coded Indian Tribal Councils and related establishments in the private sector.

As a result of the new law, CEW data reflects significant shifts in employment and wages between the private sector and local government from 2000 to 2001. Data also reflect industry changes. Those accounts previously assigned to civic and social organizations were assigned to tribal governments. There were no required industry changes for related establishments owned by these Tribal Councils. These tribal business establishments continued to be coded according to the economic activity of that entity.

To insure the highest possible quality of data, State employment security agencies verify with employers and update, if necessary, the industry, location, and ownership classification of all establishments on a 3-year cycle. Changes in establishment classification codes resulting from the verification process are introduced with the data reported for the first quarter of the year. Changes resulting from improved employer reporting also are introduced in the first quarter. For these reasons, some data, especially at more detailed geographic levels, may not be strictly comparable with earlier years.

County definitions are assigned according to Federal Information Processing Standards Publications as issued by the National Institute of Standards and Technology. Areas shown as counties include those designated as independent cities in some jurisdictions and, in Alaska, those areas designated by the Census Bureau where counties have not been created. County data also are presented for the New England States for comparative purposes, even though townships are the more common designation used in New England (and New Jersey).

Data for the Job Openings and Labour Turnover Survey (JOLTS) are collected and compiled from a sample of 16,000 business establishments. Each month, data are collected for total employment, job openings, hires, quits, layoffs and discharges, and other separations. The JOLTS programme covers all private nonfarm establishments such as factories, offices, and stores, as well as Federal, State, and local government entities in the 50 States and the District of Columbia.

The JOLTS sample design is a random sample drawn from a universe of more than eight million establishments compiled as part of the operations of the Quarterly Census of Employment and Wages, or QCEW, programme. This programme includes all employers subject to State unemployment insurance (u0 laws and Federal agencies subject to Unemployment Compensation for Federal Employees (UCFE).

The sampling flame is stratified by ownership, region, industry sector, and size class. Large firms fall into the sample with virtual certainty. JOLTS total employment estimates are controlled to the employment estimates of the Current Employment Statistics (CES) survey. A ratio of CES to JOLTS employment is used to adjust the levels for all other JOLTS data elements. Rates then are computed from the adjusted levels. The monthly JOLTS data series begin with December 2000.

Not seasonally adjusted data on job openings, hires, total separations, quits, layoffs and discharges, and other separations levels and rates are available for the total nonfarm sector, 16 private industry divisions and 2 government divisions based on the North American Industry Classification System (NAICS), and four geographic regions. Seasonally adjusted data on job openings, hires, total separations, and quits levels and rates are available for the total nonfarm sector, selected industry sectors, and four geographic regions.

Establishments submit job openings information for the last business day of the reference month. A job opening requires that (1) a specific position exists and there is work available for that position; and (2) work could start within 30 days regardless of whether a suitable candidate is found; and (3) the employer is actively recruiting from outside the establishment to fill the position.

Included are full-time, part-time, permanent, short-term, and seasonal openings. Active recruiting means that the establishment is taking steps to fill a position by advertising in newspapers or on the Internet, posting help-wanted signs, accepting applications, or using other similar methods. Jobs to be filled only by internal transfers, promotions, demotions, or recall from layoffs are excluded.

Also excluded are jobs with start dates more than 30 days in the future, jobs for which employees have been hired but have not yet reported for work, and jobs to be filled by employees of temporary help agencies, employee leasing companies, outside contractors, or consultants. The job openings rate is computed by dividing the number of job openings by the sum of employment and job openings, and multiplying that quotient by 100.

Hires are the total number of additions to the payroll occurring at any time during the reference month, including both new and rehired employees and full-time and part-time, permanent, short-term and seasonal employees, employees recalled to the location after a layoff lasting more than 7 days, on-call or intermittent employees who returned to work after having been formally separated, and transfers from other locations.

The hires count does not include transfers or promotions within the reporting site, employees returning from strike, employees of temporary help agencies or employee leasing companies, outside contractors, or consultants. The hires rate is computed by dividing the number of hires by employment, and multiplying that quotient by 100.

Separations are the total number of terminations of employment occurring at any time during the reference month, and are reported by type of separation—quits, layoffs and discharges, and other separations. Quits are voluntary separations by employees (except for retirements, which are reported as other separations). Layoffs and discharges are involuntary separations initiated by the employer and include layoffs with no intent to rehire, formal layoffs lasting or expected to last more than 7 days, discharges resulting from mergers, downsizing, or closings, firings or other discharges for cause, terminations of permanent or short-term employees, and terminations of seasonal employees.

Other separations include retirements, transfers to other locations, deaths, and separations due to disability. Separations do not include transfers within the same location or employees on strike. The separations rate is computed by dividing the number of separations by employment, and multiplying that quotient by 100. The quits, layoffs and discharges, and other separations rates are computed similarly, dividing the number by employment and multiplying by 100.

The JOLTS data series on job openings, hires, and separations are relatively new. The full sample is divided into panels, with one panel enrolled each month. A full complement of panels for the original data series based on the 1987 Standard Industrial Classification (SIC) system was not completely enrolled in the survey until January 2002.

The supplemental panels of establishments needed to create NAICS estimates were not completely enrolled until May 2003. The data collected up until those points are from less than a full sample. Therefore, estimates from earlier months should be used with caution, as fewer sampled units were reporting data at that time.

The inclusion of transfers in the JOLTS definitions of hires and separations is intended to cover ongoing movements of workers between establishments. The Department of Homeland Security reorganization was a massive onetime event, and the inclusion of these intergovernmental transfers would distort the Federal Government time series.

Data users should note that seasonal adjustment of the JOLTS series is conducted with fewer data observations than is customary. The historical data, therefore, may be subject to larger than normal revisions. Because the seasonal patterns in economic data series typically emerge over time, the standard use of moving averages as seasonal filters to capture these effects requires longer series than are currently available.

As a result, the stable seasonal filter option is used in the seasonal adjustment of the JOLTS data. When calculating seasonal factors, this filter takes an average for each calendar month after detrending the series. The stable seasonal filter assumes that the seasonal factors are fixed; a necessary assumption until sufficient data is available.

When the stable seasonal filter is no longer needed, other programme features also may be introduced, such as outlier adjustment and extended diagnostic testing. Additionally, it is expected that more series, such as layoffs and discharges and additional industries, may be seasonally adjusted when more data are available.

JOLTS hires and separations estimates cannot be used to exactly explain net changes in payroll employment. Some reasons why it is problematic to compare changes in payroll employment with JOLTS hires and separations, especially on a monthly basis, are: (1) the reference period for payroll employment is the pay period including the 12th of the month, while the reference period for hires and separations is the calendar month; and (2) payroll employment can vary from month to month simply because part-time and on-call workers may not always work during the pay period that includes the 12th of the month.

Additionally, research has found that some reporters systematically underreport separations relative to hires due to a number of factors, including the nature of their payroll systems and practices. The shortfall appears to be about 2 per cent or less over a 12-month period.

Compensation and waged data are gathered by the Bureau from business establishments, State and local governments, labour unions, collective bargaining agreements on file with the Bureau, and secondary sources. The Employment Cost Index (ECI) is a quarterly measure of the rate of change in compensation per hour worked and includes wages, salaries, and employer costs of employee benefits. It uses a fixed market basket of labour—similar in concept to the Consumer Price Index's fixed market basket of goods and services—to measure change over time in employer costs of employing labour.

Statistical series on total compensation costs, on wages and salaries, and on benefit costs are available for private nonfarm workers excluding proprietors, the self-employed, and household workers. The total compensation costs and wages and salaries series are also available for State and local government workers and for the civilian nonfarm economy, which consists of private industry and State and local government workers combined.

The Employment Cost Index probability sample consists of about 4,400 private nonfarm establishments providing about 23,000 occupational observations and 1,000 State and local government establishments providing 6,000 occupational observations selected to represent total employment in each sector. On average, each reporting unit provides wage and compensation information on five well-specified occupations. Data are collected each quarter for the pay period including the 12th day of March, June, September, and December.

Beginning with June 1986 data, fixed employment weights from the 1980 Census of Population are used each quarter to calculate the civilian and private indexes and the index for State and local governments.

These fixed weights, also used to derive all of the industry and occupation series indexes, ensure that changes in these indexes reflect only changes in compensation, not employment shifts among industries or occupations with different levels of wages and compensation.

For the bargaining status, region, and metropolitan/non-metropolitan area series, however, employment data by industry and occupation are not available from the census. Instead, the 1980 employment weights are reallocated within these series each quarter based on the current sample. Therefore, these indexes are not strictly comparable to those for the aggregate, industry, and occupation series.

Total compensation costs include wages, salaries, and the employer's costs for employee benefits. Wages and salaries consist of earnings before payroll deductions, including production bonuses, incentive earnings, commissions, and cost-of-living adjustments. Benefits include the cost to employers for paid leave, supplemental pay (including nonproduction bonuses), insurance, retirement and savings plans, and legally required benefits (such as Social Security, workers' compensation, and unemployment insurance).

Excluded from wages and salaries and employee benefits are such items as payment-in-kind, free room and board, and tips. The series of changes in wages and salaries and for total compensation in the State and local government sector and in the civilian nonfarm economy (excluding Federal employees) were published beginning in 1981.

Employee benefits data are obtained from the Employee Benefits Survey, an annual survey of the incidence and provisions of selected benefits provided by employers. The survey collects data from a sample of approximately 9,000 private sector and State and local government establishments. The data are presented as a percentage of employees who participate in a certain benefit, or as an average benefit provision (for example, the average number of paid holidays provided to employees per year).

The survey covers paid leave benefits such as holidays and vacations, and personal, funeral, jury duty, military, family, and sick leave; short-term disability, long-term disability, and life insurance; medical, dental, and vision care plans; defined benefit and defined contribution plans; flexible benefits plans; reimbursement accounts; and unpaid family leave. Also, data are tabulated on the incidence of several other benefits, such as severance pay, child-care assistance, wellness programs, and employee assistance programs.

Employer-provided benefits are benefits that are financed either wholly or partly by the employer. They may be sponsored by a union or other third party, as long as there is some employer financing. However, some benefits that are fully paid for by the employee also are included. For example, long-term care insurance and postretirement life insurance paid entirely by the employee are included because the guarantee of insurability and availability at group premium rates are considered a benefit.

Participants are workers who are covered by a benefit, whether or not they use that benefit. If the benefit plan is financed wholly by employers and requires employees to complete a minimum length of service for eligibility, the workers are considered participants whether or not they have met the requirement. If workers are required to contribute towards the cost of a plan, they are considered participants only if they elect the plan and agree to make the required contributions.

Defined benefit pension plans use predetermined formulas to calculate a retirement benefit (if any), and obligate the employer to provide those benefits. Benefits are generally based on salary, years of service, or both. Defined contribution plans generally specify the level of employer and employee contributions to a plan, but not the formula for determining eventual benefits. Instead, individual accounts are set up for participants, and benefits are based on amounts credited to these accounts.

Tax-deferred savings plans are a type of defined contribution plan that allow participants to contribute a portion of their salary to an employer-sponsored plan and defer income taxes until withdrawal. Flexible benefit plans allow employees to choose among several benefits, such as life insurance, medical care, and vacation days, and among several levels of coverage within a given benefit.

Surveys of employees in medium and large establishments conducted over the 1979-86 period included establishments that employed at least 50, 100, or 250 workers, depending on the industry (most service industries were excluded). The survey conducted in 1987 covered only State and local governments with 50 or more employees. The surveys conducted in 1988 and 1989 included medium and large establishments with 100 workers or more in private industries. All surveys conducted over the 1979-89 period excluded establishments in Alaska and Hawaii, as well as part-time employees.

Beginning in 1990, surveys of State and local governments and small private establishments were conducted in even-numbered years, and surveys of medium and large establishments were conducted in odd-numbered years. The small establishment survey includes all private nonfarm establishments with fewer than 100 workers, while the State and local government survey includes all governments, regardless of the number of workers. All three surveys include full- and part-time workers, and workers in all 50 States and the District of Columbia.

Data on work stoppages measure the number and

duration of major strikes or lockouts (involving 1,000 workers or more) occurring during the month (or year), the number of workers involved, and the amount of work time lost because of stoppage. Data are largely from a variety of published sources and cover only establishments directly involved in a stoppage. They do not measure the indirect or secondary effect of stoppages on other establishments whose employees are idle owing to material shortages or lack of service.

Number of stoppages: The number of strikes and lockouts involving 1,000 workers or more and lasting a full shift or longer. Workers involved: The number of workers directly involved in the stoppage. Number of days idle: The aggregate number of workdays lost by workers involved in the stoppages. Days of idleness as a per cent of estimated working time: Aggregate workdays lost as a per cent of the aggregate number of standard workdays in the period multiplied by total employment in the period.

Price data are gathered by the Bureau of Labour Statistics from retail and primary markets in the United States. Price indexes are given in relation to a base period—December 2003 = 100 for many Producer Price Indexes (unless otherwise noted), 1982-84 = 100 for many Consumer Price Indexes (unless otherwise noted), and 1990 = 100 for International Price Indexes.

CONSUMER PRICE INDEXES

DESCRIPTION OF THE SERIES

The Consumer Price Index (CPI) is a measure of the average change in the prices paid by urban consumers for a fixed market basket of goods and services. The CPI is calculated monthly for two population groups, one consisting only of urban households whose primary source of income is derived from the employment of wage earners and clerical workers, and the other consisting of all urban households.

The wage earner index (CPI-W) is a continuation of the historic index that was introduced well over a half-century ago for use in wage negotiations. As new uses were developed for the CPI in recent years, the need for a broader and more representative index became apparent.

The all-urban consumer index (CPI-U), introduced in 1978, is representative of the 1993-95 buying habits of about 87 per cent of the non-institutional population of the United States at that time, compared with 32 per cent represented in the CPI-W. In addition to wage earners and clerical workers, the CPI-U covers professional, managerial, and technical workers, the self-employed, short-term workers, the unemployed, retirees, and others not in the labour force.

The CPI is based on prices of food, clothing, shelter, fuel, drugs, transportation fares, doctors' and dentists' fees, and other goods and services that people buy for day-to-day living. The quantity and quality of these items are kept essentially unchanged between major revisions so that only price changes will be measured. All taxes directly associated with the purchase and use of items is included in the index.

Data collected from more than 23,000 retail establishments and 5,800 housing units in 87 urban areas across the country are used to develop the "U.S. city average." The area indexes measure only the average change in prices for each area since the base period, and do not indicate differences in the level of prices among cities.

Producer Price Indexes (PPI) measure average changes in prices received by domestic producers of commodities in all stages of processing. The sample used for calculating these indexes currently contains about 3,200 commodities and about 80,000 quotations per month, selected to represent the movement of prices of all commodities produced in the manufacturing; agriculture, forestry, and fishing; mining; and gas and electricity and public utilities sectors.

The stage-of-processing structure of PPI organizes products by class of buyer and degree of fabrication (that is, finished goods, intermediate goods, and crude materials). The traditional commodity structure of PPI organizes products by similarity of end use or material composition.

To the extent possible, prices used in calculating Producer Price Indexes apply to the first significant commercial transaction in the United States from the production or central marketing point. Price data are generally collected monthly, primarily by mail questionnaire. Most prices are obtained directly from producing companies on a voluntary and confidential basis. Prices generally are reported for the Tuesday of the week containing the 13th day of the month.

Since January 1992, price changes for the various commodities have been averaged together with implicit quantity weights representing their importance in the total net selling value of all commodities as of 1987. The detailed data are aggregated to obtain indexes for stage-of-processing groupings, commodity groupings, durability-of-product groupings, and a number of special composite groups. All Producer Price Index data are subject to revision 4 months after original publication.

The International Price Programme produces monthly and quarterly export and import price indexes for nonmilitary goods and services traded between the United States and the rest of the world. The export price index provides a measure of price change for all products sold by U.S. residents to foreign buyers. ("Residents" is defined as in the national income accounts; it includes corporations, businesses, and individuals, but does not require the organizations to be U.S. owned nor the individuals to have citizenship.) The import price index provides a measure of price change for goods purchased from other countries by residents.

The product universe for both the import and export indexes includes raw materials, agricultural products, semifinished manufactures, and finished manufactures, including both capital and consumer goods. Price data for these items are collected primarily by mail questionnaire, In nearly all cases, the data are collected directly from the exporter or importer, although in a few cases, prices are obtained from other sources.

To the extent possible, the data gathered refer to prices at the border for exports and at either the foreign border or the border for imports. For nearly all products, the prices refer to transactions completed during the first week of the month.

Survey respondents are asked to indicate all discounts, allowances, and rebates applicable to the reported prices, so that the price used in the calculation of the indexes is the actual price for which the product was bought or sold.

In addition to general indexes of prices for exports and imports, indexes are also published for detailed product categories of exports and imports. These categories are defined according to the five-digit level of detail for the Bureau of Economic Analysis End-use Classification, the three-digit level for the Standard International Trade Classification (SITC), and the four-digit level of detail for the Harmonized System. Aggregate import indexes by country or region of origin are also available.

BLS publishes indexes for selected categories of internationally traded services, calculated on an international basis and on a balance-of-payments basis. The export and import price indexes are weighted indexes of the Laspeyres type. The trade weights currently used to compute both indexes relate to 2000. Because a price index depends on the same items being priced from period to period, it is necessary to recognize when a product's specifications or terms of transaction have been modified.

For this reason, the Bureau's questionnaire requests detailed descriptions of the physical and functional characteristics of the products being priced, as well as information on the number of units bought or sold, discounts, credit terms, packaging, class of buyer or seller, and so forth. When there are changes in either the specifications or terms of transaction of a product, the dollar value of each change is deleted from the total price change to obtain the "pure" change. Once this value is determined, a linking procedure is employed which allows for the continued repricing of the item.

The productivity measures relate real output to real input. As such, they encompass a family of measures which include single-factor input measures, such as output per hour, output per unit of labour input, or output per unit of capital input, as well as measures of multifactor productivity (output per unit of combined labour and capital inputs). The Bureau indexes show the change in output relative to changes in the various inputs. The measures cover the business, nonfarm business, manufacturing, and nonfinanc-ial corporate sectors.

Corresponding indexes of hourly compensation, unit labour costs, unit nonlabor payments, and prices are also provided.

Output per hour of all persons (labour productivity) is the quantity of goods and services produced per hour of labour input. Output per unit of capital services (capital productivity) is the quantity of goods and services produced per unit of capital services input.

Multifactor productivity is the quantity of goods and services produced per combined inputs. For private business and private nonfarm business, inputs include labour and capital units. For manufacturing, inputs include labour, capital, energy, nonenergy materials, and purchased business services. Compensation per hour is total compensation divided by hours at work.

Total compensation equals the wages and salaries of employees plus employers' contributions for social insurance and private benefit plans, plus an estimate of these payments for the self-employed (except for nonfinancial corporations in which there are no self-employed). Real compensation per hour is compensation per hour deflated by the change in the Consumer Price Index for All Urban Consumers.

Unit labour costs are the labour compensation costs expended in the production of a unit of output and are derived by dividing compensation by output. Unit nonlabor payments include profits, depreciation, interest, and indirect taxes per unit of output. They are computed by subtracting compensation of all persons from current-dollar value of output and dividing by output.

Unit nonlabor costs contain all the components of unit nonlabor payments except unit profits. Unit profits include corporate profits with inventory valuation and capital consumption adjustments per unit of output. Hours of all persons are the total hours at work of payroll workers, self-employed persons, and unpaid family workers. Labour inputs are hours of all persons adjusted for the effects of changes.in the education and experience of the labour force.

Capital services are the flow of services from the capital stock used in production. It is developed from measures of the net stock of physical assets—equipment, structures, land, and inventories—weighted by rental prices for each type of asset. Combined units of labour and capital inputs are derived by combining changes in labour and capital input with weights which represent each component's share of total cost. Combined units of labour, capital, energy, materials, and purchased business services are similarly derived by combining changes in each input with weights that represent each input's share of total costs.

The indexes for each input and for combined units are based on changing weights which are averages of the shares in the current and preceding year (the Tornquist index-number formula). Business sector output is an annually-weighted index constructed by excluding from real gross domestic product (GDP) the following outputs: general government, nonprofit institutions, paid employees of private households, and the rental value of owner-occupied dwellings. Nonfarm business also excludes farming.

Private business and private nonfarm business further exclude government enterprises. The measures are supplied by the U.S. Department of Commerce's Bureau of Economic Analysis. Annual estimates of manufacturing sectoral output are produced by the Bureau of Labour Statistics.

Quarterly manufacturing output indexes from the Federal Reserve Board are adjusted to these annual output measures by the BLS. Compensation data are developed from data of the Bureau of Economic Analysis and the Bureau of Labour Statistics. Hours data are developed from data of the Bureau of Labour Statistics.

The productivity and associated cost measures describe the relationship between output in real terms and the labour and capital inputs involved in its production. They show the changes from period to period in the amount of goods and services produced per unit of input.Although these measures relate output to hours and capital services, they do not measure the contributions of labour, capital, or any other specific factor of production.

Rather, they reflect the joint effect of many influences, including changes in technology; shifts in the composition of the labour force; capital investment; level of output; changes in the utilization of capacity, energy, material, and research and development; the organization of production; managerial skill; and characteristics and efforts of the work force.

The BLS industry productivity indexes measure the relationship between output and inputs for selected industries and industry groups, and thus reflect trends in industry efficiency over time. Industry measures include labour productivity,.multifactor productivity, compensation, and unit labour COSTS. The industry measures differ in methodology and data sources from the productivity measures for the major sectors because the industry measures are developed independently of the National Income and Product Accounts framework used for the major sector measures.

Output per hour is derived by dividing an index of industry output by an index of labour input. For most industries, output indexes are derived from data on the value of industry output adjusted for price change. For the remaining industries, output indexes are derived from data on the physical quantity of production.

The labour input series is based on the hours of all workers or, in the case of some transportation industries, on the number of employees. For most industries, the series consists of the hours of all employees. For some trade and services industries, the series also includes the hours of partners, proprietors, and unpaid family workers.

Unit labour costs represent the labour compensation costs per unit of output produced, and are derived by dividing an index of labour compensation by an index of output. Labour compensation includes payroll as well as supplemental payments, including both legally required expenditures and payments for voluntary programs.

Multifactor productivity is derived by dividing an index

of industry output by an index of combined inputs consumed in producing that output. Combined inputs include capital, labour, and intermediate purchases. The measure of capital input represents the flow of services from the capital stock used in production. It is developed from measures of the net stock of physical assets—equipment, structures, land, and inventories. The measure of intermediate purchases is a combination of purchased materials, services, fuels, and electricity.

The labour force statistics published by other industrial countries are not, in most cases, comparable to U.S. concepts. Therefore, the Bureau adjusts the figures for selected countries, for all known major definitional differences, to the extent that data to prepare adjustments are available. Although precise comparability may not be achieved, these adjusted figures provide a better basis for international comparisons than the figures regularly published by each country.

The foreign country data are adjusted as closely as possible to U.S. concepts, with the exception of lower age limits and the treatment of layoffs. These adjustments include, but are not limited to: including older persons in the labour force by imposing no upper age limit, adding unemployed students to the unemployed, excluding the military and family workers working fewer than 15 hours from the employed, and excluding persons engaged in passive job search from the unemployed.

Data for the United States relate to the population 16 years of age and older. The U.S. concept of the working age population has no upper age limit. The adjusted to U.S. concepts statistics have been adapted, insofar as possible, to the age at which compulsory schooling ends in each country, and the Swedish statistics have been adjusted to include persons older than the Swedish upper age limit of 64 years.

The adjusted statistics presented here relate to the population 16 years of age and older in France, Sweden, and the United Kingdom; 15 years of age and older in Australia, Japan, Germany, Italy, and the Netherlands. An exception to this rule is that the Canadian statistics are adjusted to cover the population 16 years of age and older, whereas the age at which compulsory schooling ends remains at 15 years.

In the labour force participation rates and employment-population ratios, the denominator is the civilian noninstitutionalized working age population, except that the institutionalized working age population is included in Japan and Germany.

In the United States, the unemployed include persons who are not employed and who were actively seeking work during the reference period, as well as persons on layoff. Persons waiting to start a new job who were actively seeking work during the reference period are counted as unemployed under concepts; if they were not actively seeking work, they are not counted in the labour force. In some countries, persons on layoff are classified as employed due to their strong job attachment.

No adjustment is made for the countries that classify those on layoff as employed. In the United States, as in Australia and Japan, passive job seekers are not in the labour force; job search must be active, such as placing or answering advertisements, contacting employers directly, or registering with an employment agency (simply reading ads is not enough to qualify as active search).

Canada and the European countries classify passive jobseekers as unemployed. An adjustment is made to exclude them in Canada, but not in the European countries where the phenomenon is less prevalent. Persons waiting to start a new job are counted among the unemployed for all other countries, whether or not they were actively seeking work.

The figures for one or more recent years for France, Germany, and the Netherlands are calculated using adjustment factors based on labour force surveys for earlier years and are considered preliminary. The recent year measures for these countries are therefore subject to revision whenever more current labour force surveys become available.

For the United States, beginning in 1994, data are not strictly comparable for prior years because of the introduction of a major redesign of the labour force survey questionnaire and collection methodology. The redesign effect has been estimated to increase the overall unemployment rate by 0.1 percentage point. Other breaks noted relate to changes in population controls that had virtually no effect on unemployment rates.

For Australia, the 2001 break reflects the introduction in April 2001 of a redesigned labour force survey that allowed for a closer application of International Labour Office guidelines for the definitions of labour force statistics. The Australian Bureau of Statistics revised their data so there is no break in the employment series. However, the reclassification of persons who had not actively looked for work because they were waiting to begin a new job from "not in the labour force" to "unemployed" could only be incorporated for April 2001 forward.

This reclassification diverges from the definition where persons waiting to start a new job but not actively seeking work are not counted in the labour force. The impact of the reclassification was an increase in the unemployment rate by 0.1 percentage point in 2001.

For Germany, the 1999 break reflects the incorporation of an improved method of data calculation and a change in coverage to persons living in private households only. BLS constructs the comparative indexes from three basic aggregate measures—output, total labour hours, and total compensation.

The hours and compensation measures refer to all employed persons (wage and salary earners plus self-employed persons and unpaid family workers) with the exception of Belguim and Taiwan, where only employees (wage and salary earners) are counted.

Output, in general, refers to value added in manufacturing from the national accounts of each country. However, the output series for Japan prior to 1970 is an index of industrial production, and the national accounts measures for the United Kingdom are essentially identical to their indexes of industrial production.

The output data for the United States are the gross product originating (value added) measures prepared by the Bureau of Economic Analysis of the U.S. Department of Commerce. Comparable manufacturing output data currently are not available prior to 1977. U.S. data from 1998 forward are based on the 1997 North American Industry Classification System (NAICS).

Output is in real value-added terms using a chain-type annual-weighted method for price deflation. Most of the other economies now also use annual moving price weights, but earlier years were estimated using fixed price weights, with the weights typically updated every 5 or 10 years. To preserve the comparability of the U.S. measures with those for other economies, BLS uses gross product originating in manufacturing for the United States for these comparative measures.

The gross product originating series differs from the manufacturing output series that BLS publishes in its news releases on quarterly measures of U.S. productivity and costs. The quarterly measures are on a"sectoral output" basis, rather than a value-added basis. Sectoral output is gross output less intrasector transactions.

Total labour hours refer to hours worked in all economies. The measures are developed from statistics of manufacturing employment and average hours. The series used for Australia, Canada, Demark, France (from 1970 forward), Norway, and Sweden are official series published with the national accounts.

For Germany, BLS uses estimates of average hours worked developed by a research institute connected to the Ministry of Labour for use with the national accounts employment figures. For the United Kingdom from 1992, an official annual index of total manufacturing hours is used. Where official total hours series are not available, the measures are developed by BLS using employment figures published with the national accounts, or other comprehensive employment series, and estimates of annual hours worked.

Total compensation (labour cost) includes all payments in cash or in-kind made directly to employees plus employer expenditures for legally-required insurance programs and contractual and private benefit plans. The measures are from the national accounts of each economy, except those for Belgium, which are developed by BLS using statistics on employment, average hours, and hourly compensation.

For Australia, Canada, France, and Sweden, compensation is increased to account for other significant taxes on payroll or employment. For the United Kingdom, compensation is reduced between 1967 and 1991 to account for employment-related subsidies. Self-employed workers are included in the all-employed-persons measures by assuming that their compensation is equal to the average for wage and salary employees.

In general, the measures relate to total manufacturing as defined by the International Standard Industrial Classification. However, the measures for France include parts of mining as well. The measures for recent years may be based on current indicators of manufacturing output (such as industrial production indexes), employment, average hours, and hourly compensation until national accounts and other statistics used for the long-term measures become available.

Official published data for Australia are in fiscal years that begin on July 1. The Australian Bureau of Statistics has finished calendar-year data for recent years for output and hours. For earlier years and for compensation, data are BLS estimates using 2-year moving averages of fiscal year data.

The Survey of Occupational Injuries and Illnesses collects data from employers about their workers' job-related nonfatal injuries and illnesses. The information that employers provide is based on records that they maintain under the Occupational Safety and Health Act of 1970. Self-employed individuals, farms with fewer than 11 employees, employers regulated by other Federal safety and health laws, and Federal, State, and local government agencies are excluded from the survey.

The survey is a Federal-State cooperative programme with an independent sample selected for each participating State. A stratified random sample with a Neyman allocation is selected to represent all private industries in the State. The survey is stratified by Standard Industrial Classification and size of employment.

Under the Occupational Safety and Health Act, employers maintain records of nonfatal work-related injuries and illnesses that involve one or more of the following: loss of consciousness, restriction of work or motion, transfer to another job, or medical treatment other than first aid. Occupational injury is any injury such as a cut, fracture, sprain, or amputation that results from a work-related event or a single, instantaneous exposure in the work environment.

Occupational illness is an abnormal condition or disorder, other than one resulting from an occupational injury, caused by exposure to factors associated with employment. It includes acute and chronic illnesses or disease which may be caused by inhalation, absorption, ingestion, or direct contact. Lost workday injuries and illnesses are cases that involve days away from work, or days of restricted work activity, or both.

Lost workdays include the number of workdays (consecutive or not) on which the employee was either away from work or at work in some restricted capacity, or both, because of an occupational injury or illness. BLS measures of the number and incidence rate of lost workdays were discontinued beginning with the 1993 survey. The number of days away from work or days of restricted work activity does not include the day of injury or onset of illness or any days on which the employee would not have worked, such as a Federal holiday, even though able to work.

Incidence rates are computed as the number of injuries and/or illnesses or lost work days per 100 full-time workers. Estimates are made for industries and employment size classes for total recordable cases, lost workday cases, days away from work cases, and nonfatal cases without lost workdays. These data also are shown separately for injuries.

Illness data are available for seven categories: occupational skin diseases or disorders, dust diseases of the lungs, respiratory conditions due to toxic agents, poisoning (systemic effects of toxic agents), disorders due to physical agents (other than toxic materials), disorders associated with repeated trauma, and all other occupational illnesses.

The survey continues to measure the number of new

work-related illness cases which are recognized, diagnosed, and reported during the year. Some conditions, for example, long-term latent illnesses caused by exposure to carcinogens, often are difficult to relate to the workplace and are not adequately recognized and reported. These long-term latent illnesses are believed to be understated in the survey's illness measure. In contrast, the overwhelming majority of the reported new illnesses are those which are easier to directly relate to workplace activity (for example, contact dermatitis and carpal tunnel syndrome).

Most of the estimates are in the form of incidence rates, defined as the number of injuries and illnesses per 100 equivalent full-time workers. For this purpose, 200,000 employee hours represent 100 employee years (2,000 hours per employee). Full detail on the available measures is presented in the annual bulletin, Occupational Injuries and Illnesses: Counts, Rates, and Characteristics.

Comparable data for more than 40 States and territories are available from the BLS Office of Safety, Health and Working Conditions. Many of these States publish data on State and local government employees in addition to private industry data. Mining and railroad data are furnished to BLS by the Mine Safety and Health Administration and the Federal Railroad Administration. Data from these organizations are included in both the national and State data published annually. With the 1992 survey, BLS began publishing details on serious, nonfatal incidents resulting in days away from work. Included are some major characteristics of the injured and ill workers, such as occupation, age, gender, race, and length of service, as well as the circumstances of their injuries and illnesses (nature of the disabling condition, part of body affected, event and exposure, and the source directly producing the condition). In general, these data are available nationwide for detailed industries and for individual States at more aggregated industry levels.

CENSUS OF FATAL OCCUPATIONAL INJURIES

The Census of Fatal Occupational Injuries compiles a

complete roster of fatal job-related injuries, including detailed data about the fatally injured workers and the fatal events. The programme collects and cross checks fatality information from multiple sources, including death certificates, State and Federal workers' compensation reports, Occupational Safety and Health Administration and Mine Safety and Health Administration records, medical examiner and autopsy reports, media accounts, State motor vehicle fatality records, and follow-up questionnaires to employers.

In addition to private wage and salary workers, the self-employed, family members, and Federal, State, and local government workers are covered by the programme. To be included in the fatality census, the decedent must have been employed (that is working for pay, compensation, or profit) at the time of the event, engaged in a legal work activity, or present at the site of the incident as a requirement of his or her job.

A fatal work injury is any intentional or unintentional wound or damage to the body resulting in death from acute exposure to energy, such as heat or electricity, or kinetic energy from a crash, or from the absence of such essentials as heat or oxygen caused by a specific event or incident or series of events within a single workday or shift. Fatalities that occur during a person's commute to or from work are excluded from the census, as well as work-related illnesses, which can be difficult to identify due to long latency periods.

Twenty-eight data elements are collected, coded, and tabulated in the fatality programme, including information about the fatally injured worker, the fatal incident, and the machinery or equipment involved. Summary worker demographic data and event characteristics are included in a national news release that is available about 8 months after the end of the reference year. The Census of Fatal Occupational Injuries was initiated in 1992 as a joint Federal-State effort. Most States issue summary information at the time of the national news release.

Chapter 11

Quality of Work

MORALE

Of the thousands of public sector agencies at the state and local levels of government, a very small percentage are in economic, political or legal situations that allow them to be a community, state or regional leader in terms of employee pay. Organizations that have adopted a pay or compensation philosophy as a market pay "leader" have generally come, not surprisingly, from the private sector.

It is generally difficult for public sector organizations to adopt "market leader" pay philosophies since such a philosophy would generally translate to a greater tax burden for citizens, who can be expected to harbor reservations, at the very least, about the "appropriateness" of a "market leader" pay strategy. In fact as the 1976 ICMA text on personnel administration notes, "It is doubtful that taxpayers would tolerate public employees' salaries exceeding those of their counterparts in industry."

Many or perhaps most public sector organizations are committed to a commonly accepted concept in public compensation theory, that is, to pay public sector employees at "prevailing wages." The concept of "prevailing wages" is generally defined as wages that match the external market for similar positions at approximately the 50th percentile, meaning approximately fifty per cent of similar jobs in the community have lower pay ranges and fifty per cent have higher pay ranges. This pay policy is also commonly referred to as a "neither lead nor lag" policy. Community pay leaders, on the other hand, go well beyond the prevailing wage concept and typically set employee pay ranges in the 70th through 90th percentile.

Are there advantages that accrue to an organization that adopts a community pay leader position? According to Edward E. Lawler III, there may indeed be certain payoffs from pursuing a policy of being a top-notch payer. Lawler notes that, "Such organizations as IBM and Hewlett-Packard have for a long time recognized that if they pay well, they will have very little turnover and be able to pick from among a large number of job applicants." Would public sector organizations realise any benefits if they were able to be community pay leaders? The following paragraphs describe the results for one public sector pay leader.

A PAY LEADER FROM THE PUBLIC SECTOR

As noted earlier, few public agencies are in a position to be a community, state or regional pay leader, but there are exceptions. One such exception is the municipal water utility in Denver, Colorado. This non-union organization, with approximately one thousand employees, is an independent agency of the City and County of Denver with its own policy-setting Board of Commissioners and its own civil service system.

The agency serves water to over 900,000 people, more than a quarter of the state's population, through 250,000 water taps. Its operations are funded through water rates and other fees. Essentially the agency is financially structured as an enterprise fund that does not rely on property taxes. For several years this agency has been a community pay leader and has positioned itself at approximately the 75th percentile of market pay rates. The pay leader position has brought expected and unexpected results for the agency. As expected and as private firms have found, being a pay leader has resulted in a very low employee turnover rate and has contributed to a large pool of applicants vying for job openings. The most important unexpected result has been the low level of job satisfaction expressed by the agency's employees.

In January of 1992 the Mountain States Employers Council, Inc. conducted an Employee Opinion Survey of all agency employees. The response rate for the Survey was 86 per cent. The Mountain States Employers Council had previously conducted many similar Employee Opinion Surveys in the Denver metropolitan area, therefore, the Survey used at the agency contained 34 standard questions with norms developed by previous participants.

Mountain States Employers Council divided the standard questions into several categories comparing the agency scores for these categories to the community norms that had been developed. Two points of interest emerged from an examination of the responses. First, in the category of pay-related questions and the category of benefit-related questions the agency's employees were significantly more positive about pay and benefits than the community norms. Second, in the category of questions related to employee job satisfaction the agency's employees were significantly less satisfied than the community norm.

The agency employee scores that deviated most significantly from the norms in a positive direction involved three questions pertaining to satisfaction with pay increases, satisfaction with the benefit package, and satisfaction with communication about how pay is determined. The most negative scores in terms of community norms concerned the job satisfaction issues of: opportunities for advancement; promotion policies; supervisory support of quality work; and consistency in the application of disciplinary procedures.

Analyzing the survey findings using the perspective of the community norms developed by the Mountain States Employers Council, the following points are clear.

On the positive side:

- Agency employees were generally very satisfied with their base pay and pay increases.
- Agency employees were generally very satisfied with the agency's benefit package.
- Agency employees were generally very satisfied with the equipment they use to perform their jobs.

- Employees felt that they had good job security.
- Employees were satisfied that the agency was concerned about employee safety.
- Employees felt that the amount of work they were asked to do was fair and reasonable.
- Employees felt personally responsible for "top quality" in performing their jobs.

On the negative side:

- Agency employees generally did not feel that promotions were given to the most qualified people.
- Agency employees generally felt very dissatisfied with their chances for advancement. On a related question employees believed that there were not enough opportunities for advancement for qualified people.
- Many agency employees strongly believed that "who you know" was important for getting ahead.
- Many agency employees believed that there were "communication problems" between different sections or departments of the agency.
- Comments from a significant number of employees expressed dissatisfaction with the agency's Affirmative Action policies.
- Employees were also dissatisfied with Human Resources and felt the HR department was not responsive to their needs.

Perhaps the best indicator in the Survey of overall employee job dissatisfaction involved the question "Would you accept a job at another company, doing the same job as you do here, with the same pay and benefits?" Compared to the community norm, a significant percentage of agency employees indicated they would accept another job elsewhere for similar pay and benefits.

The problem is, of course, when you work for a community pay and benefits leader and have excellent job security, the opportunity for finding a similar job elsewhere in the community (the Denver metropolitan area) with equivalent pay and benefits is very, very limited.

THE RAMIFICATIONS OF BEING A PUBLIC SECTOR PAY LEADER

The single most important consequence attributable, at least in large part, to the pay leader position has been a very low turnover of employees. The agency's turnover rate has persistently been in the two to four per cent range during much of the past decade. While on the surface a very low employee turnover rate may appear desirable, it does have its drawbacks.

For example, there are very few advancement opportunities for employees and intense interest focuses on any promotional opportunity that comes along. Additionally there is extreme unhappiness in the general employee population with any programme or civil service policy, rule or procedure seen as adversely affecting an individual's chances for advancement.

In fact a very low turnover rate makes programs to ensure workforce diversity much more difficult. In an article on turnover in the federal government, Gregory Lewis notes that although turnover may be costly for the federal government, it does have some benefits such as bringing "fresh blood" into an organization and in offering promotion opportunities for lower level employees. Lewis further notes that "turnover was key to improving the representation of women and minorities."

Exacerbating the problem of job dissatisfaction at the agency is a relatively recent change from a "promote from within" policy to one of more aggressively opening promotional opportunities to both internal and external candidates. Making job satisfaction problems worse, the agency's excellent Tuition Reimbursement Programme and nearby college campuses have motivated many employees to obtain college degrees.

A highly educated workforce may appear to be a good thing, but there now appear to be a substantial number of lower level agency employees with college degrees and very little opportunity for advancement. This combination of factors is predictably one that does not lead to a workforce with high levels of job satisfaction. There are, of course, factors other than lack of job advancement opportunities that may be contributing to employee job dissatisfaction. Three of these potential factors are discussed below.

INTERNAL EQUITY

Individuals in organizations generally make two distinct types of pay comparisons when deciding whether or not they are being fairly compensated: internal comparisons of pay with other employees within the organization and external market comparisons. Of these two types of pay comparisons Lawler believes that external market comparisons are most important.

He states that "If external comparisons are poor, an individual will usually leave as soon as he or she can find another job." While external equity is important so is the matter of internal equity. If employees perceive a lack of internal equity between jobs within the organization, morale problems will undoubtedly result.

The agency in question was aware of potential problems resulting from a lack of internal equity among the 300 plus job classifications. A point-factor job evaluation system was used to determine the relative worth of each job and to place each job in the job worth hierarchy in the appropriate pay grade. Wallace and Fay note that job evaluation systems cannot, by themselves, be the answer to all problems concerning internal equity.

Agency employees have, however, expressed very little dissatisfaction with the job evaluation system in use or with comparisons of internal equity in general. There is a job audit procedure in place at the agency so that employees or their supervisors are able to request an audit of any job they perceive incorrectly placed in a particular pay grade.

ORGANIZATION CULTURE

The agency does appear to be undergoing a gradual shift in organizational culture away from a conservative, "family-like" culture. The agency's culture has also reflected at least some of the elements of an "entitlement culture" described by

Judith Bardwick. In an entitlement culture, according to Bardwick, employees have so much security that they don't have to earn their rewards.

Bardwick states that "When people don't have to earn what they get, they soon take for granted what they receive. The real irony is that they're not grateful for what they get. Instead, they want more. It is the terrible cycle of entitlement." Pay policies can certainly contribute to a culture of entitlement. For example, if employee pays above the market rate of pay (in this case step 4 is the market step in a 9 step pay system) is not pay at risk, then it may be seen as an entitlement by employees.

It would seem logical that as the agency attempts to modify its organizational culture the level of employee job satisfaction could decrease. However, since job security at the agency remains intact, the impact of a gradual change in organization culture cannot fully explain the level of employee job dissatisfaction evidenced in the Employee Opinion Survey.

MANAGEMENT PROBLEMS

The Survey results could also be indicative of "poor" management at the agency. A large majority of respondents, however, did rate the agency Manager as doing a "satisfactory" or a "better than satisfactory" job. The agency also has a strong supervisory training programme which should, in theory at least, lead to a well-trained management team. Undoubtedly some agency managers are less than fully competent, but on the whole, the Survey does not indicate an incompetent management team or a poorly managed organization.

In reflecting on the Survey results and recent interviews with an unscientific sample of agency employees, it must be concluded that the position of being a community pay leader was primarily responsible for accomplishing the agency objective of low employee turnover. It must also be concluded that the accomplishment of the low turnover objective contributed significantly to the general level of employee job dissatisfaction the agency has experienced.

As the agency's Manager of Employment and Compensation during this period, I can certainly state that a higher-than-average level of employee job dissatisfaction was not the intended consequence of maintaining a position as a community pay leader. Edward Lawler has perhaps summed it up best when he noted that "There is some research that suggests that high pay rates can lead to high motivation.

However, motivation from this source seems to be very short-lived. Most individuals quickly decide that they deserve whatever pay rate they receive and do not try to perform better in order to deserve it." With no evidence of increased productivity at the agency it must be concluded that Lawler's words ring true for this public sector agency.

NEW DIRECTIONS - A PROPOSAL

Few public sector organizations, as noted earlier, appear to be in a position where they can legitimately pursue a strategy of being a community, state or regional pay leader. In any case, the sense is that a pay leader policy does not tend to produce desired results in public sector organizations with elabourate civil service systems. This is a private sector practice that does not translate well to the public sector.

In many organizations, both public and private, the overall aging of the workforce translates to fewer promotional opportunities and more "plateaued" employees. Even for public agencies that have the ability to pay and can afford to be community pay leaders, it would seem that there needs to be a better understanding of nonmonetary career motivators.

Being a pay leader attracts people who are interested in high pay, though they may not necessarily interested in "public service." Perry and Wise note that utilitarian incentives, such as individual pay and benefits, are not likely to be critical determinants of outputs when individuals identify with the mission of the organization, provided that the incentives are maintained at satisfactory or prevailing levels.

They also conclude that "Public service motivation is likely to be positively related to an individual's organizational commitment. Individuals who are highly committed are likely to be highly motivated to remain with their organizations and to perform."

A failure to attract employees who have at least some level of public service motivation may result in employees who are dissatisfied with their jobs in a public sector agency. The goal is not, it seems, to create utilitarian incentives that attract the "best and the brightest," but rather to provide a level of incentives to attract the best and the brightest who are motivated, for any number of reasons, to serve in the public sector. One key point is that whatever the cause of public sector employee job dissatisfaction, the use of high levels of utilitarian incentives (pay and benefits) alone cannot overcome it. The result will be highly paid, dissatisfied employees. There is a direction that seems to make more sense for public sector employers then simply "upping the ante" to compete with high flying private enterprises.

As Romzek notes, utilitarian incentives are important to attract and retain high quality public employees, but they are not enough. Of equal importance is the necessity for public agencies to foster a commitment by employees to the values and mission of the organization. In addition to fostering employee commitment to organizational values and mission, public sector managers can impact employee turnover rates through a better understanding of career dynamics.

Thomas Barth argues that the Career Anchor Theory developed by Edgar Schein could provide a conceptual framework for understanding career motivation. Barth notes that "Schein maintains that as employees progress through their careers they are engaged in a process of self-discovery that reveals career anchors of which they were not initially aware. If this discovery leads to the conclusion that they are not in the right job or career path, employees have three principal options:

- The employee leaves;
- The employee stays and represses the career anchor;
- The employee and the organization restructure the job or provide other opportunities within the organization to tap the employee's career anchor."

Public managers who seek a motivated workforce with low turnover would be wise to provide enough flexibility in their civil service policies, rules and procedures to encourage the restructuring of jobs, or the use of job rotation, or special duty assignments so that employees have an opportunity to discover their particular career anchors.

Employees who are motivated to serve in the public sector and who have found a career anchor which matches their individual needs are much more likely to express satisfaction with their jobs than public sector employees who are highly paid, but lack an appropriate career anchor and a commitment to the values and mission of their organization.

The importance of communication in organizational functioning is historically well recognized. However, a noticeable need still exists to examine organizational communication measures as they relate to other organizational concepts.

Two organizational concepts that are of interest to management practitioners and researchers are job performance and job satisfaction. Their interest emerges from the fact that the quality of job performance and satisfaction may determine the quality of organizational life and effectiveness.

Clearly communication plays a major role in one's job satisfaction (usually measured in multidimensional terms). How an employee perceives a supervisor's communication style, credibility, and content as well as the organizations communication system will to some extent influence the amount of satisfaction (morale) he or she receives from the job. Pincus, in a field study of 327 hospital nurses, found a positive relationship between communication and job performance; but the communication-satisfaction link was stronger, particularly in supervisor communication, climate, and personal feedback.

The study confirmed "the vital importance of employee-immediate supervisor communication on employee job satisfaction". Another study in the public sector reported strong positive relationships between job satisfaction and communication satisfaction with the supervisor and his or her receptivity to information.

In fact, after a review of the literature since the mid-1970's, King, Lahiff, and Hatfield report "a consistently clear and positive pattern of relationships between an employee's perceptions of communications and his or her job satisfaction". On the other hand, the influence of communi-cation upon an employee's job performance (usually measured by perceived quality and quantity of output) is not nearly as clear.

A review of the research literature suggests a general link between communication and performance; but perhaps because of varying methodologies and definitions, the results are often mixed. A study by Clampitt and Downs involving a service organization and a manufacturer has uncovered new evidence concerning the relationship.

First, their study, using both interviews and the Communication Satisfaction Questionnaire (CSQ), found that all eight communication satisfaction dimensions impacted the employees' productivity. Although such dimensions as "communication with coworkers," "meetings and memos;' and "corporate-wide information," impacted productivity somewhat, employees in both organizations perceived "personal feedback" from their supervisor to have the highest impact.

Second, satisfaction of an employee with a particular dimension of communication did not necessarily mean his or her productivity was affected. It appears that the relationship between performance and communication is more job specific than originally thought. Thus, abundant research linking communication with both job performance and satisfaction exists. What is lacking in the literature, however, is an investigation of the relationship among the three variables, particularly with communication as a moderating influence.

Zedeck indicates that the moderator approach is a systematic way of studying in what manner organizational and individual facets exert their influence and alter the relationship among target variables. Cohen and Cohen add that a moderator variable refers to "a variable V which interacts with another so as to . . . enhance predictability of criterion".

Theoretically, higher links of communication should

increase the relationship between an employee's job performance and the satisfaction with that job. Thus, this study assumes that organizational communication is one of those organizational variables that may exert a moderating effect on the relationship between job performance and satisfaction.

The primary purpose of this study is to determine the moderating effects, if any, of organizational communication upon the employee performance-satisfaction relationship. That is, if employees are exposed to appropriate communication (trust, accuracy, etc.), job performance will in turn be improved leading to increased job satisfaction. The rationale for the study and model is discussed below and gives further insight into the complex web of relationships among organizational communication, job performance, and job satisfaction.

The relationship between performance and satisfaction is highly variable. Literature reviews conducted by Brayfield and Crockett, Herzberg, Mausner, Peterson, and Capwell, Vroom, and others reflect this variability. Schwab and Cummings noted the highly variable and weak to moderate relationship between job performance and job satisfaction; they observed that these conditions may result from the impact of organizational or individual moderator. Consequently, the moderating approach to the study of the association of performance and satisfaction has emerged. However, the idea is not new.

Brayfield and Crockett criticized researchers for paying too little attention to individual and organizational factors in job performance-job satisfaction relationship studies. Researchers have already found that the relationship may be moderated by employees' self-esteem, need for achievement, organizational rewards, managerial level, job fit, and organizational pressure for performance and experienced time pressure.

Jacobs and Solomon and Bhagat have indicated a need for further research to identify other situational variables that may be moderating the relationship between job performance and job satisfaction. The current investigation proposes that organizational communication is one of those situational variables that possibly exerts an effect on the job performance-job satisfaction relationship.

Such a proposition emerges from two sources. First, Schwab and Cummings suggest that variables which differentially affect performance and satisfaction become potential moderators of performance-satisfaction relationships. Since organizational communication has been shown to be related to both job performance and job satisfaction, a likely hypothesis is that organizational communication moderates the job performance-job satisfaction relationship.

Secondly, Porter and Lawler hypothesized and found support for the proposition that variations in job performance are primarily responsible for variations in satisfaction. In a review of the literature, Schwab and Cummings also found support for this proposition. Therefore, since organizational communication has been shown to be related to job performance, it again seems appropriate to expect organizational communication to moderate the relationship between job performance and job satisfaction.

The term organizational communication, as used in this research, encompasses 7 of the 15 dimensions of communication identified by Roberts and O'Reilly: trust in superiors, perceived influence of superiors, accuracy of information, desire for interaction, satisfaction with communication, information load (underload and overload), and directionality of communication (upward, downward, and lateral). These dimensions were selected because they have been shown to be related to job performance in several ways.

First, trust in superiors, influence of superiors, accuracy of information, desire for interaction, and satisfaction with communication have shown a direct relationship with job performance. Second, studies conducted by O'Reilly and O'Reilly and Roberts indicate that communication overload tends to have an inverse and underload a direct relationship with job performance. Lastly, although conflicting results have been reported, upward and downward communication appear to be directly related and lateral communication inversely related to performance.

The preceding review concerning the relationship of job performance to job satisfaction and the association of organizational communication to performance-satisfaction serves as the basis for the two hypotheses that are tested. The first hypothesis mainly serves to replicate previous studies. The second constitutes the primary purpose for conducting this investigation.

- H_1: Job performance will be directly and moderately related to job satisfaction.
- H_2: Organizational communication - trust in superiors, influence of superiors, desire for interaction, accuracy of information, satisfaction with communication, information load, and directionality of communication - will be a moderator of the job performance-job satisfaction relationship.

Six hundred twenty-nine (629) employees from two companies were identified originally to participate in the study. Seventeen (17) of them were excluded because of business trips, sickness, or vacations. Thus 612 employees existed as potential subjects to receive the survey instruments. Companies A and B are within a diametre of no more than 40 miles in a large metropolitan area of the southern section of the United States. Company A with 27 employees is the headquarters of a firm that manufactures and markets a comprehensive line of heavy duty premium quality lubricants. Company B with 602 employees is a division of a multinational firm that deals with the research, design, engineering, and manufacturing of rotary blast hole bits, downhole percussion bits, hammers, raise reaming heads, and cutters.

Three hundred and two individuals (49.35% of the 612 potential subjects) completed and returned usable research instruments, 23 from Company A and 279 from Company B. The sample was comprised of 249 male respondents and 53 females. In terms of age, 20% were less than 30 years old, 54% between 30 and 49, and 26% were more than 49 years old. Finally, 14% of the respondents reported having worked for their employer for less than 5 years, 31% from 5 to 9 years, 22% from 10 to 14 years, and 33% for 15 years or more.

MEASURES

JOB PERFORMANCE

An overall measure of job performance was obtained by combining self-rated performance scores and supervisory rating scores from two 7-point Likert-type scales assessing performance in terms of quality and quantity. The integration of supervisory and self-ratings of performance may constitute a more objective measure of performance.

When asked to evaluate the quality of their performance, participants were requested to respond to the following two questions: (a) How would you rate the quality of your own performance in your job? and (b) How do you think your supervisor would rate the quality of your performance? Two identical questions were asked about the quantity of performance.

Supervisors were simply requested to assess the performance of their subordinates in terms of quality and quantity, separately. Both participants and supervisors rated the quality and quantity of performance using the following 7-point scale: excellent = 7; very good = 6; good = 5; average = 4; fair = 3; poor = 2; and very poor = 1.

The aggregate score of the two scales (quality and quantity) from both respondents and supervisors was taken as the measure of performance. The self-rated score of quality for each participant was determined and averaged with that provided by the supervisor. The same procedure was used to calculate the score of quantity of performance. The quality and quantity scores were then averaged to arrive at the overall measure of performance.

Data analyses yielded a significant (p [less than] .01) relationship between the self-rating of quality of performance and the supervisory rating of quality of performance (r = .32). A weaker but still significant (p [less than] .01) relationship was also found between the two measures of quantity obtained in the same fashion (r = .19). After the integration took place, the correlation between the performance dimensions of quality and quantity (r = .62) was significant at p [less than] .01.

JOB SATISFACTION

The Job Descriptive Index or JDI was the means for measuring job satisfaction. The JDI assesses five dimensions of job satisfaction:

- Satisfaction with work,
- Satisfaction with pay,
- Satisfaction with promotions,
- Satisfaction with supervision,
- Satisfaction with coworkers.

The JDI has been described as one of the most carefully developed scales for measuring job satisfaction. Its continuous validity makes it an index with the greatest acceptance among management researchers.

ORGANIZATIONAL COMMUNICATION

The Roberts and O'Reilly organizational communication questionnaire was used to measure organizational communication as operationalized in this investigation. Roberts and O'Reilly reported that their instrument had desirable psychometric properties. The mode of data collection was a pre-tested questionnaire. The readability of the instrument was tested via a graduate class in statistics at a local university.

After securing copies of the lists of employees of the participating firms, a numbered copy of the questionnaire was distributed to each member of the sample. Each individual was told that the number on the questionnaire would be used only as a means for matching statistical data and that no one else would see the number except the researchers. This number was later used to identify each respondent's supervisor.

The internal mail system of each of the participating organizations was used to deliver the research instrument and introductory letter. The completed questionnaire was to be mailed to the Department of Management of a nearby university. A total of 316 employees completed and returned their questionnaires. Of this total, seven had removed their identification numbers. Two others were improperly answered. Consequently, 307 usable questionnaires were left.

The task was then to ask supervisors to rate respondents' performance. With the assistance of the Director of Human Resources of each participating firm, the immediate supervisor of each respondent was identified using the number assigned to each returned questionnaire. Seventy-nine supervisors were identified. Again, the internal mail systems of the participating organizations were used to deliver the performance scale and related materials to the supervisors. The job performance assessments were to be returned to the University.

One supervisor of three individuals did not respond. Also, during the two weeks taken by supervisors to assess participants' performance, one of the original respondents resigned while another was dismissed. These two respondents were therefore dropped from the list of actual respondents. The elimination of these last five participants left a total of 302 participants for whom supervisors provided performance evaluations. This total of respondents represents a 49.35% rate of return.

With a span of control ranging from 2 to 8 subordinates, none of the 78 supervisors who participated in the assessment of respondents' performance accounted for a disproportionate amount of the data collected. Further, no event, project, or activity was detected that might have influenced participants' performance during the period that lapsed between the time respondents completed the research instrument and the time supervisors conducted the performance assessment.

STATISTICAL ANALYSES

Hypothesis one was tested by noting whether the correlation between job performance and job satisfaction was positive and significant. Hypothesis two, concerning the expected moderating influence of organizational communication on the performance-satisfaction relationship, was assessed by moderated regression analysis.

Since the theoretical argument that performance leads to satisfaction has been adopted in this investigation, satisfaction was treated as the criterion, with performance and organizational communication as pre-dictors.

Following Saunders and Zedeck, the basic regression equations included the interaction or cross-product of the predictors. This addition provided the following three regression equations for evaluation purposes, where Y is satisfaction, X is performance, Z is organizational communication, and a to d are constants.

- $Y = a + bX$
- $Y = a + bX + cZ$
- $Y = a + bX + cZ + dXZ$

Zedeck states that "if Equations 2 and 3 are significantly different from Equation 1, but not from each other, then the variable [the suggested moderator, organizational communication] is an independent predictor and not a moderator variable". Therefore, for this investigation, a moderator exists only in situations in which a predictor-moderator interaction term accounts for a significant amount of criterion variance after both predictor and moderator variables have entered the regression equation.

Moderated regression analyses were conducted for all organizational communication dimensions investigated. This effort also provided any predicting effects detected. The mean, standard deviation and median for each variable show high variability in participants' responses. To compare them, all scores were reduced to a seven-point Likert-type scale. More will be said about this variability in the discussion section.

Results for the relationship between performance and satisfaction show a direct and moderate relationship between them. Thus hypothesis is accepted. The highest correlation was between performance and satisfaction with work, and the lowest between performance and satisfaction with coworkers.

Assessment of the potential moderating effect of organizational communication on the relationship between job performance and job satisfaction, the central issue of this study, begins with a review of the correlation matrix. In general, the communication dimensions (potential moderators) show varying degrees of co-variance with both the independent variable (job performance) and the dependent variable (job satisfaction).

Of the seven communication dimensions investigated, directionality of communication (upward, downward, and lateral) and communication load (underload and overload) would appear to have the greatest potential as moderators. Conversely, trust in superiors, perceived influence of superiors, accuracy of information, desire for interaction, and satisfaction with communication appear to have the least potential.

The aim of this investigation is to explore the moderating influence of organizational communication on the relation-ship between job performance and job satisfaction. The study also re-examines the association between these last two variables. Results show that job performance has a direct, weak-to-moderate relationship with job satisfaction.

It also replicates the finding by Petty, McGee, and Cavender, who used meta-analysis (a statistical technique which accumulates findings across studies). Thus, previous and current findings suggest, once again, that changes in one of the two variables (performance or satisfaction) may only weakly or moderately influence the other.

Organizational communication received weak support as a moderator of the relationship between performance and satisfaction. Only 2 of the 50 interactions were significant: satisfaction with work was influenced by the interaction of accuracy of information and satisfaction with pay was impacted by the interaction of lateral communication. The correlation between performance and satisfaction with work was greater for individuals scoring high in accuracy of communication than for participants scoring low. It appears that appropriate and accurate information may enhance both performance and satisfaction with work.

This finding implies that individuals receiving proper, correct, and clear information may perform adequately, which in turn may give rise to positive feelings about their jobs, or vice versa. Supervisors might be able to promote adequate levels of job performance and job satisfaction among their employees by providing them with appropriate and accurate information.

On the other hand, individuals scoring low in lateral communication reflected a greater correlation between performance and satisfaction with pay than respondents scoring high. This finding suggests that employees subjected to low levels of lateral communication may be less inclined to make nondesirable comparisons of job related features, including pay, which in turn may negatively affect both performance and satisfaction with pay.

Such a suggestion may be especially true in places where salary or wage differences are not perceived as adequate or consistent. Ample opportunity for lateral communication may increase the possibility of perceiving pay as inadequate when compared with the contribution being made. Further investigation of this speculation may prove beneficial to management practitioners. When considering the very weak support that organizational communication received as a moderator, one question arises. Why was such support so weak? Two factors may help answer this question. First, this investigation used a very rigorous statistical procedure for detecting moderating effects - moderated regression analysis. Second, many of the communication dimensions studied received strong support as independent predictors.

Thirty of the 50 relationships investigated showed that the integrated communication dimensions acted as predictors. Zedeck suggests that moderators are very difficult to find when the change after adding the proposed moderators as a predictor to the regression equation is high to start with. In this study, the change resulting from the addition of a proposed communication moderator to a particular model as a predictor was equal to or greater than .13.

Because of this phenomenon, six of the seven communication dimensions investigated - trust in superiors, influence of superiors, accuracy of information, desire for interaction, satisfaction with communication, and communication load - received strong support as predictors of job satisfaction.

In addition, job satisfaction was treated as the dependent variable when conducting the moderated regression analysis.

Considering that virtually every dimension of communication investigated related to both job performance and job satisfaction in the same manner, it is then plausible to suggest that the main effects of organizational communi-cation are compatible with two of the central theories in the literature concerning the causal relationship between performance and satisfaction:

- Job performance - [greater than] job satisfaction,
- Job satisfaction - [greater than] job performance.

For example, high levels of accuracy of information may lead to high levels of performance, and successful performance may promote job satisfaction. The sequence may also function in reverse. High levels of accuracy of communication may lead to high levels of job satisfaction, and favourable perception of satisfaction may enhance job performance.

What appears evident from this research is that regardless of the direction of the job performance-job satisfaction relation, organizational communication appears to be an important predictor of both variables. Thus, communication can be an effective tool that practitioners may use to enhance these two dimensions. Downs, Clampitt, and Pfeiffer argue this same point.

Finally, some methodological observations should be made. Admittedly, measuring organizational and individual constructs by aggregating self-reported data from research participants, as was done in this study, is controversial. The basic criticism "is essentially that researchers using survey methods have simply combined disparate perceptions into fallacious averages".

In this study, however, the researchers are confident that the investigated measures of job performance, job satisfaction, and organizational communication are meaningful. First, these findings about the relationship between job performance and job satisfaction mirrored those of previous studies, suggesting that the variables analysed were not just fallacious or spurious averages.

Second, a graphical analysis of residuals yielded properties that suggested that the residuals were independent, had zero mean, had a common variance, and followed a normal distribution. Therefore, these reasons provide strong support for the point that the data collected adequately represent the constructs investigated in this study.

That organization communication received strong support as a predictor of job satisfaction and weak support as a moderator of the job performance-job satisfaction relationship is the major conclusion of this research. Although some relationships did not prove significant as hypothesized, communication did prove to be important in organizational functioning nonetheless.

And such importance undergirds the need for the continued investigation of communication in organizations. These findings, combined with the use of rigorous statistical procedures and the research design of relating communication to significant output variables, make this study unique in its contribution.

But more research into these complex relationships is needed by business communication scientists. Downs, Clampitt, and Pfeiffer note that, "Perhaps the opportunities are rare, and the choices few, when both objectives [performance and satisfaction] can be achieved through a single communication strategy". Business communication researchers might consider alternate strategies and combinations of strategies in future research investigations.

First, this study did not take a skills approach in defining communication and relating it to performance-satisfaction outputs. Perhaps an investigation of writing (letters and reports) and speaking in the context of this research effort might prove interesting. If specific skill levels are examined, they should be approached within the proper research context, design, and process for meaningful results to occur.

Moreover, this study used only organizational communication as defined by Roberts and O'Reilly. Other constructs of communication such as the Communication Satisfaction Questionnaire or the Interpersonal Communication Relationship Inventory could be used to determine the moderating effects of communication. Or, to determine the influence of the supervisor's interpersonal capacity on the performance-satisfaction relationship, the Index of Interpersonal Communication Competence could be used.

The various definitions of communication in the literature call for several research possibilities to analyse the performance-communication-satisfaction trilogy in organizations. The opportunities for additional research are exciting, to be sure. Business communication researchers need to tap these opportunities as they investigate the complex and dynamic process of communication in organizations.

Chapter 12

Counseling for Effectiveness

"People are our most important resource" has become far more than an obligatory line in an annual report. Organizational career development (OCD) has evolved over the last several decades and has emerged as a competitive strategy for enhancing organizational effectiveness through a well-developed workforce.

Before painting an accurate picture of how OCD has changed over the last few decades, we need to set the context by sketching various "big-picture" transformations that have occurred in the business landscape. First, bottom line margins of success can no longer be guaranteed by technological advances; competitiveness means mastery of interpersonal communication, teamwork, and critical thinking.

New information and communications technologies, along with harsh global economic realities (e.g. downsizing), now require new ways of looking not only at career development but also at the appropriate balance between individual and organizational needs. Finally, career development is increasingly taking place in a context of systems that connect such development with other HR initiatives and practices. In order to assess the impact of these changes, we decided, in the early 1990s, to embark on a full-fledged reexamination of OCD. Our aim was to determine how far the field has come, attitudinally and practically, since 1978—the year in which the American Management Association sponsored a major survey of OCD practice. That study revealed "widespread support" for career planning but also a "wide gap" between actual and ideal practice.

The essential questions prompting our own investigation were these: What is the current state of the practice of career development in larger organizations? How have things changed since 1978? And what new ideas or trends are in the offing—that is, what is the state-of-the-art of OCD?

Our study, sponsored by the American Society for Training and Development and presented in detail in our book, Organizational Career Development, made use of both broad-based surveys and structured telephone interviews. We conducted a random sampling of 1,000 corporations and 96 federal agencies; in addition, our survey targeted samples of between 500 and 1,000 European, Australian, and Singaporean corporations.

Because the career development systems of large organizations are typically more visible than those in smaller organizations and thus afford richer data, we concentrated on large entities (over 40 per cent of which were international) in diverse industries. Our survey had a healthy 26 per cent response rate, and we believe that the results (although unstratified) offer a meaningful representation of OCD trends in bigger organizations. Directed at HR executives, our survey instrument (like that of the 1978 study) included questions on the following issues:

- The prevalence of career development systems (defined as "processes and practices that link individual career goals with the organization's HR needs");
- System "drivers" (factors prompting system design and implementation);
- Corporate attitudes toward OCD;
- Implementation (audiences and structures);
- Perceived effectiveness; and
- Outcomes and assessment.

OCD PRACTICE: FINDINGS FROM OUR RECENT

Nearly 70 per cent of our U.S respondents had or were launching career development systems; most of those systems were either less than a year old or over six years old. (We suspect that this prevalence rate is above average for large U.S. organizations overall because of the self-screening involved in choosing to be a respondent.)

Organizations without systems cited three main reasons for this lack: insufficient top-management support, inadequate budgetary resources, and lack of organizational capability or interest.

FACTORS THAT ENCOURAGE CAREER DEVELOPMENT SYSTEMS

Why do organizations have or start career development systems? We asked respondents to indicate the top three factors that influenced the development of their career development systems. Surprisingly, the two reasons most often cited by our survey respondents had to do with upward mobility:

- A desire to promote from within (23 per cent)
- A shortage of promotable talent (14 per cent).

A third often-cited factor, organizational commitment to development, actually ranked considerably higher among government respondents. Significantly, the development of an organization's strategic plan was cited nearly as frequently (i.e., by 12 per cent of all respondents) as a shortage of promotable talent.

To our surprise, only 8 per cent of all respondents alluded to the desire to motivate employees under conditions of limited growth—and a mere 2 per cent cited a desire to improve worker productivity. These findings were the first of several signals indicating the durability of a traditional view of career growth as synonymous with upward mobility. In developing their systems, most respondents believed that their main audience was salaried (i.e., exempt) employees.

Almost 75 per cent targeted "fast-track" management candidates or "high-potentials," and over half targeted management trainees. Again, the major emphases seemed to be on enhancing upward mobility and building bench strength (i.e., the ability to replace departing employees quickly and effectively).

ATTITUDES TOWARD OCD

With regard to our respondents' attitudes toward OCD, several themes emerged from the survey. Organizations, managers, and employees alike viewed career development as important. Supervisors were seen as playing a vital but problematic developmental role. Career development was viewed as directly relevant to strategic business planning: fully 85 per cent of our survey respondents agreed with the statement that career development programs must be linked with strategic planning.

Finally, career development was perceived as having many of the positive effects (such as enhanced skills) but few of the negative ones (such as loss of good employees through movement to other employers) sometimes associated with it. Significantly, the "drivers" or prompts for career development did not always mesh logically with attitudes toward it.

Thus, while neither motivational or productivity-related reasons were cited by our survey respondents as major drivers for the design and implementation of their systems, respondents nonetheless stated that career development enhances job performance and should be tied to strategic plans.

It appears that assumptions about the benefits of a career development system are not what drive system design and implementation; once the system is in place, however, it tends to engender positive attitudes and garner managerial support. The actual impetus for system development seems to be quite specific to individual organizations and their cultures and business needs.

OCD SYSTEM AUDIENCES, TOOLS, AND TECHNIQUES

As noted earlier, salaried employees were the main target of most respondents' developmental efforts. Interestingly, more than twice as many governmental respondents than private-sector ones (i.e., 75 per cent) targeted new employees. Although this finding surprised us, it seems likely that within the private sector, as both the projected number of available new entrants and their skills decrease, organizations will have no choice but to attend more closely to the new employee and his or her developmental needs.

Traditional career development practices predominated in our survey pool. Nearly 60 per cent of all respondents had development programs, including training/development and tuition reimbursement (as well as job enrichment and redesign). Over half had job matching programs, and roughly 45 per cent offered individual career development discussions. Processes for assessing organizational potential and tools for employee self-assessments were available in roughly 30 and 45 per cent, respectively, of all organizations. Internal labour-market information exchanges were present in about one-quarter.

The emphasis on internal promotion and development of bench strength was clearly evidenced by the prevalence of development programs (broadly defined) and job matching programs. Yet it remains unclear, in our view, how such programs can succeed over the long term. Without a heavier use of employee and manager self-assessments and without access to career and organizational information, how can individuals undertake job moves (either upward or lateral) effectively? In the end, our findings on common career development practices seem to beg the basic question of what really constitutes development in today's organizations.

IMPLEMENTATION OF OCD SYSTEMS

About half of all our respondents used a task force or advisory group to design or implement their systems. Staffing was generally lean: less than 25 per cent of all systems had a full-time staff person devoted to career development. Typically, the responsibility for development was viewed as one shared by employees, managers, and the organization—with the employee, however, bearing the largest share (i.e., over half of the responsibility).

Significantly, less than 50 per cent of all respondents were training their line managers to hold career discussions. In our minds this finding raises important questions about how effectively OCD systems can be implemented when neither training nor accountability are consistent features of the manager's role.

PERCEIVED EFFECTIVENESS OF OCD PRACTICES

Among our respondents, the three practices with the highest effectiveness ratings were tuition reimbursement, internal training and development programs, and external seminars and workshops. These are all traditional training and development activities not necessarily linked to a career development strategy. The same holds true for employee orientation and job posting programs, which also received high effectiveness ratings.

Tools that we had thought were commonly accepted components of career development systems - including career planning workshops, stand-alone career workbooks, and computer software - received surprisingly low prevalence and effectiveness ratings. (Only 34 per cent of our respondents used career planning workshops; only 15 per cent offered workbooks; and a mere 13 per cent had computer software for career development.) Perceptions of low effectiveness may be attributable to the fact that often these tools are not formally linked to systems or HR initiatives, leaving tool usage as an isolated activity.

Although a notably high percentage of respondents reported that line managers were holding career discussions with their employees, less than 25 per cent described those discussions as effective. This perception of ineffectiveness may well stem from the fact, noted earlier, that fewer than half of the respondents were actually training their managers to hold career discussions.

RESPONDENTS' ASSESSMENTS OF THEIR SYSTEMS

Although government respondents were somewhat more inclined to evaluate their processes, the organizations we surveyed had few formal means of determining whether their career development systems were achieving their aims. The most common evaluation method was informal verbal feedback with nearly two-thirds of respondents relying on that method.

From an informal standpoint, we asked respondents to assess their systems through a series of open-ended questions. Less than one-third of the corporate sample rated their systems as effective or very effective—in marked contrast to respondents in the government sample, whose effectiveness ratings were about 20 points higher. In fact, nearly half of the corporate respondents were only lukewarm about their systems.

Despite these results, most respondents expressed the belief that their systems produced positive outcomes and recognized the need for greater accountability, formality, and systemization. Overall, two variables that seemed to influence positive perceptions of effectiveness were the length of time in which a system had been in place and the number of full-time staff devoted to career development.

These findings buttressed our belief that systems take time to develop and need sufficient resources to thrive. We also believe that as line managers become more integral to a career development system's implementation (and are held accountable for their role in the process), they will contribute directly and continuously to its effectiveness and thereby positively influence the perceptions of all the players in the system.

In 1978, over 1,100 members of the AMA (half of whom were from manufacturing) were mailed a questionnaire regarding their career planning and management practices; 225 organizations responded to this questionnaire. The survey instrument was similar to that used in our 1990 survey. To our surprise, the results of the two surveys were strikingly similar despite downsizing, delayering, and other significant changes in the overall business climate. The state of the practice underwent few radical transformations in the 1980s.

Both the 1978 and 1990 survey respondents named the desire to promote from within and a shortage of promotable talent as key drivers of their career development efforts. Thus, "climbing the corporate ladder" persists as a goal in a variety of organizational cultures, despite mounting evidence that this notion is no longer as realistic or relevant as it once was. This finding surprised us in light of the currently pressing need to motivate employees in conditions of limited growth; the two emphases seem at odds. (It may be, however, that attitudes about upward mobility take time to catch up to economic reality.)

Career counseling by line managers increased (from 56 to 83 per cent), as did training for these managers (from 25 to 44 per cent); however, the 1990 survey sample reported continued dissatisfaction with the manager's role. One might speculate that although a growing number of organizations view their managers as crucial to any formalized, integrated, and strategically oriented OCD effort, not all organizations are clear on how to prepare and use their managers in developmental activities.

Computer software for career development, expected by many to become very popular during the 1980s, fared poorly in ratings by the 1990 survey respondents: only 13 per cent reported using such software, and of those users, less than half rated it effective or very effective. Job posting was the only practice that grew significantly from 1978 to 1990 and was seen positively by respondents—probably because of shifts toward openness and ongoing communication in many corporate cultures.

What about attitudes toward OCD? It appears that they, too, have not changed drastically from 1978 to the present. As noted, the latest survey respondents, like their predecessors, stressed the problematic role of the manager in the development process as well as the burdensome nature of the process for supervisors. In our view these findings once again imply a need for more and better training of managers in their multiple roles as coaches, developers, and creators of links to business strategy.

Regardless of perceived problems, the respondents in both surveys stated that they were witnessing an increase in the systemization of career development practices and a burgeoning range and efficiency of tools and techniques. It thus seems that although certain trends exist, the field of OCD has by no means settled into a uniform or predictable future direction. It remains a "work in progress," powerfully influenced by specific circumstances and conditions.

FOREIGN VERSUS DOMESTIC OCD PRACTICES AND ATTITUDES

The European, Australian, and Singaporean samples of our survey were by no means a homogenous group; they differed from one another and, as a whole, from the U.S. sample. The European sample comprised 70 respondents in several different countries, whereas the other two samples comprised 200 respondents from each country (Australia and Singapore). As in the United States, the desire of foreign companies to develop people from within and to make an organizational commitment to career development were major factors contributing to system design and implementation. Development of the organization's strategic plan was a third top-ranked factor.

What basic beliefs were shared by survey respondents in all four samples? Most respondents reported a belief in some version of the following:

- Senior management values career development and seeks to link it with the organization's strategic plan.
- Career development enhances the use of employee skills and helps people deal with a low-growth environment; however, most supervisors aren't equipped to conduct career discussions.
- Employee participation in career development should be voluntary, not mandatory.

The latter belief was held especially strongly among American respondents, who tended to focus on the role of the individual employee. American respondents also had weaker perceptions of senior managerial "buy-in" to career development and to the strategic link than did their foreign counterparts. An emphasis on in-house training and development and on external seminars or workshops—

coupled with the relative lack of practices that help "solid citizens" as well as high-potential employees—characterized all four samples. Despite the fact that the global business environment may not be one in which "up" is the only or best direction for career growth, organizations are apparently still clinging to the traditional notion of development as upward mobility within a clearly defined corporate hierarchy.

How do domestic and foreign attitudes compare with regard to outcomes? Only 29 per cent of American respondents rated their systems as effective or very effective, as opposed to 52 per cent in Australia, 58 per cent in Europe, and 62 per cent in Singapore. This attitudinal divergence may be reflected in these relevant facts: fewer full-time career development staff are available in most American organizations, fewer career discussions are held between employees and their managers, and the link between strategic planning and career development is weaker.

Across the board, respondents cited several benefits of career development systems—regardless of either their effectiveness ratings or specific prompts for their design. Among the key benefits named were the following:

- Better planning and management of human resources;
- Increased competitive advantage; and
- Enhanced skills, motivation, and employee retention.

When asked what they would do differently, respondents around the world often cited more systemization, accountability, and evaluation as well as more training and involvement of managers. Most also reported a need for greater commitment of resources. Future plans typically included strategies to expand current programs and increase systemization and linkages. Respondents also reported that managers would be receiving greater support in their crucial role in the developmental process.

Index

A

B

C

D

E

F